AMERICAN BY PAPER

AMERICAN BY PAPER

How Documents Matter in Immigrant Literacy

KATE VIEIRA

 University of Minnesota Press
Minneapolis
London

Support for this research was provided by the University of Wisconsin–Madison Office of the Vice Chancellor for Research and Graduate Education with funding from the Wisconsin Alumni Research Foundation.

Parts of chapters 1 and 2 were published as "American by Paper: Assimilation and Documentation in a Biliterate Bi-ethnic Immigrant Community," *College English* 73, no. 1 (2010): 50–72; copyright 2010 by the National Council of Teachers of English; reprinted with permission. An early version of chapter 3 was published as "Undocumented in a Documentary Society: Textual Borders and Transnational Religious Literacies," *Written Communication* 28, no. 4 (2011): 436–61.

Published by the University of Minnesota Press
111 Third Avenue South, Suite 290
Minneapolis, MN 55401-2520
http://www.upress.umn.edu

Library of Congress Cataloging-in-Publication Data
Names: Vieira, Kate.
Title: American by paper : how documents matter in immigrant literacy / Kate Vieira.
Description: Minneapolis ; London : University of Minnesota Press, [2016] | Includes bibliographical references and index.
Identifiers: LCCN 2015022460 | ISBN 978-0-8166-9751-9 (hc) | ISBN 978-0-8166-9752-6 (pb)
Subjects: LCSH: Literacy—Social aspects—United States. | Immigrants—Legal status, laws, etc.—United States. | Legal documents—Social aspects—United States. | Azorean Americans—Massachusetts—Social conditions. | Brazilian Americans—Massachusetts—Social conditions. | Brazilians—Massachusetts—Social conditions.
Classification: LCC JV6475 .V54 2016 | DDC 305.9/069120973—dc23
LC record available at http://lccn.loc.gov/2015022460

Printed in the United States of America on acid-free paper

The University of Minnesota is an equal-opportunity educator and employer.

22   21   20   19   18   17   16   10   9   8   7   6   5   4   3   2   1

For Amália

CONTENTS

PREFACE

An American with Papers

It is 2011, three years after primary data collection in "South Mills," the pseudonym I have given my hometown for this book. I am preparing to bring my three-year-old daughter to visit her family in Brazil. As the date for our trip gets closer, I have to think of our visas. My heart beats faster, in a worried rhythm. I lie awake at night.

I think of the many interviews I conducted with documented and undocumented immigrants, during which people wept as they told me of family they could not see because of their legal status. As they spoke, I offered tissues with one hand and felt for my daughter's reassuring kick inside my belly with another. In such moments, it became clear that to understand the significance of literacy in immigrants' lives, I first had to understand the significance of legal papers, the way papers loomed.

In comparison, my worries about my own family's upcoming trip are vague, ridiculous even. I am a third-generation Azorean American, I have had two other Brazilian visas, and my daughter is the daughter of a Brazilian citizen. There is nothing at stake.

Still, I apply for our visas by the books. I notarize, take standard-size photos, fill out forms in my most legible print, and sign, careful to reverse the order of day and month. I enclose in a large certified envelope our passports, my daughter's birth certificate, a $320 money order, and a folded, stamped, self-addressed certified return envelope. I breathe. I give the documents to the kindly man at the post office, the branch about whose potential closing there is a community meeting that evening. This is an act of trust. A trust in the infrastructures built on paper that have, for the last century and a half, ferried writing across geographical space. A trust in the legibility of one government's documents to officials of another. A trust that someone behind the Brazilian consulate's walls will find us worthy of a visa and will send our papers back, intact, with the promise of mobility stamped in their pages.

I have the privileged document of the U.S. citizen, passport of passports, allowing mobility so free in the world that as an American I am, I admit, also a bit indignant to have to be inconvenienced to apply for a visa, as do so many for entry into my country. Yet what I feel in the moment of placing my and my daughter's birth certificate and passports into an envelope is not the certainty of privilege, but its fragility. I am, to echo the words of a research participant and the title of this book, just American by paper. Papers define the legal terms of my inclusion in, or exclusion from, the nation.

In speaking to other women who do research in their own communities, I have been struck by a common theme. We do research because we know it could be us: pregnant too soon, in jail, or otherwise stuck. There but for the grace of God go I, said a friend, describing her work with Chicana inmates. And there but for the grace of God go I, said a graduate student, describing the Latinas in her home community who could not go to college. There but for my passport go I, I think, as the balding white man hands me over a tracking number.

I became a mother amid wrenching stories of family separations that should be a national shame. I became a wife in a similar way, holding tight to the marriage certificate, love letters, photos, leases, and shared bank statements that would allow my partner to stay in the United States. I waited in line for hours along with hundreds of others one hot Texas Saturday for free immigration advice from a priest, who called me *m'ija* and showed me an insider's way around red tape. He blessed me as I walked out the colorful doors of the community center, back into the hostile sun. Three years later, as my partner and I sweated through our official interview, the immigration officer asked us if we were communist, and I laughed, thinking we were all on the same side. But he was not joking. He repeated the question, a standard one, I suppose.

You seem like you've done this before quite a bit, I say to the postal worker.

Yep. Can't lose these, he tells me, and in his voice is a reassuring midwestern competence.

I want his assurance, his blessing, his collusion. To connect with this partner in bureaucracy, this ally in regimes of print, this comrade in the circulation of documents. This human being beyond the humorlessness of paper.

I leave my papers to be sorted and sent, pushing back fears that my humanity will be disregarded along the way, my papers misplaced, my presence in this or that country vilified, my baby lost, my life stretched out across national borders until it shreds into flurries of confetti. I remember that I am American and this cannot happen to me.

Which is to say, it can and does happen to many.

I feel privileged to share some of their stories in this book, from the perspective of how papers and literacy, literacy and papers, sometimes motivate movement, sometimes facilitate it, and sometimes stall it.

ACKNOWLEDGMENTS

I am deeply grateful to the communities and families of the South Mills region for supporting this project. Those who opened their lives to me for the purposes of this book often did so at great risk, with the belief that sharing their stories could serve a larger good. Without their bravery, this book would be inconceivable. My aunt and uncle, Maria and David Beshara, graciously housed me, fed me, connected me with community members, and provided crucial insights during data collection. Frank F. Sousa and Maria Gloria de Sá of the Center for Portuguese Studies at the University of Massachusetts Dartmouth encouraged me to pursue work on Portuguese Americans in this project's early stages and offered useful advice along the way. *Muito obrigada.*

Many patient readers have helped shape this book. Annette Vee, Timothy Laquintano, and Rebecca Lorimer Leonard have seen draft after draft from the beginning, lending the project their irreplaceable expertise. My revisions were kept on track by several writing groups at the University of Illinois in Urbana–Champaign: in the English Department, Spencer Shaffner, Melissa Littlefield, and Justine Murison; in the Education Department, Alecia Magnefico and Elizabeth Bagley; and in Latino/a Studies and Anthropology, Gilberto Rosas. Thanks to writing partners Sandra Fitzgerald and Cynthia Marasigan, who at different stages made the writing process a joy. I am indebted to many other readers as well: Janet Eldred for her unflagging belief in intellectual projects with personal roots; Christa Olson for our weekly writing meetings; Christina Haas for her exacting attention to chapter 3; Nancy Abelmann for her mentorship on book writing and publishing; Catherine Prendergast for her clear-eyed assessment and on-the-mark advice; Lalita duPerron for her enthusiastic engagement with the book's larger intellectual and political implications; Mary Fiorenza for writing advice that was both wicked smart and profoundly human; Margaret Bertucci Hamper for her fine-grained attention to the final manuscript; Pieter Martin and Kristian Tvedten of the University of Minnesota Press for their involvement, responsiveness, and professionalism; my dissertation committee, Michael Bernard Donals, Ellen Sapega, Susan Stanford Friedman, and Morris Young, who helped me design this study early on; and the many anonymous readers whose comments clarified the book's argument and enriched its theory making. I also appreciate the many conversations about this book I have had over the years, especially talks with Ralph Cintrón, Maisha Winn, and Paul Prior, whose questions have furthered my thinking about literacy, papers, and the state. Thank you to Leonardo Cardoso, who saved me many hours by transcribing interviews in Portuguese, and to Andrew Leinberger for expert technical help. Deepest thanks to Deborah Brandt, who saw where this project could go before it was a project, and who offered direct, demanding, and generous advice at many crucial stages. Any errors are, of course, my own.

I have been honored to participate in several enriching intellectual environments during this book's composition. From 2010 to 2012 at the University of Illinois in Urbana–Champaign I took part in the Center for Writing Studies, whose broad vision of "writing" and interdisciplinary conversations sharpened the book's direction. Working with the talented graduate students at the University of Illinois and the University of Wisconsin in our seminars on the social history of literacy, research methods, and literacy and migration, has made this a better book. I am grateful, as well, to have worked for institutions that recognize that writing books takes time: the University of Illinois provided me with a Humanities Released Time grant, and the University of Wisconsin offered me a semester leave and summer salary support. Finally, a Federal Language and Area Studies Grant supported Portuguese classes—thank you to Severino Albuquerque for helping transform my limited heritage Portuguese into a research tool.

And my family. Thank you to Joan and Jerry Vieira, without whose abiding belief in the value of academic pursuits I could not have written this book. Thank you to the many caregivers and teachers who nurtured my daughter while I wrote. And thank you to Amália, whose joy has lifted me and whose love has grounded me during all stages of this project. *Te amo muitão.*

INTRODUCTION

How Documents Matter in Migrants' Lives

José is a Brazilian man who, at the time of our interview in 2008, had lived undocumented in the United States for twenty years. As a nurse in Brazil, he struggled to support his family, ultimately making the difficult decision to leave his wife and infant son for the United States in the hopes that his remittances from abroad could sustain them. When the tourist visa he used to enter the United States expired, he found himself unauthorized to work, reenter the country, or legally sponsor his family to join him. To make a modest living without a work permit, and to avoid the mistreatment he received from employers who exploited his legal status, he painted houses as an independent contractor. As we spoke, he took his wallet out of his paint-splattered overall pockets to show me his individual taxpayer number, describing the irony of paying taxes on money that he was forbidden to earn. He also showed me his driver's license, expired in 1988, which he could not renew without a social security card. "Everything you want to do," he told me, leaning over the table that separated us in the dark church hall where we conducted our interview, "you depend on a document you don't have." Having been reunited with his wife and son, who made the life-threatening illicit journey on foot across the Mexican border, he held out hopes for a moment of political amnesty. He held out for papers.

Visas, passports, and green cards mattered a great deal to the people featured in this book, the Azorean and Brazilian migrants and Azorean Americans, both young and old, who shared their lives with me for this project. For many, these papers could mean the difference between work offering a living wage and work that exploits, family unification and separation, respect and disrespect, belonging and exclusion, life and death. Legal papers could facilitate social movement into better jobs and ease physical movement across national borders. Without papers, mobility could be limited, and many were stuck. For these reasons, papers reverberated with the immense bureaucratic and military strength of the United States, with opportunities offered or foreclosed. Papers coursed through migrants' lives and inner worlds. It is no surprise, then, that in the interviews I conducted with scores of documented and undocumented migrants between 2008 and 2010, people repeatedly and at length spoke of papers.[1]

I did not set out to write a book about papers. My interviews originally addressed another long-standing marker of national belonging, literacy. After all, scholars and policy makers alike have long touted literacy as the key to upward social mobility, national belonging, civic participation, and ultimately "assimilation" (a term I discuss in chapter 1). To assess whether such claims held water, I conducted interviews, collected writing samples, and took reams of ethnographic notes about "literacy." The result was, to me, perplexing: When I asked about literacy, participants instead often shared their experiences of papers. In living rooms, parking lots, kitchens, and cafés, the documented and undocumented alike spoke of papers with an urgent intimacy that conferred to me, as researcher, a responsibility to take them into account. It was only after I completed two rounds of analysis of these interviews that I could do so. Papers and literacy, I found, were intimately linked. I came to realize, and I hope to convince readers in the course of this book, that to understand the role of one in migrants' lives, we also need to understand the role of the other.

For José, as for others in this book, literacy's value for enfranchisement, opportunity, and belonging shifted in relation to papers. José, for example, spoke, read, and wrote English, but because he did not have a work permit he could not leverage his literacy for the upward social mobility he came to the United States to pursue. As a result, he wrote and read not primarily in a civic or professional realm, but instead in one of South Mills' Brazilian evangelical churches. There, he composed religious songs and sermons in Portuguese, proselytizing in environments where he needed not a green card but a missionary card. Likewise, papers shaped how, why, and with what consequences for their U.S. lives others wrote and read. Those who were in reach of legal status often painstakingly wrote letters, filled out documents, and took tests to attain legal papers, leading not to assimilation into an American identity, but to more ambivalent, bureaucratic affiliations, what one participant called "American by paper." And for the young people who traveled through school in fear that their documentary status would be found out, the social value of literacy and papers merged, as they wrote to pass both their classes and the border checkpoints that pervaded their educational experiences. For them, the difficulty in achieving the upward social mobility for which they longed was not English. "The English," in the words of one young woman, "was not the problem." The problem was papers.

For most, the weightiest papers, with the most significant consequences for their literacies, were the immigration documents that legitimized their presence in the United States and promised them rights. But the meanings attached to immigration documents also infused other papers. People spoke of the power of diplomas, certificates, and time sheets. For the purposes of this book, then, papers are textual objects, artifacts, and technologies that link migrants to larger institutions, such as the state, the school, and the workplace, and that allow them to move up, to move around, and to get by. Papers, this book argues, mediate literacy's promise as a way for migrants to make it in the United States.

Papers clearly matter for migrant literacy. The central question I ask, and answer, in this book is how. Education scholars have rightly and conscientiously examined effective and inclusionary methods for immigrant English literacy attainment, methods I have taken to heart in my experiences as an elementary, high school, and university teacher of composition and English as a second language. Yet without a theorization of papers' role in literacy access and use, we are missing a crucial aspect of migrants' educational experiences and desires. At a moment when a full 25 percent of the United States' forty million migrants is undocumented, and at a moment when both civic and economic demands mean we should be investing fully in the educational potential of all who choose to be here, accounting for papers in migrants' literacy lives is critical.[2] I wrote this book to respond to this call.

In doing so, my hopes are that it achieves three goals. The first is to offer an updated account of literacy in migrants' lives. Upward mobility and social inclusion for migrants is tied to literacy in ways that are much more complex than we often think. Popular thinking often holds that English literacy can unlock the door to the American Dream. For the documented and undocumented people in this book, sometimes this was true, and they were able to deploy individual literacy practices to achieve *uma vida melhor*, a better life. Yet their ability to profitably leverage such practices often hinged on ideologically loaded literacy artifacts, specifically immigration papers. Papers and literacy. Literacy and papers. These two objects of national identity alternately promoted and constrained opportunities, and in doing so, further shaped how and why migrants wrote and read. This book offers an ethnographic explanation of this social process. It tells the story of how migrants wrote to attain papers, how they wrote when they could not attain papers, and how their writing functioned *as* papers. It describes how migrants in two communities—one from the Azores, largely documented, and one from Brazil, largely undocumented—came to experience literacy not as a means toward assimilation, as educational policy makers often believe, nor as a means of resisting oppression, as literacy scholars often hope, but instead as tied up in *papers*, those authoritative bureaucratic objects that have come to be the currency of highly literate societies, and that often promise a better life not only within borders but also across them.

Second, I hope to answer a more academic question—one in which, as a literacy scholar, I am invested, and one that I hope both specialist and nonspecialist readers will find compelling: What do migrants' experiences with papers reveal about the nature of literacy itself? To answer this question, I draw from both migrants' experiences and literacy scholarship to develop a sociomaterial theory of literacy. This theory draws together several aspects of literacy highlighted in transnational lives: literacy as a skill, resource, and social practice that aids in interpreting and composing texts; literacy as a material product or technology (like papers) exchanged in bureaucratic and interpersonal interactions; and finally, literacy as a sociohistorical trend circulated through texts, readers, writers, and their practices, which has become "infrastructural" to communication and social control in many contemporary societies.[3] Seen sociomaterially, literacy is both a social practice and a material product coursing through institutions, lives, and history. This book tracks literacy as it moves, illuminating how it accrues meaning and force.

Finally, in examining the literacy experiences of migrants living under a regime of paper, *American by Paper* seeks to contribute to the social history of literacy, which in turn has implications for more informed literacy pedagogy and policy. I believe that regardless of whether we are cognizant of it, when teachers and administrators

intervene in a person's literacy development we are also interven-
ing in history, aligning ourselves with particular ideologies of literacy
and distancing ourselves from others, with consequences for how students use literacy. By detailing the contours of literacy, documents,
and bureaucracy at a moment of rapid globalization, I hope to unravel
part of the story of what literacy is, how it acts, whom it benefits, whom
it hurts, and under what conditions. The particular understanding I
put forth here—that both literacy's materiality and sociality powerfully act on everyday lives—is both theoretical and intended to be of
use, as educators and learners rise to the challenges and opportunities
posed by transnational migration.

In service of this last goal, this chapter's remaining pages intro-
duce readers to the role of literacy and papers both globally and for
the Azorean and Brazilian communities under consideration here. I
detail the larger social trends shaping papers' dominance in transnational lives, the place of these trends in literacy's longer social history
and debates about its nature, and finally broad characteristics of the
Azorean and Brazilian communities of South Mills and how I engaged
with them.

The Textual Conditions of Globalization

The Azoreans and Brazilians who traffic in papers in this book offer
a rare glimpse into the hostile textual conditions of globalization that
regulate the lives of many. The 33.7 million Mexican nationals and
their descendants within the United States have come to represent the
racialized face of undocumented migration and disproportionately
suffer from what some have called "the Latino education crisis."[4] But
such problems are not limited to Mexicans, Latinos, or the United
States. Public debates about migrant groups' social exclusion are rag-
ing in Europe, Japan, and elsewhere, often careening toward those
charged terms, literacy and legality. Azoreans and Brazilians are much
less nationally visible than other migrant groups, numbering within
the United States approximately 190,000 and 335,000, respectively.
And like any other group, they lay claim to irreducibly particular histories, migration trajectories, and cultures. Yet many of the challenges
they face, encapsulated in *papers*, are widely shared.

I will shortly offer details about the specific Azorean and Brazilian communities that contributed their experiences to this research.

But first let's consider two pervasive contemporary trends that impinge on transnational lives more broadly: the thickening borderland and documentary society. Coined by anthropologist Gilberto Rosas, the "thickening borderland" captures a crucial fact about U.S. immigration enforcement: Document checkpoints do not exist only on the physical border marked on a map.[5] They pervade migrants' experiences in the United States, where documents are demanded in workplaces, in schools, on the road. For example, the thickening border is apparent in "secure communities," implemented in 2008 and expanded until 2013, which includes efforts to use local jurisdictions to deport the undocumented. It is evident in a 2011 law in Alabama that required elementary schools to gather students' immigration information. And in Georgia, which passed a law in 2010 that would ban the undocumented entry to its most prestigious public universities.[6] And it is evident in states across the United States, where the undocumented cannot get driver's licenses. The local Department of Motor Vehicles, the elementary school, and the university all become, in effect, borders.

Even moves to liberalize immigration policy can thicken the border. Consider what is known as DACA, the Deferred Action for Childhood Arrivals memorandum that the Obama administration authored and whose enforcement began in 2012. Composed in response to the repeated failure to pass the Development, Relief, and Education for Alien Minors Act (the DREAM Act) that would have provided a route to permanent residence for many undocumented youth, DACA promised to halt deportation proceedings and provide a two-year employment authorization for many who entered the country unauthorized as children. For many, DACA was a welcome compromise, as was the new immigration reform announced by President Obama in 2014, to cease deportations of citizens' parents, among other measures. But even *not being deported* requires encountering the border: To benefit from DACA and other such reforms, qualifying individuals must identify themselves to immigration services. In interacting with these new reforms, people encounter the border, as it wends its way into their employment options, their imagination of the future, and their families, who may still be at risk.

In a moment of a "thickening border," enforcement comes to be diffused through federal agencies, like immigration services and local citizenry, like school secretaries or civil servants at the DMV. Cultural geographers have called this dispersal of state power a "flattened scale," whereby power is exercised not from the top down, but rather horizontally.[7] It is across this "flattened" scale that migrants move both transnationally and regionally. But far from the borderless flows of people and information that scholars once imagined characterized the global 1990s, current theories of globalization account for "stoppages" within networks of movement.[8] Such stoppages, in this account of migrants' lives, are often bureaucratic. States, and their regulatory apparatus of texts, pervade not just official offices, such as embassies and border checkpoints, but everyday sites of bureaucratic interactions where papers are demanded.

Which brings me to the second trend—"documentary society."[9] In a documentary society, a term introduced by sociologist Dorothy Smith and writing studies scholar Catherine Schryer, texts are so ubiquitous as arbiters of daily life that they often go unnoticed. We fill out forms for employment, we send e-mails, and we sign for our medical prescriptions. Even those who have difficulty with the filling out, the sending, and the signing still must contend with these literate acts. In fact, as literacy scholar Deborah Brandt has shown, as demands on literacy outpace skills, those previously considered literate can easily be rendered *il*literate.[10] Bureaucracy, after all, as one anthropologist of papers has pointed out, means "writing desk."[11] This kind of textual saturation constitutes "documentary society." Writing, in our late stage of mass literacy, is a potent regulatory mechanism. It is the beating heart of large modern bureaucracies.

The thickening border brings documents into bright relief, as migrants move between one documentary society and another. In the United States, papers have regulated national borders at least since the Chinese Exclusion Act of 1882.[12] In response to the act, many migrants forged "paper sons," fictional descendants that secured them legal entry.[13] In the early twentieth century, migrants were required to present health certificates and head-tax receipts. More famously, 1924 saw the initiation of visa requirements and literacy tests. Currently, subjects carry passports and identity cards that, in the words of migration scholar John Torpey, "sort out 'who is who.'"[14] To enter into a new textual regime, some migrants develop elaborate "file selves" to gain entry to host countries.[15] Others wield multiple passports as evidence of a privileged "flexible citizenship."[16] And still others forge documents to escape the state's grasp.[17] Immigration documents, in sum, constitute what sociologist Smith calls "active texts" that shape social action, "like a crystal which bends light as it passes through."[18] Filling out and compiling the right papers are essential parts of the migration process, with far-reaching consequences stateside and in homelands.[19] While Immigration and Customs Enforcement (ICE) is improving its digital databases and while our fingerprints may soon deny or admit us entry to another country, as of this writing papers play a central role in transnational lives. And, this book will argue, in transnational literacies.

Writing and Being Written

Papers and literacy practices in the lives of migrants in this book were tightly knotted, as they wrote to gain legitimacy, to pass checkpoints, and to fulfill other goals that resonated with the role of official documents in their lives. Practicing literacy in the textually anxious conditions of globalization, migrants often wrote in response to being written. The condition of *being written* is a bureaucratic one, gesturing to key moments in the social history of writing. Examples of the relationship of bureaucracy to literacy abound: accounting in ancient Mesopotamia; conscription in Athenian democracy; record-keeping in the Middle Ages; census taking to develop the modern nation-state; colonizing to extend church and state; documenting state enemies to uphold the Reign of Terror; using "files" to develop the basis of modern law; and constructing race through immigration law, to name just a few.[20] For the late anthropologist Jack Goody, bureaucracy was one of the central domains of literate society in the ancient Near East, one of the very foundations of civilization.[21] This historical and geographic sweep is clearly not exhaustive, but it speaks to writing's central role in managing complex information and populations. Not infallible for large-scale state projects, literacy nonetheless appears to be the best tool bureaucrats have. Documents, in particular, make subjects "legible" to the state.[22] And passports and visas, as particular kinds of identification documents, seek to control the unwieldy movement of bodies across national borders. Bureaucratic uses of writing often appear as fundamentally impersonal interactions in which we are no more than a piece of paper, a file, a number, a bad photograph. And yet bureaucracy is nothing if not personal. In fact, it is often invasively so. We are *written* and are thus classified and managed.

The bureaucratic conditions that manage transnational lives, even at the cusp of a supposedly paperless age, may be much more fundamental to everyday literacy than scholars have previously appreciated.[23] Because of their histories with official papers, members of the communities under consideration here often experienced writing as a technology of oppression. Such associations differ from what studies of migrant and minority literacies have emphasized over the last fifteen years, in which migrants use literacy strategies to contest the injustices connected to minority status.[24] While I did interview activist journalists and priests, and while forgeries and other subversive acts of writing peppered migrants' accounts of their writing lives, migrants often wrote not to resist power, but more mundanely and more pragmatically to comply with it, that is, to attain the privileges associated with that oft-uttered word, "papers."

By "comply" I mean that migrants often wrote under the auspices of large bureaucratic institutions.[25] Even the most expressive writing I encountered in South Mills, that being the religious writing done in the Brazilian evangelical and Catholic communities covered in chapter 3, was nonetheless circumscribed by an institution (transnational churches) that rivaled the state for bureaucratic power. Migrants complied with bureaucracies such as state, church, school, and workplace by grounding their writing within the documentary infrastructures of these institutions. Their meanings and words were their own, certainly, but they were also regulated by and recruited into the larger mechanisms of bureaucracies that trade in documents. Migrants often wrote, sometimes with more agency and sometimes with less, to inscribe their positions within these institutions and to gain some advantage.

Papers, in the communities under consideration here, acted as material linchpins in the process of writing and being written. They functioned on three levels. First, papers were simply papers, artifacts made from wood pulp or plastic, inked, laminated, encrusted with an electronic chip, embossed, stamped, signed. Second, as they circulated between subject and state, they were tools by which states legitimized those lucky enough to have them and disenfranchised those who didn't, and by which subjects petitioned for particular bureaucratically granted privileges. That is, these material artifacts had real-life consequences. On a third level, as migrants wrote to achieve papers, wrote in light of not having papers, or wrote to gain privileges associated with papers, papers attained the status of what theorist Pierre

Bourdieu has called symbolic capital—a kind of power assumed when other forms of capital (such as economic, cultural, and social) are socially recognized as legitimate.[26] Such legitimacy, Bourdieu points out, is often conferred by documents. In many migrants' lives, papers leached bureaucratic meanings, such as officialdom, authority, and regulation, meanings activated in part through migrants' everyday bureaucracy- and paper-infused acts of writing. Papers fairly vibrated with these associations. As material artifacts, they took on larger social meanings adumbrated through their use. They acted in a way I will later describe as sociomaterial. For this reason, one undocumented young woman described seeing her name printed on her diploma as the highlight of her studies. More than a particularly influential class or an inspiring book, her diploma—the paper document—symbolized legitimacy, belonging, possibility. These meanings, in turn, came to characterize how many approached everyday acts of writing and reading and what they believed such acts would achieve. Literacy and papers. Papers and literacy. When migrants traded in one of these resources, they also traded in the other.

Azoreans, Brazilians, and the Documentary Border

The experiences of Azoreans and Brazilians are so telling of these phenomena, because despite their many similarities, at the time of this study they were divided by a documentary border. Living in a former mill town in Massachusetts that I call South Mills, members of these groups shared a common language, Portuguese, the unofficial second language of the city. They also shared economic struggles. Well-paying jobs were scarce in South Mills, one of the United States' many mid-sized former manufacturing centers picking its way through the ruins of a drawn-out process of deindustrialization. And they shared similar goals. Members of both groups came in search of, in the words of so many, *uma vida melhor*, a better life, the promise of the American Dream.

Yet they were often positioned differently in relation to the law. Azoreans, from the Atlantic Islands 930 miles off the coast of Portugal, arrived in the largest numbers to South Mills between the 1960s and 1980s to work in the area's factories, often with official papers in hand.[27] They benefited from the family reunification clause in the 1965 Hart–Cellar Act, which allowed many to sponsor family members' migration, creating an Azorean community in South Mills. Many

Brazilians, on the other hand, were offered few to no paths to legalization. The very same act that facilitated Azoreans' legal migration
also included quotas for the Americas for the first time, criminalizing
Mexican migration and by extension Latin American migration more
broadly.[28] Brazilians, then, often came to South Mills by other means:
overstaying a visa or paying a coyote (human smuggler) to sneak them
across a deadly border.

To be clear, the very category of illegality is a historical construct;
the term "illegal" only began to apply to groups of people as recently
as 1950.[29] And in making a distinction between documented Azoreans
and undocumented Brazilians, I do not want to reify the categories
of "legal" and "illegal" along hemispheric or racial lines. In fact, in
other areas of the United States, the Portuguese, not Brazilians, are
the larger undocumented group.[30] Yet the fact remains that the legal
status granted to many Azoreans in South Mills and withheld from
many Brazilians had wide consequences. Without legal status, one was
not permitted to drive, take out federal school loans, work, vote, or
sponsor family members to migrate. All of these rights—without which
families were torn apart, daily activities induced anxiety, and upward
mobility was near impossible—were conferred through papers. For
documented Azoreans, legal papers were revered as textual evidence
of their journey toward U.S. national belonging. For undocumented
Brazilians, papers were textual evidence of their exclusion.

For these reasons, among others, attaining the right papers was
at least as important for many migrants as was acquiring literacy in
English—that panacea so often offered in relation to migrants' social
and economic struggles. Give them literacy, the policy makers say,
offering state-sponsored GED, ESL, and computer literacy classes.
Give us papers, comes migrants' unheeded response.

Strong Texts

How do migrants put reading and writing to work—how do they
practice literacy—in a context so stringently circumscribed by literate
products, that is, papers? And what do such practices teach us more
broadly about how literacy works in an age of papers?

To answer these questions, I bring together two opposing literacy
theories—"strong text" theories and "New Literacy Studies" theories—
that have dominated literacy research for the last decades, in order to

develop a sociomaterial theory of literacy. Recent literacy theorists have rebutted what have been called "strong text" theories of literacy. Popularized by Deborah Brandt in 1990, the term "strong text" summarized what was wrong with previous theories of literacy: They fixated on writing's power as a technology, they gave undue weight to writing as an object that could outlive its author, and they underscored writing's ability to act independently from its social context.[31] For recent literacy scholars, those early theories of literacy wrongly abstracted the writer and reader out of the communicative, contextualized, and interpersonal acts of writing and reading. That is, "strong text" theories focused on the strength of literate products, texts, as opposed to the meaning made dialogically through literate processes. Such theories have been replaced with a view of writing and reading as meaning-making practices wedded to the specific sociohistorical contexts of both writers and readers. This New Literacy Studies approach, most prominently forwarded by scholars including Shirley Brice Heath, James Gee, and Brian Street, has offered crucial insights into literacy practices, particularly of marginalized populations.[32] It has shown how the acts of reading and writing are never detachable, isolated skills. Instead, they are complexly embedded in lived experiences, in relationships, and in power, insights that have transformed literacy pedagogy and theory.

When I first set out to answer the question of how migrants practice literacy, I took this New Literacy Studies, context-based approach. In interviews and in note taking, I listened carefully for the situation in which people read and wrote (With whom? Why? At whose behest? With what materials?), for the way larger systems of power (such as social class, race, gender, nationality, legal status, historical legacies) intervened in writing and reading, and for how participants' early childhood, family, and school experiences of literacy echoed in their contemporary uses of reading and writing. In other words, I sought to understand how, as Brandt puts it, "writing pulls into sharp focus the means by which we make the world together."[33]

This approach, however, continued to lead me back to earlier, strong text theories of writing. Consider the comment that opened this introduction, made by a Brazilian migrant, José, and repeated in so many different ways by so many people I encountered in my fieldwork: "Everything you want to do, you depend on a document you don't have." José's experiences with these literate artifacts had less to do with a negotiated meaning-making activity and more to do with force, with compliance, with threats of punishment. As a technology, as a thing with a status that could outlive its author, as an object through which the state conferred legal power, the document José didn't have was strong, in many of the senses that earlier literacy theorists meant it.

At the same time, it was clear to me that texts were not autonomously strong. They were only as strong as the strongest made them. Put another way, José's experiences of strong texts were conditioned by larger geopolitical trends. And here my analysis realigns with the social practice views forwarded by New Literacy Studies. Papers do not *a priori* embody state authority. Histories of the passport in the United States and Europe show that this document arrived at its supremacy through contested historical processes, that people had to learn to trust paper.[34] Likewise, one of the processes this book highlights is how such a mundane artifact as paper comes to embody such intense symbolic power. That the authority of passports and other papers is socially constructed, however, does not mitigate their power. Quite the opposite: Texts are strong, because some of the most powerful contemporary institutions, whose authority is supported by constellations of state enforcers, say they are. For these profoundly social reasons, for many migrants, *everything you want to do depends on a document you don't have*.

Put simply, the experiences of migrants such as José demanded that I link older, widely criticized, "strong text" or "autonomous" theories of literacy with more recent, context-sensitive approaches. Bringing these opposing views of literacy together sheds light on what happens to literacy practices in a context managed by its product, that is, in a documentary society in which the border is thickening. The result is a sociomaterialist theory equipped to explain some crucial aspects of literacy in transnational lives.

To develop this sociomaterialist perspective, I attempted to uncover under what social conditions and in what ways literacy's materiality came to gain importance for transnational migrants in South Mills. By literacy's materiality, I mean the surfaces, tools of inscription, scriptural systems, and bodies people use to write and read, as well as the infrastructures that facilitate writing's dispersal.[35] These aspects of literacy are irreducibly material, but they are also irreducibly social. First, they are social, because they are developed from a series of social practices: Immigration papers, for example, are the result of what Latour calls "congealed labor," including voting, law making, and printing, among many other processes.[36] They become a "technical delegate," in which the actions of a potentially "long disappeared" actor, sedimented in papers, shape migrants' lives. They are also social, then, because they act on society. In this way, texts, in the words of Brandt and Clinton, mediate "larger and longer pieces of the social world, holding them in connection, across contexts."[37] For migrants, papers hold together the nation, allowing or denying access to nation-related rights and privileges. Finally, literacy's materiality interacts with social processes to gain meaning, as migrants write to attain papers or write in light of not having papers. This interaction is what some have called the *immateriality* of literacy, in which the "material conjures the immaterial, which relies on the material for its salience."[38] Papers, in sum, are strong texts, because subjects and state engage in everyday activities, including reading, writing, and deporting, which contribute to and reify the social belief in texts' power. The sociomaterial theory of literacy developed throughout this book highlights how these aspects of literacy inter-animate one another. To develop this theory, I follow in the tradition of literacy ethnographers, who trace the everyday practices and meanings of literacy in ordinary lives.[39]

An Ethnographic Approach to Literacy in South Mills

In carrying out and writing up this research, I am bridging two worlds: the academic audience that I imagine as readers of this book and the migrant communities who are its subject. While sometimes members of these communities overlap, more often they do not. In what follows, then, I disclose why and how I used the stories of those who, often at personal risk, participated in this project. In doing so, I hope to make clear the terms on which this book's claims can be assessed and interrogated.

First, a fuller picture of South Mills: At the turn of the twentieth century, South Mills, then a booming mill town, boasted the largest percentage of foreign-born inhabitants of any city in the United States. A full one-fifth of the population was Portuguese, largely from the archipelago of the Azores. Isolated from the Portuguese continent by nearly one thousand miles of ocean, most Azoreans worked as subsistence farmers, and the men were often sent to fight in the Portuguese kingdom's wars. Following the paths established by earlier whalers and the stories of America told by those who returned, many immigrated to the United States.[40] As a result, South Mills' Portuguese population grew so rapidly (and so apparently problematically) that it warranted a book-length ethnography, published in 1923, documenting Portuguese illiteracy and the community's shockingly high rates of infant mortality.[41] A combination of racial quotas and literacy tests instituted in 1924 stemmed migration from southern Europe. And soon after, the Great Depression saw the return of many Azoreans to the Azores.

Despite its diminished numbers the community persisted, and due to legislative changes stateside coupled with difficult conditions in the Azores, it even grew in subsequent years. In the 1950s a volcano erupted on the Azorean island of Faial, leading John F. Kennedy, then a senator, to author the bill that would give Azoreans refugee status in the United States. (One participant, whose parents emigrated from Faial, told of the crushed velvet portrait of JFK that hung in her family's living room.) In the following decade, immigration law continued to work in the Azoreans' favor. Though the Immigration and Nationality Act of 1965 did not benefit all groups equally, it was a boon for Azoreans: The family reunification clause facilitated the largest wave of migration of Azoreans to the United States, which lasted until the mid-1980s. In the Azores, for those who lived outside the capital, many were still eking out livings on the land under quite rustic conditions: no running water, no electricity, and, to make things worse, under Portugal's right-wing dictatorship (which lasted until 1974) young men were conscripted to fight in imperial wars. Stateside, life looked rosier. Factory jobs in South Mills were plentiful and relatively well paid, and Azorean migrants were able to work and save. During this time, an estimated 226,000 Azoreans migrated to the United States, a considerable number for an archipelago with a population that currently hovers around 250,000.[42] Subsequently, Azorean migration waned, in part because many factories closed in South Mills and in part because, with Portugal's accession to the European Union, life on the Azorean islands improved. Still, at the time of this study those claiming Portuguese descent made up 43 percent of South Mills' population. Portuguese flags waved from the awnings of houses; some of the local architecture mirrored exactly that found on the largest Azorean island, São Miguel; signs claiming "Falamos Portugués" (Portuguese spoken here) hung in shop windows; and even the local Walgreen's sold Portuguese sweet bread.

As Azorean migration to South Mills dwindled, Brazilian migration to the city grew. Brazil has long served as a host country for migrants, as opposed to a sending country.[43] And although some Brazilians migrated earlier, Brazilian out-migration is a relatively new phenomenon, growing on the heels of the demise of Brazil's military dictatorship in the mid-1980s and the subsequent period of instability and inflation that priced out many of middle-class lifestyles. Unlike Azorean migrants, who often had completed no more than fourth grade in the Azores, Brazilians often (though not always) came from more urban areas and had completed high school and sometimes technical schools and university. But they found their advancement in Brazil's infamously entrenched class system stymied. As a result, many came to the United States—often first to Florida, New York City, or other larger cities in Massachusetts, and then to South Mills, drawn there by a combination of its cheap rents, Brazilian religious institutions, and links, familial or more casual, to the local Portuguese-speaking community. In South Mills, many worked in service jobs (caring for children or the elderly, housecleaning, fast-food restaurants) or manual labor (construction, factory work). These positions did not pay well enough to allow most Brazilians to enter the middle class in the United States, but many sent remittances home, where they supported families, paid for their children's educations, and sometimes funded the building of houses.

The precise number of Brazilians in South Mills, or nationally, is impossible to pinpoint. Census calculations are problematic. Because of the undocumented status of many Brazilians, they may not have claimed Brazil as a country of origin. Moreover, because Brazilians are of a variety of ethnicities, including European, African, Indigenous, Asian, and Arab, Brazilian nationals might have answered the census ancestry question in a number of different ways besides "Brazilian."[44] In fact, to address the undercounting of Brazilians, the census launched a Brazilian-specific publicity campaign in 2010. All over town, posters pictured a chubby toddler in a Brazilian soccer jersey framed by the words, "Eu também conto!" (I count, too!). The poster warned that failure to "be counted" would mean cuts in the educational services that use census numbers to justify their continuation. So, while the U.S. census reported a small Brazilian population in South Mills at the time of the study, the actual population was larger—large enough, in any case, to ensure the survival of Brazilian restaurants, religious institutions, travel agencies, community organizations, and products in local grocery stores in a city of the modest total population of eighty-eight thousand. In subsequent years, as the Brazilian economy improved, as the U.S. economy worsened, and as restrictions on the undocumented tightened, many returned home. But at the time of the study, and as of this writing, a significant core community remained. These, then, are the larger trends shaping Brazilian and Azorean migration to South Mills.[45]

My primary aim in South Mills was not to exhaustively describe Azoreans' and Brazilians' cultures or ways of life, the traditional goals of ethnography. More centrally, I was after the meanings and uses of one very specific sociohistorical phenomenon—literacy—as experienced by these particular groups of people.[46] This project is best characterized, then, not as ethnography, but as an ethnographic approach to the study of literacy. To understand the way literacy and papers intertwined for Brazilians and Azoreans, I collected more than fifty literacy history interviews, lasting between one and three hours, about half in Portuguese and half in English, with members of both groups, of diverse ages and backgrounds, in 2008 and 2010. Though interviews rely on participants' imperfect memories and retellings, such data nonetheless offered an understanding of how participants experienced literacy and the larger ideologies swirling around its use. The subjective nature of these narrative accounts ultimately became a strength, helping me to develop an emic understanding of what literacy meant to particular people, as well as a larger composite sense of how literacy, as a macrosocial force, appeared across stories.[47] These interviews also allowed me to approximate before and after pictures of participants' migration to the United States, a comparison that became important in the analysis, since participants' literacy practices changed as they became documented or undocumented. In this way, I was able to track continuities between early home-country education and literacy practices stateside, and also ruptures, as many found the value of their literacy resources recalibrated in relation to their documentary status stateside. To triangulate these accounts, I also collected participants' writing—including sermons, songs, poems, essays, articles, letters, and written preparations for oral performances. Finally, over a six-week period I took field notes in community centers, such as ethnic cafés, churches, and the local immigration office.

I located participants through a snowball sample, which provided a way to meet with a range of community members. The center of the "snowball" was my Aunt Tequila, a first-generation Azorean immigrant who has lived in the United States since the late 1960s and who has close ties to both Brazilian and Azorean communities, and with whom I lived during my field research. She made use of her extensive social network to help me interview Azorean participants from a range of occupations, experiences, and educational backgrounds. These initial participants, in turn, often referred me to other potential participants. Because the Portuguese community makes up close to half the population of South Mills, it was relatively easy to find first- and second-generation Azoreans and Azorean Americans who were willing to speak with me. Plus I had an in: a web of familial relationships made me legible to many in this community, in which extended families often live in close proximity, from the first floor of the tenement buildings that line the city streets to the third. I formally interviewed twenty-five Azoreans and Azorean Americans, all except for four in English, some on multiple occasions, and had informal interviews with a handful more.[48]

My snowball sample of Brazilian research participants also began with Aunt Tequila, who introduced me to two Brazilian South Millsites, who in turn provided an entry into the Brazilian South Mills community. My aunt's upstairs Brazilian neighbor, Paulo, was a nurse's assistant and nondenominational evangelical Christian. In my first week in South Mills he granted me my first interview and brought me to two evangelical Christian churches—the Igreja Universal do Reino de Deus (Universal Church of the Kingdom of God) and the Igreja de Assembléia de Deus (Church of the Assembly of God)— where he introduced me to the pastors, who generously put in a good word for me with congregants. In turn, I taught a weekly conversational English class at the Igreja Universal for a small group of congregants and also offered to help members of the Assembly of God Church with writing or reading in English. Renata, another Brazilian friend of my aunt's, who often stopped by for a coffee and a chat, helped me widen this circle. I was introduced to the Brazilian Catholic Community and their religious leader, Padre Pedro. Additionally, Renata introduced me to the proprietors of two Brazilian stores in

South Mills, who then introduced me to customers. I interviewed twenty-two members of the South Mills Brazilian community, all except for one in Brazilian Portuguese, some on multiple occasions, representing a range of races, ages, home states, education levels, and occupations.[49]

As an Azorean American married to a Brazilian at the time of the study, my interactions with participants were sometimes of close identification and other times of suspicion and distance. On the one hand, as a small, visibly pregnant woman with typical Portuguese features (dark hair, white skin), my body resonated with South Mills' dominant racial, cultural, and religious meanings. Moreover, I speak Brazilian Portuguese in an accent picked up from my in-laws from Brazil's rural interior, resulting in a kind of comfortable country twang that some would call hick. For these reasons, to many participants who made themselves vulnerable before my digital recorder, I believe I appeared safe. A churchgoer wanted to baptize my baby, traffic stopped for me as I crossed a busy street, and participants told me the excruciating details of their travels. Some days, with some people, I was the ethnographic "insider."

Other days, as an educated, middle-class woman who had flattened her native South Mills accent into the hardened r's of the Midwest, I was also suspect. One Azorean American woman, for example, shared so many demographic characteristics with me that to list them here would betray her identity. She referred to me as the "lady" and "the writing lady," a gendered and classed appellation that showed respect for my education and also maintained social distance between us. Another Azorean American participant tested my identity by gesturing to the trope of the ethnically authentic Portuguese grandmother, or *vovó*—Catholic, proper, and knowledgeable in the making of *bacalhau*: "So your grandmother, was she a *real* Portuguese lady?" she asked suspiciously. "Oh yes," I said. Then the digital recorder registers an uncomfortable silence. I had accumulated such a privileged distance from South Mills that even my grandmother was suspect! Such moments shaped data collection, in ways that I attempted to remain aware of, both in ethnographic encounters and in analysis.

In some ways, the larger goals of the project were forwarded by my documentary and educational privilege in relation to many participants. One day, after an especially long and moving conversation with an undocumented Brazilian man, he thanked me. For what? I asked.

You are the one helping me. He thanked me for listening to, with the goal of eventually publicizing, the daily injustices he faced. No one would listen to him, but someone might listen to me, he said. I left his apartment ethnographically entangled, newly aware of the privilege and responsibility of research. I proceeded with analysis, then, firm in my conviction that if the seeds of this book grew from personal affinities and connections, it should ultimately grow into a public document.

To analyze the interviews, writing samples, and ethnographic observations, I examined the interaction among three different instantiations of literacy: literate artifacts, as in documents and pieces of writing; literacy practices, as in people's literacy activities and beliefs; and national and international infrastructures, such as state and church bureaucracies, that rely on the technology of writing. Taken together, these broad categories of literacy coalesced around the regulation of mobility—as bureaucracies issued documents that allowed one to move or restricted one from moving, and as people leveraged their writing within these textual systems to move up or move elsewhere. I then examined how literate regulation of mobility worked differently for three key groups: the documented, the undocumented, and young adults. The picture that resulted from this analysis was not uplifting. For many, writing was not primarily about home language mainte- nance or ethnic expression or resistance to oppressive structures, as I had initially hoped. It was rather about how papers, as literate objects imbued with authority by powerful institutions, came to suffuse migrants' everyday literacy practices.

To represent this analysis as clearly and convincingly as possible, I use two strategies in this book: At some points, I offer extended narratives of individual participants whose experiences offer telling cases of larger trends. Their stories, I hope, offer readers a way to anchor the arguments this book makes in actual lives. At other points, I offer brief extracts from various participants' lives, sometimes in rapid succession. This method, I hope, shows readers how the trends I document vary among and are represented by a range of participants. In other words, I have attempted to provide the detail and explanatory power of narrative depth with what I hope is the persuasive potential of breadth.

The story this book tells, then, is as follows: Literacy has historically been used to attempt to culturally *assimilate* immigrants into the nation, and popular belief still holds that it paves the way to the

American Dream. The people with whom I spoke, however, did not associate literacy with cultural assimilation. Instead, they linked literacy to mobility—mobility that bureaucratic institutions, demanding *both* literacy skills and papers, alternately facilitated or impeded. Chapter 1 shows how, as Azoreans and Brazilians sought to maximize their mobility, they recalibrated the value of literacy and papers in relation to each other. Brazilians sought immigration papers and U.S. diplomas to make their literacies legible to potential employers; and Azoreans, struggling with a legacy of limited educational attainment, relied on their permanent resident cards and passports as markers of legitimacy.

If chapter 1 argues *that* papers and literacy mediated migrants' physical and social mobility, the rest of the book examines *how* papers and literacy interacted for three different groups: documented Azoreans and Azorean Americans (chapter 2); undocumented Brazilians (chapter 3); and documented and undocumented Azorean and Brazilian young people (chapter 4). In chapter 2, Azoreans' transnational letter writing and other literacy practices become entangled in state bureaucracies, as they write to achieve papers. In these efforts to become "American by paper"—American by virtue of the literacy labor required to attain papers attesting to legal status—state and individual uses of writing comingled, associating papers with mobility and legitimacy. For the undocumented featured in chapter 3, texts represented their disenfranchisement. In this context, many documented themselves in ethnic religious institutions, which provided the textual legitimacy they were denied in secular contexts. Written out of one documentary society, they wrote their ways into another, emphasizing the importance of a sponsoring bureaucracy, and its attendant textual regime, in everyday writing practices. If the documented wrote to attain papers, and the undocumented wrote when they could not attain papers, for the young adults in chapter 4 writing functioned *as* papers, as they wrote to pass the checkpoints that pervaded their educational experiences. They laid their hopes and dreams on the immigration papers, certifications, and diplomas that (sometimes falsely) promised both upward mobility and transnational mobility. For them, the American dream was primarily a promise on paper.

In light of these findings, the conclusion suggests that whatever empowering or uplifting function literacy is thought to have, it is seen quite differently through transnational eyes. If literacy is widely thought to be a *contextualized* social practice, for many migrants it was also a technology of *decontextualization*. If literacy is thought to be a site of *identity* negotiation, for many it was also a tool of *identification*. If literacy is thought to *humanize* or *empower*, as those of us who are literacy educators often so deeply desire, for many it also *alienated*. To reconcile these seemingly conflicting views, the conclusion points toward a sociomaterialist theory that illuminates how literacy, as both a social practice and a material object, accrues meaning and power as it circulates through the lives of people and the institutions that attempt to regulate their movement. Ultimately, literacy does not make immigrants American. Viewed sociomaterially, however, it can make them American by paper.

1 LITERACY AND ASSIMILATION IN AN AGE OF PAPERS

The View from South Mills

"YOU HAVE UNDERSTOOD, BY NOW, that we are without papers," said Sandra, her gaze lighting on my digital recorder and then meeting my eyes. We were sitting at her kitchen table on a warm summer day in 2008, having come to the end of our first interview. Sandra, a former Portuguese teacher in Brazil, led Sunday school classes at South Mills' Brazilian Catholic congregation and worked at a local factory on weekdays. Her husband, a former banker, washed dishes in a restaurant. And her two daughters were students, one in high school, the other in college.

The family's undocumented status posed challenges. The ineligibility of Sandra and her husband to work in their professions or under the protection of minimum wage laws created financial difficulties; both of their daughters held full-time jobs while attending high school and college. Moreover, Sandra's oldest daughter, an adept reader and writer in English, faced discrimination at school for her undocumented status. She proceeded to college, where documents were needed to register for classes, to commute by car, to take part in an internship, to graduate, and to apply for jobs, under a haze of fear. By the end of our first interview, I knew that Sandra's family was undocumented without their having to tell me. The anxiety of "illegality" permeated their lived experiences, including their ability to trade on their literacy skills for social mobility stateside.

Across town, I sat at another kitchen table to speak with another mother, Tina, whose parents migrated to the United States from the Azores before she was born. Tina recited to me the chain of official "invitation letters" from an aunt to her mother to her father that made their migration possible, resulting in their permanent resident status and ultimately Tina's birth as a U.S. citizen in South Mills. Her papers, mythologized in family lore, set her apart from the other Portuguese-speaking groups in the area. "No green cards here," she told me a friend liked to say when she encountered Brazilians on the street. For Tina, legal documents evidenced her national belonging, over and above other newly arrived groups.

Yet as a single mother working as a caregiver for the elderly, Tina like Sandra felt alienated from the social mobility the United States promised *her* mother, who recalled seeing U.S. planes fly above the island of São Miguel while she was hanging laundry. The planes became a symbol for her desire to live in the prosperity of an imagined United States. Such prosperity, and the education required to achieve it, proved elusive. In need of money, Tina left school at age fifteen to work in the area factories and was subsequently laid off. At the time of our first interview she was attending state-sponsored GED classes in the hopes of finding better work, but two years later she had dropped out because the hours conflicted with another low-paying job. For her daughter she encouraged "books," so that she wouldn't "do what Mommy did" and could instead achieve what the first and second generation failed to.

Both Tina and Sandra wanted the mobility that the United States seemed to promise, ends they promoted by earnestly following the advice of so many policy makers, teachers, and scholars: to pursue literacy education, if not for themselves then for their daughters. Both, like many who spoke with me, were nonetheless stymied. Although Tina had papers, she did not have the right literacy. And although Sandra had literacy, she did not have the right papers. Under conditions of political, economic, and educational disenfranchisement, to reap the potential benefits of one, both women needed the other.

I open this chapter with these two women because their situations stand in for a bigger question at the heart of this book. Under what conditions can literacy help migrants meet their goals? To address this driving question, this chapter offers readers an overview of Azorean, Azorean American, and Brazilian literacy lives in South Mills at a moment in which unemployment and restrictive immigration laws conspired to devalue their literacy skills and resources. In doing so, it reevaluates both what constitutes "literacy" for migrants and what is often believed to be their "goals." Specifically, I seek to replace popular conceptions of literacy's association with cultural *assimila-tion*, an association that has haunted immigrant education for over a century, with a more nuanced understanding of literacy's and paper's connection to *mobility*, the social, economic, and physical movement that characterized both migrants' pasts and their dreams for their futures.

Immigrants' goals are often believed to be assimilation, that is, becoming similar to a mainstream. Popular conception and a tena-cious historical legacy hold that literacy, often defined as English lit-eracy skills, is the way to get there. To offer some early, and by no means exhaustive, examples: During the Americanization campaigns of the early twentieth century, immigrant workers attended compul-sory evening literacy classes (where some were told to write on the "American chalkboard" with "American chalk"!), schoolchildren heard lectures on cleanliness and had their mouths forcibly washed out (with nonkosher soap), students composed patriotic poems, teachers encour-aged group read-alouds to homogenize accents, and heritage language education was seen as political aggression.[1] Later, immigrants' liter-acy was tested at the border, with the goal of keeping out groups deemed racially undesirable.[2] While theories about migrants' transna-tionalism—movement across borders—have, in some circles, replaced theories about their "assimilation," I revive assimilation here because its ideological grip on education policy still informs much pedagogy, policy, and popular thinking.[3] For example, assimilative uses of liter-acy are visible in English-only campaigns, the monolingualist goals of even many bilingual education programs, public rhetoric about immi-gration, and education scholarship that uses literacy as a measure of whether immigrant groups have assimilated.[4] This widespread asso-ciation between literacy and assimilation bears examining from the perspective of migrants themselves.

As this chapter will detail, for the people with whom I spoke the relationship between literacy and assimilation was neither simple nor direct. Literacy appeared to lead to assimilation only insofar as it prom-ised to ease migrants' access into the powerful national bureaucracies that regulated mobility, such as state and school.[5] Such access, more-over, required not only literacy, but also papers. For these reasons, participants did not associate literacy with cultural assimilation, but rather with the mobility that bureaucratic institutions, demanding both literacy and papers, alternately facilitated or impeded. Against a backdrop of undocumented status (for many Brazilians) and limited educational access (for many Azoreans and Azorean Americans), the value of papers and literacy shifted in relation to each other. For many Brazilians, papers were needed to make good on literacy's potential. For many Azoreans and Azorean Americans, lack of access to literacy education heightened the value of papers as a form of literacy- and nation-related social capital. Literacy and papers, their values and meanings mutually calibrating and recalibrating in light of harsh political, social, and economic realities, mediated the fulfillment of migrants' aspirations, not necessarily to assimilate, but to *move*.

To understand the relationship of literacy to assimilation from the perspective of migrants, then, demands two moves: First, it requires a sociomaterial understanding of literacy, in which both literacy practices *and* products, both literacy skills *and* papers, are leveraged to navigate host-country institutions. And second, following from this sociomaterial understanding, it requires examining how literacy and papers link migrants not primarily to *cultural* aspects of the nation, but more dramatically to *bureaucratic* ones. Understood sociomaterially, literacy becomes associated not with assimilation, but with the mobility that bureaucratic institutions alternately offer or deny and that many migrants so profoundly desire. Migrants' stories, in sum, complicate long-standing equations of literacy and cultural assimilation. As readers will see, for migrants to effectively move through the literate infrastructures of the nation at a moment of rapid globalization and the textual policing of borders, they had to present both their literacies and their papers. Subsequent chapters will detail with more precision *how* literacy, as a social practice, and papers, as material products, interacted in migrants' lives. This chapter, as an overview of South Mills' migrants' educational terrain, establishes *that* they worked together to mediate migrants' larger goals, laying the groundwork for the sociomaterial theory of literacy that the rest of the book develops in more detail.

To meet these goals, I detail the unique social and educational backgrounds of each group, dividing the chapter in four. The first section addresses Brazilians; the second addresses Azoreans and Azorean Americans; the third brings both groups together to examine how papers gained status as markers of privilege under conditions in which migrants' literacy skills were devalued; and the fourth offers an extended narrative of one undocumented Brazilian woman to give ethnographic texture to these claims.

Literacy without the Right Papers: Tracking Brazilian Mobility

Many Brazilians spoke to me not of cultural assimilation, but of mobility: economic, social, and physical. When set alongside their actual experiences, the notion of cultural assimilation became an abstraction and, worse, a distraction from more pressing issues: Will I be arrested and deported? How will I find work without papers? If I can't move up here, then where? Many Brazilians in South Mills had the educational qualifications for better jobs than they actually worked. For them to achieve upward mobility stateside, however, their advanced literacy resources had to be certified and legitimized by literacy products—papers. In this section on Brazilian migrants, I show why assimilation is the wrong frame for understanding Brazilian migration experiences, detail the relationship between Brazilians' educational goals and their migratory trajectories, and describe how such trajectories were thwarted by their lack of papers.

The traditional heuristic, assimilation, cannot account for the experiences of the nascent South Mills Brazilian community for a host of reasons. First, assimilation often tracks the 1.5 (those who arrived in the United States as children) and second generation, whose numbers are small (but growing) among Brazilians in the United States.[6] Assimilation also implies a long-term project of settling in. And according to recent scholars of Brazilian migration to Massachusetts and elsewhere, many Brazilians (like other groups) would prefer to earn money and return home.[7] What's more, "assimilation" suggests a racial identification congruent with how the host country understands race. And given the racial diversity of Brazilian migrants, their position within the U.S. racial landscape is not only unclear, as it is for Azoreans, but also varies from individual to individual.[8] Finally, assimilation addresses overall trends in a population, and identifying trends among Brazilian migrants is difficult, because little reliable data exists about how many Brazilians are living in the United States.[9] Many Brazilians I spoke with wanted, instead, economic mobility, aspirations they projected transnationally. They were making their way in the world, and they hoped to use literacy to do so, though as readers will see, lack of papers often impeded their goals.

Migrating for Education

Like other immigrant groups, many Brazilians brought with them to the United States the belief that they could use education to move up economically, a belief that may have been especially tenacious since most Brazilians in Massachusetts come from Brazil's lower middle class, where material affluence is often visible but just out of reach.[10] The very poor often had no way to finance the trip to the United States (either by buying a visa and a plane ticket, or paying a coyote), and the rich had no need to. There were, of course, exceptions: For the two participants who spoke to me of their poverty in Brazil, one had cousins living in South Mills who lent her money for her migration, and the other had an employer line up a coyote to smuggle her across the border. For the three wealthy participants I interviewed, one was fleeing a bad marriage, another moved to be closer to his children, and one held out hopes that an American environment would be a positive influence on her troubled teenage son, who migrated with her. Two of these wealthy participants described family members who had completed college, although they themselves hadn't managed to, suggesting that they may not have been in a position in Brazil to reap the benefits otherwise available to those of their class status. The majority, though, were educated lower-middle-class Brazilians who believed that hard work and further education would offer upward mobility, in North or South America.

In Brazil, upward social mobility is intertwined with an educational system that many see as rigged to keep out the lower classes. While wealthy children often attend private schools geared to prepare them for competitive university entrance exams, lower-middle-class and poor children go to public schools, putting them at a disadvantage to enter the best universities—which in Brazil are public and free. Often, then, children of the lower middle class decide against college or work full-time to pay tuition at less prestigious private colleges or technical institutes. Even if they succeed in graduating from these private colleges, they must compete for jobs with high-status counterparts who completed state-sponsored educations. Jumping social classes is rare and difficult in Brazil. Many try and many fail.

For many Brazilians with whom I spoke, the United States seemed to offer a way out of the stalled mobility that plagued the lower middle class in Brazil, primarily via education. With the money earned stateside, many hoped to pay for their children's or their own studies. To offer a few examples: Fábio, a construction worker in his early thirties, left his three children (the youngest one was five) in the care of in-laws to migrate with his wife to the United States. *His* father's dream, unfulfilled at the time of his death, was for his children to finish school. A delivery person in Brazil, Fábio himself didn't graduate but held similar hopes for his own children, whose education he was supporting through remittances. Rafaela, a middle-aged single mother, whose extended narrative readers will encounter later in the chapter, left a teenage son in Brazil in order to pay for his attendance at a military school, a common path to the middle class. Her salary in Brazil was too low to pay for the required uniform, but her remittances subsequently made his studies possible. And Washington, a refrigeration technician in Brazil who worked double shifts for five years in South Mills, left his children and wife in Brazil to pay for their education. He had dreams of becoming an engineer. "After they study, it will be my turn," he said. Another young man with whom I spoke was on the receiving end of such remittances until he reunited with his mother in South Mills. He stayed with friends in Brazil while his mother worked and recalled receiving school supplies and clothes from her during her five-year absence. These transnational migrants moved outside of Brazil to educate themselves and their children by remitting tuition dollars. They crossed borders in hot pursuit of their own and their children's education, a commodity whose value shifted in relation to the borders they inhabited and the papers they held. Education, including literacy, was linked for Brazilians not with assimilation but with mobility, pervading their motivations for moving and their plans for the future.

How Papers Certify Literacy

Despite their educational motivations and often relatively high educational attainment, Brazilians' mobility was often blocked by their ineligibility to attain two kinds of papers: nationally certified diplomas and immigration documents. To leverage their literacy skills for the upward mobility they desired, the Brazilians with whom I spoke needed papers.

The certification of their home-country education, literally their Brazilian diplomas and certificates of educational achievement, were often illegible to U.S. authorities, causing many to experience not upward mobility stateside, but downward. To offer again an incomplete list: Fábio's wife traded a teaching position in Brazil for that of housekeeper in the United States. Washington went from a respected trade to unskilled factory work. José, a nurse in Brazil, painted houses in South Mills. Paulo, an obstetrician in Brazil, was a nurse's assistant stateside. Sandra, who was a Portuguese teacher, labored in a South Mills factory. Márcio, a private detective in Brazil, cleaned cars. Rafaela, a nurse's assistant in Brazil, cared for the elderly. Renata, a federal employee in São Paulo, cleaned houses. Despite the advanced literacy skills they certified, educational credentials from Brazil failed to translate.

This downward mobility for migrants is a well-documented phenomenon. In early studies of Brazilian migration to New York in the 1980s and early 1990s, scholars highlighted migrants' disappointment that while in Brazil many *had* maids, in the United States they *were* maids.[11] Offering a different perspective on this phenomenon, Martes reports that Brazilian migrants are largely satisfied with their lower-status work, because they are able to buy more in the United States than they could buy in Brazil, leading to upward mobility if they returned. She notes that another happy consequence of migration is that in Brazil it is seen as chic to live in the United States.[12] But despite the cultural capital and economic capital that may accrue in the process of living in the United States, many expressed ambivalence, and often dismay, at their lower status.

This status, incommensurate with their educations, was often linked to problems with papers. What's more, in attributing their socioeconomic disappointments to lacking the proper papers, many Brazilians elevated the practical and symbolic value of papers for upward mobility. Consider, for example, Paulo. He had been an obstetrician in Brazil; and when I met him, he had been studying to pass his medical boards in the United States for ten years. He lived by himself in a small attic apartment (just above my Aunt Tequila's house) littered with medical books and unwashed dishes. So committed was Paulo to his medical studies that he often turned down work to spend more time with his books, often earning too little to fully pay his rent. An eager student of English, Paulo took advantage of multiple opportunities to enhance his literacy: browsing the academic book stores of nearby Brown University, engaging conversation partners, apprenticing with established doctors. He clearly felt he had taken a step down in the United States but was buoyed by the hope of retaining his former profession. Unfortunately, four years later, he continued to fail the boards, never gaining the professional standing he so earnestly desired. Or consider Renata. Renata was a federal employee in São Paulo, a prestigious position to attain, which she earned thanks to a top score on a competitive national test. Renata's high scores did not translate to an equivalent position in the U.S. context, however, and she found herself cleaning houses to support herself and her school-aged son. Respected and valued in a Brazilian market, Renata's and Paulo's professional certificates were illegible in the United States. The value of the training, test-taking, and other literacy resources that their diplomas certified depreciated once they crossed the border, necessitating new, difficult-to-attain papers to revalue them.[13] From Paulo's and Renata's point of view, it was not primarily incommensurate home- and host-country language and education that blocked their upward social mobility stateside. It was, instead, papers. It was in pursuit of a new, American paper that Paulo (in vain) exerted his academic energy, and it was in despair that she would never again achieve such a paper that Renata made a living cleaning houses.

Most of the people I spoke with did not try to regain the professional standing they had held in Brazil, because they lacked a more important kind of paper, the paper that allows one to legally work at all: a work visa or green card. Sandra, whose narrative opened this chapter, was attending a public GED class—not for her own professional advancement, impossible in the United States given her legal status, but to be able to engage more fully in the academic life of her daughters. Another undocumented participant, Juliana, who had worked in Brazil as a salesperson on commission, had begun work at a factory job, the kind often held by documented Azoreans. When she was asked to bring her social security card, she began to panic about handing over a forged document, so she quit the job to clean houses. Without legal papers, finding employment commensurate with Brazilians' educational backgrounds was nearly impossible.

Some undocumented migrants were able to make horizontal professional moves by owning small businesses, yet entrepreneurship still represented a move downward for many. José went from being a nurse in Brazil to contracting his services as a painter, a change he treated with ambivalence. He remarked to me that if he were in Brazil in his painting clothes, he would be considered lower class and not be well attended in stores or cafés. Here, he said, despite his appearance as part of the working class, he feels he is treated with respect. While sociologist Martes reads similar stories as evidence of migrants' overall satisfaction with downward social mobility stateside, I see these testimonies as registering discomfort.[14] For José, the difference between wearing nurse's scrubs and paint-spattered overalls was significant. One signals education and one doesn't. Another small business owner, Dominico, who did not reveal his legal status, served as a pastor in Brazil and in the United States opened a small store selling Brazilian specialty foods. Although he had no congregation in Massachusetts, he maintained his (high) social status as pastor by keeping a room in the back of his store for theological consultations, leading his store to go by the informal name of "loja do pastor," the pastor's store. He was able to mitigate a loss in social status by practicing his profession, even if for free. Even among these most entrepreneurial undocumented migrants, such as José and Dominico, and the best educated, such as Paulo and Sandra, downward movement in class status in the United States was nearly inevitable for those lacking appropriate documents.

If lack of papers could limit how migrants leveraged literacy education for mobility in the United States, it could also limit their very access to literacy education. For those who were too young to have professions in Brazil before moving, many could not continue the studies they hoped to when they arrived stateside: Neither Jocélia nor Graziela, both young Brazilian women in their twenties with a deep desire to learn English and graduate from a U.S. university, was eligible to take out loans to pay for college. For Jocélia, because undocumented status forced her into low-paying work, she needed multiple jobs to stay afloat and remit money to her mother, still living in Brazil, leaving neither time nor funds for further schooling. For older undocumented immigrants, their precarious employment situations restricted literacy access. For example, Celia, whose oldest son was deported twice, owed eleven thousand dollars to pay for his thwarted passage via coyote. She worked two jobs to pay this debt, often going straight from an eight-hour factory shift to her job at a fast-food restaurant (she changed into her uniform in the car). This punishing schedule left little time for

English, though when she finishes paying the debt, she told me, she hopes to take classes. That day might be a long way off, however, as at the time of our interview she was paying only the interest on her loan and had not begun to pay the principal. Similarly, Fábio noted that being undocumented restricted him to low-paying manual work alongside or under other Portuguese and Brazilians, limiting his exposure to English, and enforcing his dependence on an unscrupulous Portuguese-speaking boss. State immigration regulations, embodied in papers, essentially stripped literacy opportunities from these undocumented migrants—migrants who were otherwise education-minded and motivated, many of whom migrated to the United States in pursuit of educational goals in the first place.

Brazilians brought a wide range of literacy skills and credentials with them to the United States in the hopes that they could leverage them for social mobility. They found, however, that the difference between upward social mobility and downward social mobility rested only partly in their skills. Brazilians' skills and credentials had to be made legible to officials and employers stateside through appropriate diplomas and visas. Even if Brazilians' literacy skills were to translate into marketable skills stateside—and research in immigrant literacy suggests that homeland literacy repertoires can and should be profitably built on—they often could not leverage such literacies for upward mobility without papers. For these purposes, their literacy was only as valuable as the papers that attested to their value. In this context of political disenfranchisement, the Brazilian migrants who shared their stories with me sought to use their literacies not for assimilation but for social mobility—mobility that was blocked without the papers that certified them and their skills as legitimate, in the eyes of national bureaucracies.

Papers with Limited Literacy: Tracking Azorean and Azorean American Mobility

Consider, now, a different context, this time one in which literacy is restricted but papers are abundant, as was the case for many Azoreans and Azorean Americans in South Mills. This section details why literacy has not led to "assimilation" in South Mills for Azoreans and Azorean Americans. It tells the story of Azoreans' educational underachievement, describing how many have experienced the resulting stigmatized literacy practices as limiting their mobility, thereby increasing their reliance on papers as markers of legitimacy.

Much like for Brazilians, the goal of assimilation did not resonate for many Azoreans and Azorean Americans. In many ways, however, assimilation as a model fits Azoreans' experiences better than it does Brazilians'. As a group, Azoreans and Azorean Americans are more established, more readily seen as white, and more easily folded in to dominant narratives of European immigration and assimilation. Following this logic, for ninety years scholars have been calling for Portuguese American assimilation in Massachusetts, a process whose failure to be realized has led most to prescribe more and better literacy education. A 1923 ethnography of the Portuguese in Massachusetts, originally an inquiry into the unusually high rate of infant mortality in the community, pursued the following research question: Was Portuguese ignorance due to their illiteracy or the "Negroid" blood of the Azoreans?[15] So common (and apparently shameful) was illiteracy that many considered it impolite to ask a neighbor if he had read the newspaper the night before, for fear of exposing him.[16] Many early twentieth-century cohorts of European immigrants were less literate than is popularly imagined. But unlike other white ethnics, the Portuguese of southeastern Massachusetts continued to struggle educationally. In 1989 a report on the Portuguese of the area pointed out that it was "remarkable" that between 1909 and 1989 there had been no educational improvement for the group.[17] A follow-up study in 2005 reported that Portuguese rates of high school and college completion remained low, arguing that as the Portuguese improved their English language abilities and committed themselves not only to high school but also to college, they could assimilate.[18]

At the time of this study, assimilation via education, called for since 1923, had simply not come to fruition; many remained without the educational credentials they desired. Portuguese Americans in Massachusetts continued to underperform educationally compared to white peers: 22.7 percent of Portuguese Americans in Massachusetts had less than a high school diploma (compared to 8.1 percent of whites), 77.3 percent had a high school degree or higher (compared to 91.9 percent of whites), and 20.6 percent had a bachelor's or higher (compared to 40.9 percent of whites).[19] In the otherwise educationally saturated state of Massachusetts, the Portuguese remained locked out of the educational achievement that scholars and policy makers suggested would promote their assimilation. In sum, whether further education would facilitate assimilation was an open question.

In the meantime, however, pressing issues remained: Azoreans and Azorean Americans continued to lack access to education, a problem whose urgency, as readers will shortly see, was heightened by closing factories and high unemployment. In this context, those who spoke with me seemed unconcerned with assimilation. Rather, much like Brazilians, they described their educational hopes in terms of the mobility they needed both literacy and papers to achieve. In this process, the value of literacy and papers were recalibrated, both in relation to each other and in relation to shifting political, social, and economic circumstances.

"When We Came from There, We Just Worked, Worked, Worked":
Factories and Educational Attainment

Azoreans and Azorean Americans have long associated literacy with mobility, in ways that shed light on their legacy of educational underachievement and their relationship with papers. Due to the availability of blue-collar work in South Mills at the time of migration in the 1960s to 1980s, they often had to sacrifice literacy education for the upward mobility they came to the United States to pursue. This relationship reversed when, as factories closed in the 1990s and 2000s, many sought out and often failed to achieve the standard literacies they hoped would lead to employment.

Educational scarcity often began in the Azores. Many Azoreans in South Mills came from rural Azorean villages and left school after the fourth grade. Conditions outside Ponta Delgada, the Azorean capital, were often rustic at least until the late 1970s: no running water, no electricity, livings eked out through farming and fishing. Literacy resources in the Azores were equally humble. Public schools provided slates and chalk; the Catholic Church gave girls a missalette upon their confirmation; and a mobile library (i.e., a "book van") offered reading materials once every few weeks. Many described not having enough money for books: One participant recalled that her family was able to purchase their first Bible only after having moved to South Mills. Likewise, educational opportunities were often out of reach. To complete an education beyond the eighth grade, those from rural areas needed to travel to Ponta Delgada. To complete an education beyond high school, one would have to travel farther, to continental Portugal, an investment beyond the means of most. As an autonomous region of Portugal, nine hundred miles across the Atlantic Ocean from the cultural center of Lisbon, the Azores had few educational resources.

Upon arrival in Massachusetts, Azorean immigrants found educational resources scarce for a second reason: Often they worked instead of studied, earning a living wage in factories that did not require education. Nearly every Azorean I interviewed had either worked in the factories (in local parlance, the "shops") or had a close family member who did. Workers cut sleeves, packed cosmetic bags, rolled bolts of fabric, stitched curtains. While other white ethnics, such as Poles and French, worked in the factories prior to the 1960s, the Portuguese soon became the majority group, earning a reputation for their "Portuguese work ethic"—a stereotype of a hardworking manual laborer that one second-generation Azorean American told me was the nicest thing anyone ever said about the Portuguese while she was growing up in South Mills in the 1980s. More than a cultural trait, however, hard work was born of necessity. One participant had wanted to go to school to study to be a nurse, but she pointed out that when she arrived, "It was not the time to do that . . . To go to work, yeah. Of course. To school, no." As another said, "When we came from there, we just worked, worked, worked." Even those who arrived in the United States as children often left school for the factories. "Because I was young, I couldn't go to the machines," explained one woman who left school as soon as she legally could, in eighth grade. Her job instead was to cut threads. Others who left school in subsequent decades followed a similar trajectory. The availability of well-paying factory work ultimately depressed Azorean education in the United States.[20] Migration, undertaken to climb out of poverty circumstances, ultimately resulted in attrition and underachievement.

The consequences of attrition differed for the generation who came of age before the recent decline of the factories, and for those who, in their prime working years at the time of data collection, were facing under- or unemployment. The retired people I interviewed often earned a living wage in the factories, usually without a high-school diploma, often without English, and sometimes without basic literacy. That is, they accomplished what they had hoped to with their migration, essentially sacrificing literacy education for mobility. For example, one retired woman, who arrived in South Mills in the 1960s and remained monolingual in Portuguese at the time of our interview in 2008, told of going directly to work in the United States doing "piecework," stitching pockets and sleeves that she was paid for by the piece. Having made a living in the Azores selling corn and home-made wine, within five years of piecework in the United States she and her husband were able to buy a three-tenement house, including one apartment for their family and the other two to rent. The factories may have blocked educational attainment, but at least they offered a livelihood.

Among members of this generation, those who attempted to study instead of work not only lost income, they also paid an interpersonal price. Anthony, who immigrated to the United States at age seventeen in 1963, had attained a student visa, which his relatives stateside be-lieved he was going to use to work, not to study. But he had other plans:

> I couldn't understand the sort of pressure I was getting from my relatives here . . . Their idea was you gotta go to work, I don't know why you're going to school, where none of them went to school. For them, work was the norm . . . The same thing happened in the community. In other words, who's this guy who's going through higher education? Because at the time most of the people didn't even finish high school, much less go through higher education.

Anthony could not escape the factories altogether, though. The institu-tion he attended, with the sponsorship of a local Portuguese priest, was a textile college. Overall, the presence of the factories made choosing to study instead of work such an unattractive option that a well-known adult education program, SER Jobs for Progress, found that one way to keep the Portuguese in school was to offer families money to par-tially replace lost salary if their children turned down paying jobs.

While it is perhaps predictable that upon arrival many first-generation immigrants went directly to work, more striking is that the presence of the factories also depressed the educational attainment of many second-generation Azorean Americans. More than a stopgap measure for new immigrants who needed transitional work, factory work became an integral part of pulling one's economic weight in a Portuguese American family with modest means. Joanne, a second-generation woman in her mid-fifties, left school in the tenth grade in order to help her parents:

> I was sixteen. My mother told me I could stay in school. She didn't tell me I had to leave. She said no, no, you can stay in school until you're eighteen. And you know maybe you can get a little part-time job in the summer, but

I just felt guilty staying in school when I could be working. So I left school at sixteen and I went to work in a shop that made sweaters . . . I think it's just something that, you know, it's just drilled in to you, you need to carry your share of the load. Your part as well.

This notion that doing one's part meant physical work, and that education was *not* work, pervaded participants' discussions with me about their educational histories. If "hands-on, blue-collar work" was available, in the words of a second-generation young man who idolized the work ethic of the Portuguese "old-timers," staying in school was often seen as indulgent, and even for some a threat to class-based claims to Portuguese-ness. Doing one's "part," carrying one's "share of the load," engaging in "hands-on work"—these words, spoken with pride, equate blue-collar work with the community survival that trumped education.

In this labor context, the community pressure to work also entailed gender-specific educational sacrifices. The domestic labor that made a twelve-hour shift possible often fell to the daughters—who were sometimes kept from completing homework because of time-consuming domestic responsibilities, such as cooking, cleaning, and child care. When asked if she did any reading and writing after school hours, Tina, the second-generation Portuguese American woman whose story opened this chapter, replied, "The only thing I did after school, my love, was clean the house. It was nuts, I'm telling you. It was clean the house. My mother used to work a twelve-hour shift. It was make food for my father, and take care of my sister, and make sure my brother's lunch is ready." While Tina at the time of our last interview worked as a caregiver for an elderly woman, when she left school at fifteen she, like her mother, went to work in a factory that is now closed. The gendered domestic work that underwrote factory work, in other words, also detracted from educational achievement.

These educational sacrifices mattered, financially speaking, less for older generations, for whom factory work provided the mobility they sought in the United States (as readers have seen).[21] For those of working age at the time of data collection, however, factory jobs were becoming more and more difficult to find, making education more crucial for the upward social mobility for which many hoped. A rash of factory closings that began in the 1980s culminated in 2007, leaving thousands without work and devastating the city. While many had made the difficult choice to sacrifice education for mobility in the boom years of factory growth, they now faced a different economic reality as factories closed. The conditions of deindustrialization and the new information economy demanded investment in literacy education.

Such a shift proved difficult for many, as the stubborn promise of well-paying blue-collar work persisted, continuing to detract from educational opportunity. Such was the case for Timothy, a second-generation Azorean American man in his thirties who started his career in the factories. Having completed high school, he was able to work his way up from the factory floor, where he weighed and carried reels of fabric, to an office, where he entered data on a computer. Like other workers, he was laid off when the business closed its doors. He subsequently enrolled in a state-sponsored program to gain advanced computer skills, with the goal of improving his prospects. But when the factory temporarily reopened and he was called back to work with the promise of a dollar more an hour, he quit the computer-literacy program and returned to his job. A few months later, however, he was laid off again, this time having forfeited his chance at a free education. As he put his reaction, "I could have kicked myself." Timothy's situation in 2008 recalls the concerns voiced by anthropologist Donald Taft in 1923: "Is the educational problem [of the Portuguese in New England] to make 'educated' people love to tend looms? Or is it to make them dissatisfied with the cotton mill, and if so, who is to tend the looms?"[22] Factories benefited from a pool of available labor, though the Azoreans and Azorean Americans who staffed factory floors appeared to no longer benefit from employment with them, particularly as layoffs continued.

To this end, in place of factory work, many laid-off South Mills Azoreans often attended state-sponsored education programs, with the rationale that advanced literacy skills would help them secure employment. This investment may or may not bear fruit, as many would require years of schooling to attain rare professional-sector jobs. Consider Gloria, an Azorean woman in her forties, who was taking GED classes at the time of our interview. She showed me an essay assignment, whose goal was, tellingly, to practice the past tense to describe her former job:

> I used to work at [the large textile manufacturer that has since closed]. I was a machine operator. It took me a few weeks to learn that job. In the beginning it was hard, but after it was ok. Since I was more or less experienced.

I got lay-off. First when I got there, I had to punch my id card and after we
did five minutes of exercises, I checked the machines. I inspected all the
fabric. I had to see if I ran with the right color and the right design. That
was my job, but I can't explain it better than this. Now I have the opportunity to be in school to learn English and again it's very hard for me to
learn English. I try very hard.

In the margins of this essay her teacher had written, "You're doing
very well . . . Great job description!" But Gloria's essay is more than
a simple job description. It is a narrative of a professional trajectory
that emphatically does not show increasing stability and professional
status. Rather, Gloria's description of her career path works backward.
It begins with Gloria being "more or less experienced." It is then punctuated by the shortest, most poignant sentence of the essay: "I got lay-
off." Finally, it ends with Gloria in the position of a novice attempting
to learn English, a goal yet to be accomplished: "Again it's very hard
for me to learn English. I try very hard." Yet Gloria and I conducted
our entire interview in English (she saw it as an opportunity to practice). What was hard about learning English "again" was that Gloria
had not mastered the elusive English held out as the key to attaining
jobs that did not exist. The factory boom that for decades employed
immigrants from the Azores in southeastern Massachusetts had not
been replaced by other industry—and even if it were, it was uncertain
whether the kind of literacy skills certified by a GED would offer
entrance into their doors.

Limited resources in the Azores coupled with regional labor conditions in the states conspired to weaken the educational attainment
of Azoreans and their descendants in South Mills. For earlier generations, work's payoff for mobility was greater, and education cost what
many could not afford. But for those of working age, further economic
mobility necessitated further educational attainment—attainment that
remained out of reach of many.

"Village Talk": Consequences for Mobility

As a result of the limited educational attainment described above,
many Azoreans and Azorean Americans told me they lacked fluency
in standard English and Portuguese literacy. Lacking the privileged
national literacy did not necessarily call into question their similarity to or difference from other Americans, as assimilation models suggest. Instead, it made many worry about their ability to move through

institutions associated with the nation, anxiety that readers will later see was partly alleviated through appeals to papers.

For many, literacy's relationship to the "nation" mattered not primarily culturally, as it does in theories that suggest English literacy leads to national assimilation, but instead bureaucratically. Consider Manuel, a middle-aged Azorean American who arrived in South Mills as a teenager in the late 1960s. He told me he was "possibly illiterate." In the Azores, he often skipped school, with the village priest in hot pursuit on his moped. He arrived in the United States at age twelve after brief stays in Bermuda and Canada, two other common destinations for Azorean migrants, where his family worked in agriculture. In the United States, Manuel went to middle school briefly, leaving in eighth grade for a job in the factories. He worked in maintenance at the time of our interview, owned a house, and had a family. When he had to drive somewhere for his job, he navigated by recognizing the first letter of street names. And when he was watching TV and something printed appeared on the screen, he asked his wife to interpret. On a pragmatic level, then, his possible illiteracy did not block him from participating in popular culture, the economy, and social life. His limited literacy, however, did prevent him from freely moving through the civic institutions of the nation. He told me he feared being called for jury duty, during which he imagined he would not be able to read the documents put in front of him. "That would put me in a corner," he said. In impeding bureaucratic participation, his limited literacy, Manuel imagined, would leave him trapped.

Likewise, many described how limited English literacy impeded their mobility in schools. David, a 1.5-generation Azorean immigrant in his forties, felt behind in school because of his Portuguese: "I didn't go to preschool or anything. I went right to kindergarten. And when I went, I only knew how to speak Portuguese . . . I always felt like I was behind because I had to learn from the beginning." Although David reported using Portuguese and English in both his work and social life, in his narrative Portuguese made him vulnerable to bullying and held him back educationally. Like Manuel, David turned to a metaphor of mobility to express the relationship between Portuguese language literacy and institutional demands, describing being "behind," unable to catch up.

For these reasons, for many, Portuguese retained associations with educational underachievement and marginalized status, causing some

Azorean Americans to attempt to reject Portuguese outright. Such was the case with Tina. In a discussion of whether she spoke Portuguese with her daughter, she told me the following:

> I stay away from Portuguese. . . . My mother gets so upset. I'm like, Ma, thank God, I had enough of that when I was living with you. Nothing, no, no . . . I don't care for it. I was around it all my life. And I want my daughters to live different.

Tina relegated Portuguese to the world of factories, immigrant parents, and what Tina described as her confining childhood, where she cooked and cleaned instead of studying and playing. Restricting her from the "different" life that she hoped her daughter would lead, Portuguese became the language of a difficult and limiting past, whereas English became the language of a wider, "different" future.

If for Tina and David Portuguese seemed to inhibit movement through schools, for others it limited mobility among larger social circles. Such was the case for Manuel, whom readers encountered above. He described his Azorean Portuguese dialect, in comparison to dialects from the continent or from Brazil, as regional, local, and limiting:

> M: It's just village talk, like the way your parents talk. You know, they talk and nothing's really like school. . . .
> K: But do you use it to communicate? Do you use it on a regular basis?
> M: Portuguese? Oh yeah. Because some of the Portuguese around here. Some of them are like village talk and all that. And some are educated Portuguese and all that. But to understand what they're saying, some words you might not, but you get away with it. They understand what it is. They know automatically that I'm village talking and they're not.

"Village talking" encapsulates a logic in which rural Azorean roots, educational limitations, and marked class status are intertwined, conveying marginalized status in the very pronunciation of particular words.[23] Whereas Manuel imagined other varieties of Portuguese would allow wider movement, village talk was located in a limited geographical space, the village.

This association of Azorean Portuguese with the circumscribed locale of the "village," as opposed to other, more mobile varieties of Portuguese, was repeated even among those who had taken Portuguese in school—an activity that research suggests often helps heritage language speakers value their language and ethnicity.[24] For example,

Timothy took a Portuguese class in high school in order to "broaden everything, a lot more that maybe I didn't know of. . . . Because the way I speak Portuguese and the way my relatives speak Portuguese is kind of like a slang version of Portuguese." Timothy wanted a Portuguese that could reach wider than his "slang" home dialect. Likewise, Joanne saw her Portuguese as limited to home and village: "I can still remember the very first word that turned me on to the fact that my parents and grandparents didn't speak correctly." She ultimately challenged her mother's pronunciation of the word in Portuguese. "So I showed her my book. And she said you know . . . you're right. This is the correct way to say it. But you know we grew up in the *village* and this is how we say it" (emphasis mine). The conflict between school and home was settled, then, when Joanne's book trumped her mother's Azorean Portuguese, rendering it "village talk." Joanne put Azorean Portuguese in its place, aligning with the language promoted by the institution of the school, one that promised wider mobility outside the ethnic enclave.

Until the recent economic decline, "village talk" sufficed in South Mills for the purposes of many, who could conduct their social and work lives locally and in Portuguese. As one participant described the conditions surrounding her elderly mother's lack of English literacy, "By the time we got here [in 1969], they already had built the Portuguese community. It was already built . . . They had feasts, so they had the Portuguese church, if they wanted to go . . . The *missa* [mass] was in Portuguese. [My mother] had a profession. She did everything. . . . She became very satisfied because she encountered things that were just like in the Azores." As a result of what migration scholars call deterritorialization—a process by which the social life of one territory is unhinged from its geographical location and reproduced elsewhere— Portuguese was used on the factory floor, in places of worship, in stores, in banks, in hospitals, in restaurants, on the street.[25] Far from feeling isolated, many first-generation migrants participated in robust social lives without ever learning much English, except for a few choice phrases. One woman, whose family member I interviewed, worked her whole adult life in the United States and, according to her daughter, only knew one English word: sonabitch, as in *"aquel* sonabitch!" (that there sonabitch!). But as factories closed, working-age people needed more than one or two useful phrases to accomplish the upward mobility they desired.

As economic conditions in South Mills changed, so, too, did literacy standards.[26] As an Azorean woman who had lived in the United States for forty years and did not speak much English said, "For me it's good to know how to read and write in Portuguese, but for young people it's worth it to learn English." As readers have seen, those of working age, such as Manuel, Tina, David, Timothy, and Gloria, agreed. Deindustrialization put a new premium on literacy and education, precisely the resources that had in the past been unnecessary, and in fact *withheld*, as Azoreans and Azorean Americans toiled in local factories, worshipped in local churches, and socialized with families that often lived in the same three-tenement apartment buildings.

Perhaps, for many South Mills Azoreans and Azorean Americans, literacy has not led to assimilation because it has been withheld from many or because those who have achieved higher educations have left South Mills. What was clear from my interviews and observations, however, was that migrants did not primarily associate literacy with assimilation. Like Brazilians, Azoreans and Azorean Americans hoped to attain and leverage literacy to alleviate more immediate concerns, namely un- and underemployment, as the factories that depressed education levels in South Mills closed, one by one. In this context, many working-age Azoreans and Azorean Americans associated non-standard literacies—as useful as they had been for older generations to simultaneously pursue upward mobility and participate in local socioeconomic circles—as circumscribing their movement through school and state, beyond the economically and educationally struggling Portuguese archipelago of Massachusetts. For those who "village talked," such mobility appeared out of reach. It was in this context that papers, as textual objects that promised mobility, came to matter more profoundly.

Papers and Privilege

Thus far this chapter has offered an overview of South Mills Brazilian and Azorean and Azorean American educational trajectories, through the lens of the literacy practices and literacy products that alternately facilitated and compromised their attempts to reach their goals. To recap, for Brazilians, lacking the right papers devalued their literacies, threatening their upward mobility.[27] Azoreans' upward social mobility was also threatened, but for different reasons. Educational attainment was withheld from Azoreans in line with regional labor needs, leaving many underprepared for new employment and with nonstandard literacies that they experienced as parochial and limiting. For both groups, papers took on a heightened social power, symbolizing the social status and promising the mobility that was otherwise threatened by stigmatized language and literacy practices (in the case of Azoreans and Azorean Americans) and political disenfranchisement (in the case of Brazilians).

In light of their legacy of educational underachievement, Azoreans often reinforced their social position through their papers, a literacy resource that set them apart from undocumented groups. Papers allowed Azoreans and Azorean Americans a kind of mobility often denied the undocumented: as citizens or permanent residents, they populated the immigration office, hospitals, police force, schools, and banks. As Brazilian migrant Rafaela noted, "There is always someone who speaks Portuguese." She mentioned that when she needed to go to the hospital, the majority of nurses were "Portuguese or the daughters of Portuguese, who speak a little Portuguese," who facilitated her communication with doctors. Likewise, Brazilian migrant Fábio described how during a car wreck, the police officer called to the scene was a Portuguese speaker, as were two witnesses, who told him they would testify that he was not at fault. Thanks to their legal papers, Azoreans and Azorean Americans were police, witnesses, and nurses, circulating in realms of officialdom.

Across the terrain of shared language and different legal status, Azoreans shored up their papers, as members of both groups scrambled to attain the upward mobility that, for different reasons, eluded them. Legal status allowed some Azoreans to assert superiority over other newly arrived groups with whom they shared an uncomfortable linguistic similarity, leading to intergroup discrimination—not surprising, given the racial status of Azoreans as "not quite white," South Mills' economic depression, and the longer history of colonization that animated their relationship.[28] A snapshot of this complex context appeared in the form of an editorial cartoon in *O Jornal*, the newspaper serving the Portuguese readership of the South Mills region (Figure 1). The cartoon depicts the manager and cook of a Portuguese restaurant.[29] The manager says to the cook, "Maria, no more potatoes and fish, now we sell cassava root and Brazilian bean stew." *Chicharros*, small fish popular in the island of São Miguel, and potatoes are staples of the Azorean diet, just as bean stew characterizes typical Brazilian food. In the cartoon, Maria's eyebrows furrow in a horizontal line. Both a question mark and an exclamation point are pictured above her head in a thought bubble. The cartoon leads readers to believe that Maria is Portuguese and has long been serving fish and potatoes to clientele in South Mills. Yet this fish-and-potatoes tradition, symbolic of this established ethnic enclave, is disrupted by a new culinary tradition, a new economic reality, and a new group of Portuguese speakers, whose popular culture takes delight in mocking the fish-loving Portuguese, all of whom seem to be named Maria. Without reading too much into the cartoon, I want to note that cassava root and Brazilian bean stew originate in the African communities of the northeast of Brazil, a nod to the Portuguese role in the shamefully

Figure 1. In this cartoon, a Portuguese waitress shows dismay at catering to Brazilian customers. Drawing by Jota; courtesy of O Jornal.

vast Brazilian slave trade. And here is Maria, descended from colonists, serving descendants of the colonized on U.S. soil, where both groups labor under literacy ideologies that have promulgated racial abuse throughout the twentieth century.[30] One young Brazilian woman, Jocélia, put her relationship with the Portuguese in the following, telling terms: "I always lived in houses owned by Portuguese, because they have been here for quite a bit more time than Brazilians have. I think that they almost colonized [South Mills]. Just like they colonized Brazil, they colonized the U.S. There are no Americans here. Only Portuguese!" Or as another Brazilian woman, Renata, put it, "We're not in the U.S. We're in the Azores." Jocélia's and Renata's words speak to an assimilationist ideology by which Americans are defined as white and English-speaking. Such ideologies reverberated across these two migrant groups, yoked together by a violent history of colonization, one of the results of which was a shared stigmatized language.[31]

Disparate legal status reinforced these ideologies. As Brazilian-born Rafaela remarked, "But it's not the Americans who discriminate. I have noticed that it's not the Americans. The Americans are nice, treat you well, try to help. It's the very Portuguese who become *naturalized* Americans and become ashamed of their language." Whether Portuguese speakers in fact discriminated against Brazilians more than Americans did is a question beyond the scope of this study. Important here is how, in light of language tethering these groups together as inferior to "Americans," legal status differentiated them, perhaps allowing Azoreans to bolster what some have called their "fragile whiteness" over and above newly arrived Brazilians.[32] For Rafaela, the status of many Portuguese as naturalized—that is, having been born elsewhere but achieved citizenship papers in the United States—interacted with their linguistic and educational marginalization.

In this multiethnic and economically strapped environment, legal status—concretized through legal papers—seemed to compensate for many Azoreans' and Azorean Americans marginalized literacies. Tina, whose anecdote opened this chapter and who, as readers have seen, struggled with attaining standard literacy, told me how she disliked the way Brazilians spoke Portuguese, a theme that came up repeatedly in discussions with both groups, members of which sometimes even claimed they couldn't understand the members of the other. She laughed when she recounted her friends' comment upon seeing a group of Brazilians: "No green cards here." If Tina, and other Azoreans and

Azorean Americans like her, faced regionally specific impediments to educational attainment that blocked their mobility, they at least had green cards and citizenship papers with the promise of mobility etched on their surfaces, partially alleviating their social exclusion. Papers certified belonging in a context where belonging was in question. They promised social mobility in a context where many felt stuck.

In fact, in my interviews, it was only in conditions of unusual privilege that papers did *not* seem to carry such social heft. Consider here one Brazilian and one Azorean example. For Brazilians, perhaps only racial privilege and native-like fluency in English could mitigate papers' hold on literacy's value. I met one undocumented Brazilian woman, Maria Clara, who spoke English fluently, had a European phenotype and blonde hair, and acted unafraid of officials. For these reasons, she explained, she had never been asked for documents for a job. And as jobs for the undocumented go, she had had a series of good ones, as an administrative assistant in various local firms. Still, her modest monthly income meant that her standard of living in the United States was lower than it was in Brazil, where her father had been a prominent public official. In a limited way, she had "assimilated" via English literacy, perhaps not to the American Dream, but to an American reality in which lower-middle-class employment often barely covers expenses. But even such compromised social mobility was not available equally to all Brazilian immigrants, who did not share her racial privilege.

Likewise, consider how advanced literacy attainment among the Portuguese in South Mills could override the need for papers to certify national belonging. Lavinia, a middle-aged bilingual journalist, emigrated from the continent of Portugal as a teenager, where her father owned a bookstore. She spoke, read, and wrote privileged dialects of Portuguese and English. She had permanent resident status, meaning she could freely enter and leave the country, could work, and could drive but could not vote, a privilege reserved for citizens. "My kids have been bothering me to get my citizenship papers for years," she told me. Lavinia already had the privileges that Americanness promises: She worked at a stable job and commanded professional respect. Moreover, her literacy practices—standard, widely understood—traveled, offering her transnational mobility within communities of English and Portuguese readers. What more could citizenship offer? Compared to Manuel, whose possible illiteracy trapped him in a "corner," Lavinia's literacy allowed her an expansive, transnational, and *mobile* notion of where she belonged. In the privileged position of an educated transnational writer, papers could be an afterthought. Likewise, for Maria Clara, while she would have liked to legalize her status, her racial and linguistic privilege allowed her to successfully negotiate the dangers of being undocumented.

But for most Azoreans and Brazilians in South Mills, for different reasons, papers were front and center. In a context of educational, economic, and political injustice, in which home literacies were institutionally and economically stripped of material worth, members of both groups valued not only literacy but also the papers that could certify those literacies or stand in for them when they were lacking. The symbolic weight of papers and literacy shifted in relation to each other and in relation to the larger social conditions in which migrants swam, promising, sometimes symbolically, sometimes materially, and sometimes both, the mobility that many migrants I spoke with had been denied. People did not look to literacy and papers for cultural assimilation. Rather, they clung to them to help them get ahead, in otherwise unpromising circumstances.

Rafaela: A Tourist Visa, Two Crossings, and a Wedding

Readers have seen how literacy and papers interact to mediate migrants' goals for a composite of South Mills Brazilians, Azoreans, and Azorean Americans. I close this overview of the South Mills educational landscape with an extended narrative of Rafaela, an undocumented Brazilian migrant whose experiences exemplify many of the trends I've broadly documented here. Her story makes clear the consequences of papers and literacy for mobility, both across borders and within them.

Two factors influenced Rafaela to migrate to the United States: the national news and the need to pay for her son to go to school. Watching a news show in Brazil about New York, Rafaela's mother exclaimed of the Americans on TV, "Do you see that? All colorful, all red, from eating good meat!" Rafaela, mother of four and aged sixty at the time of our interview, took a good hard look. "They showed the American life, and even my children remember this, I said, 'One day, I'll go to America.'" She had been working as a nurse's assistant in a local hospital in Rio, cleaning houses on her days off, and selling cosmetics on the side. All this, and she couldn't both pay her mortgage and eat, never mind pay for her youngest son to attend college. When she heard that an acquaintance was headed to the United States, she asked her for help arranging work. Like other participants described in this chapter, she undertook migration to accomplish the upward social mobility that included the education of her son.

Her first step on her journey was to travel to the U.S. consulate in Rio de Janeiro to apply for a tourist visa. To receive such a visa, would-be tourists usually have to prove that they have money in the bank, family members who need them in Brazil, and/or property in Brazil—a supposed guarantee to immigration services that they will not overstay. Rafaela had older teenage sons and no money in the bank. In fact, she could barely afford her Brazilian passport, which she needed for the application process. Her family and friends tried to persuade her not to waste her time and money applying. But Rafaela told them, "I'm going to get a visa. I'm going to get a visa. Do you know why? . . . Because it's not them [the Americans] who are going to give the visa. It's God." Sure enough, Rafaela, with no money in the bank, no property, and no husband to keep her tied to Brazil, was granted—either inexplicably or miraculously, depending on your point of view—a multiple-entry, ten-year tourist visa. She was on her way to the land of the red-faced Americans.

Despite this auspicious beginning, Rafaela misinterpreted the visa, leading to a devastating string of events, all tied up in the relationship of literacy and papers to both physical and upward social mobility. A multiple-entry visa generally means that one can enter the United States legally for periods of ninety days but then *must leave again* for at least ninety days. That Rafaela's visa lasted for ten years meant that she was allowed, in the next ten years, to visit for periods of time lasting no longer than three months. Rafaela mistakenly assumed, however, that she could stay in the United States legally for ten years. Under this assumption, she rented an apartment, got a job working for and living with an Azorean American woman who ran an in-home care facility for the mentally ill, and began sending money back to her youngest son so that he could continue his studies. When her son fell sick, she took a six-week leave of absence from her job to visit him in Brazil. On her return-trip layover in Miami she had a rude awakening. Due to her misunderstanding of the U.S.-authored visa rules, she had overstayed her visa and was deported back to Brazil.

Her misinterpretation of visa rules—and ultimate deportation—indicts both her English literacy skills and her lack of appropriate papers. To delve more deeply into the literacy event of deportation, the intended audience of Rafaela's tourist visa was not Rafaela, the migrant, but instead other bureaucrats and border guards, who shared and enforced similar understandings of a ninety-day multiple entry visa. The literacy of the bureaucrats and border guards was much more heavily underwritten than was Rafaela's; indeed, they were compensated for it. Rafaela protested that she held a different understanding of the ambiguous terms of her visa. But such protestations held no water, because she was not a reader of the visa, but instead was *read* by it. In other words, she could not negotiate the competing meanings evoked by the text of her visa because she was not the audience for the visa, but instead was its object. The text represented her body and the geographical location that it could or could not inhabit. Perhaps her body, racially marked as Latin American, was also being read at the moment of deportation. Her visa colluded with instances of individual racial discrimination, abstracting these events into the realm of bureaucratic rule, under the conditions of which, Rafaela, as a Latin American, could stay within the United States only for a limited time, not long enough to claim it as a home. Her reading of the card (her interpretative literacy practice) was trumped by papers (literacy products) that rendered her not an equal dialogic partner in the literacy event, but instead an alien subject to forcible deportation.

Labeled an illegal alien, Rafaela was sent back to Brazil. Desperate to continue earning money to provide for her son's education, and with no possibility to attain legal papers, she turned to her employer for help, who lent her $8,000 to pay a coyote to make the dangerous trip on foot across the Mexican border back into the United States. To pay off this loan, she became an indentured servant for eight months; $1,000 of each monthly $1,600 paycheck was remitted to her employer. Such conditions speak to the interplay of literacy and papers in the upward mobility Rafaela desired but could not achieve: One could argue that during her servitude her literacy skills were useful—she leveraged her nurse's assistant background in Brazil to read prescriptions and accurately administer drugs to patients. Yet such usefulness was limited. Without papers, she felt she could not appeal to the law, find another job, attain more marketable skills, or remit the money to her son that he needed for his studies. She was on call twenty-four hours a day. Her employer, Rafaela told me, would not even allow her to take time off to go to English classes, worried that she would learn English and leave the job. In this context, her literacy could not lead to cultural assimilation. Assimilation was not on her agenda. She needed papers—immigration papers—to escape.

She achieved this longed for mobility when she left her job, having fallen in love with a South Mills Azorean American man, Humberto, a retired factory worker in his sixties, who proposed to her and planned to legalize her status through marriage. In fact, he naturalized as a U.S. citizen for that express purpose. He had never learned English, having made a living, like so many others, in the factories. Because of his age, and his longtime residence in the United States, he was able to take his citizenship test in Portuguese, and now proffered his abundance of papers to his fiancée: "You need documents?" he said jokingly to Rafaela during our interview. "Here, I have two." He put two social security cards on the table, one old card and one newly minted as a result of his recent citizenship test. "I'll take one, and you can have the other," he said. For his part, Humberto evinced not a sense of cultural assimilation to the United States, but rather a pragmatic orientation to the national bureaucracies that demanded papers. Through the logic of family reunification laws, he could share the privileges of those papers with his future wife, who would likely become a permanent resident. With papers, she planned to continue her education, in order to become a nurse's assistant in South Mills.

Rafaela's story had an ostensibly happy ending. Wedding bells would ring in South Mills! Nonetheless, her narrative highlights the unjust grip of literacy and papers on many migrants' lives, and the vulnerability of transnational migrants without sufficient literacy or sufficient papers to attain the mobility that the United States, at least in the images it broadcasts across national borders, would seem to promise. Rafaela had sufficient English literacy to work productively and to be such a valued (or discounted) employee that her employer lent her thousands of dollars to make the life-threatening trip back to the United States. Once reestablished at work, however, Rafaela did not have the sufficient papers to escape a deeply exploitative position, nor to further her education, until she was able to appeal to another institution, that of heterosexual marriage to a U.S. citizen, which could provide the papers that would, she hoped, unlock the potential of her literacy for further upward social mobility.[33]

Papers, Literacy, and Mobility

Papers and literacy, in the lives of those with whom I spoke, chased each other. Papers could imbue individual literacies with value, making them legible to U.S. employers and to the state that regulates employment. Without papers, homeland literacies often lay underutilized and host-country literacies often remained out of reach, complicating many migrants' education-driven quests for upward social mobility. Papers underwrote, and sometimes stood in for, other meanings and potentials of literacy: literacy as a marketable skill, an individual resource, a social practice, or a marker of social status. In the trying economic and political conditions of South Mills, the way people experienced the *practice* of literacy depended greatly on how they experienced those ubiquitous *products* of literacy—papers—and vice versa.

For migrants, who were moving from one "literacy regime" to another, both practice and product had to be in place if literacy was to have any chance of fulfilling its promise as a catalyst to upward social mobility.[34] Literacy, scholars have shown, does not do much as an independent variable, but interacts with countless variables in its social context to have particular effects.[35] Put another way, for literacy to be useful, it must be accompanied, its power unlocked, by a host of other sometimes seemingly unrelated factors.[36] In the context of South Mills, the key factor was papers—textual objects which promised not assimilation into a national culture, but movement through powerful national bureaucracies.

The way that literacy and papers mediated migrants' goals in this community reflects larger, national trends, as evidenced by their ubiquitous presence in immigration policy.[37] Consider immigration-reform plans forwarded under George W. Bush and Barack Obama. In the summer of 2007 President Bush called for a two-tiered system of immigration, in which those immigrants with a high level of education, including English fluency and literacy, would be eligible to apply for permanent residence. The other tier would include a temporary-worker program, in which those who could not earn enough points through literacy and other means would work in low-wage jobs for two years at a time, for up to three two-year stints. Applicants would leverage their literacies to earn papers that would provide them entry to particular class positions. This version of immigration reform never passed, yet new immigration reform with striking similarities would be proposed in the next administration. In 2012 President Obama announced that the United States would cease deportations of undocumented people under the age of thirty, who arrived in the country before the age of sixteen, and were attending school. These particular migrants were seen as distinct from other classes of migrants in part due to their educational attainment, including English literacy. Much like in Bush's plan five years prior, this group's papers, certifying they had the appropriate literacy education within the United States, would allow them more mobility than presumably less deserving migrants, who would continue to face deportation.

Much like for those in this chapter, in these plans literacy and papers interact, both serving as coarse yet expedient filters of who stays and who leaves, of who does the clean work and who does the dirty work, of who gets to move up and who stays put. Following this logic, papers can symbolically mask educational underachievement, offering proof of belonging and a ticket to move, as in the case of many South Mills Azoreans. And following this logic, literacy without the papers that certify it is not a literacy that is worth much economically at all, as in the case of many South Mills Brazilians.

These experiences redefine outdated notions of literacy's relationship to assimilation. Becoming culturally similar to groups within a host-country populace, that old goal of assimilation, was not on the agendas of Azoreans and Brazilians. This is not to say that Azoreans and Brazilians disliked the United States, wanted to leave, or hadn't settled in. Azoreans, as a longer established and often quite patriotic group, were entrenched in their stateside community, and many Brazilians hoped to find ways to stay. Yet in the interviews I conducted with Azorean and Brazilian migrants, literacy accumulated associations not with cultural assimilation, as is often thought, but with the bureaucracies that regulate mobility. Migrants hoped to leverage the often-limited literacy resources at their disposal—both their practices and their products, both their literacy educations and their papers—for social and economic mobility. Institutions, such as the state, the school, and the workplace, mediated this mobility through a combination of requiring particular literacies and demanding particular certifications through papers. In this sense, migrants practiced literacy not in the service of national ideals, but instead to achieve social and economic success for themselves and their families. Few held lofty sentiments about a national language and literacy. Instead they had more practical concerns: What will I have to know and what certificate will I have to present in order to move up? Literacy practices and literacy products, their value calibrated and recalibrated in relation to one another, were exchanged, in a way best described as sociomaterial, for mobility.

Unlike "assimilation," "mobility" anchors migrants to pasts shot through with movement. Most spoke in detail and at length of their migration journeys, which for some meant running scared across a desert in the dark and for others meant witnessing the thrilling electric lights of a Boston night sky as their plane landed. For many, the moment of crossing a border turned their narratives, changing what happened afterward. The fact of migration followed them inside the United States, as participants leveraged what they had for what they could get, for where they could go, and for whom they could bring along. As readers will see in the rest of the book, at every step of the way these travels were negotiated via papers and literacy. For example, one migrant entered the United States via the Mexican desert because she had been denied a visa on five separate occasions and wanted to reunite with her husband. Others, who were legally documented within the United States, issued official documents to sponsor family members to join them. The young, for their part, longed for diplomas to reach the goals their families brought them to the United States to achieve. Migration organized participants' lives, and papers organized migration. Papers suffused migratory pasts, shaping migrants' understandings and uses of literacies in the present, and their dreams for future mobility.

For this reason, when I asked in interviews about literacy *practices*, participants often called attention instead to the literacy *products* that resulted from or otherwise shaped their practices—the diaries, personal letters, school essays, driver's licenses, poems, official documents, diplomas, certificates, sermons, time sheets, job applications, songs, and visas that entered into their lives or remained out of reach. These texts were exchanged, guarded, displayed, gestured with, held close to bodies, and urgently desired. Papers carried a heavy load in their lives, both materially and symbolically. Materially, they were indispensible for everyday interactions. Symbolically, they became associated with the regulatory bureaucratic realms in which they circulated.

In this chapter's overview of Brazilians', Azoreans', and Azorean Americans' literacy experiences in South Mills, readers have seen *that* papers and literacy interacted to facilitate or prevent migrants' mobility. But *how* precisely did papers come to hold such profound value in immigrants' literacy lives? The next chapters answer this question by examining the literacy histories of documented Azoreans and Azorean Americans (chapter 2), undocumented Brazilians (chapter 3), and finally documented and undocumented young people (chapter 4), further developing the theory of sociomaterial literacy that chapter 1 has, in broad strokes, posited.

2 "AMERICAN BY PAPER"

Azorean and Azorean American Literacy Lives

MY AUNT TEQUILA, with whom I lived during my field research, is "a paper person."[1] I would often come back to my aunt's house after an interview or observation to find her seated at the large table on the porch, surrounded by newspapers, magazine articles, scratch paper, her calendar. The papers seemed to grow from the table, to flutter organically around her body. They were her research. She read about weight loss, poverty in Central America, spiritual healing, and new recipes, clipping articles here and there, jotting things down for friends and family. She often looked at me, in her view a real researcher, wistfully. The opportunities I had, the privilege of writing papers. Then she would get on the phone, set up an interview for me, ask me about my findings, offer some commentary, make some notes, file them away. She had learned to read and write Portuguese as a girl in the Azores, was punished for writing on church doors, learned English when her family migrated to Bermuda and then Canada, and finally settled in Massachusetts as a teenager, where she left school to work in the factories, later completing her GED and a technical degree. Her literacy practices and accomplishments were married to literacy's incarnation in papers: the U.S. passport, the diplomas, the articles and notes that flowed into and out of her house, creating, in writing studies scholar Charles Bazerman's words, their own seemingly irrefutable "social facts."[2]

Here, for example, is her response to a question I asked her about when different islands on the Azores got electricity and running water. She asked my uncle to scan it for her, send it to me, then return the paper copy to her (Figure 2).

My aunt's jotting reveals how papers can maintain primacy even in a digital age. In fact, digital technology facilitated her accumulation

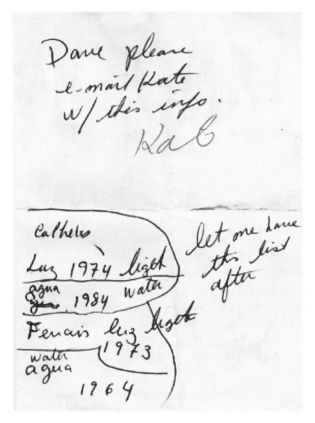

Figure 2. In this biliterate note, Tequila indicates that she would like the paper copy to be scanned and returned to her. Photograph by the author.

of papers. She did not have to send this note in an envelope through the post. It could be scanned and promptly returned to her files. For my aunt's purposes, moreover, the materiality of the paper seemed to matter even more than the language in which it was written. Penned in Portuguese and English to an audience with differing levels of biliteracy (herself, my uncle, me, posterity?), the note moves between languages, what scholars have called "translanguaging."[3] But my aunt did not emphasize language. She was entirely casual about her biliteracy, having scribbled "water" near "agua," where she found some space. The translation was an afterthought. What took precedence instead was the paper. She wanted it back.

Like my Aunt Tequila, other documented Azoreans and Azorean Americans spoke to me of papers, the most prominent of which were the papers that underwrote their transnational mobility and national belonging. When I asked about their literacies, they described personal letters that maintained transnational familial ties, the official forms that plea for legalization, and the written tests required to naturalize. Papers, immigration papers in particular, mattered for Azorean literacy not because Azoreans lived in fear of deportation, as did many Brazilians with whom I spoke.[4] Instead, papers mattered for Azoreans because the literacy-saturated process of attaining them was married to migration paths that for many had defined their lives. In other words, they wrote to attain the papers that offered them and their families transnational mobility.

In this chapter, I trace this process across Azoreans' migration histories: from writing letters to recruit immigrants, to issuing official letters of invitation for legal family reunification, to taking tests in order to naturalize, to writing to achieve papers for an "alien" relative. Coordinated via the state infrastructures that regulate migration, this constellation of high-stakes literacy practices imbued papers with symbolic capital in migrants' lives and literacies. Papers became sedimented with the social meanings of mobility, regulation, and belonging, meanings created as participants wrote within state infrastructures to facilitate migration.[5] As a result, papers spoke. *I belong,* they said *I am legible. I can pass.*[6] Given the legacy of limited literacy in South Mills, such associations rang loudly. They emanated from papers' otherwise mundane functionality, connecting meaning, matter, and literate action in a way I have come to think of as sociomaterial. Here I extend research on literacy's materiality to show how literacy practices and literacy products can be imbricated in the larger (bureaucratic) systems of power that manage migrants' lives.[7] For many Azoreans, the state underwrote the consequences of individual literacy practices, lending literacy products high value. In this way, people wrote to attain papers, a process at every turn mediated by the state, and a process in which families, lives, and livelihoods hung in the balance.

I first show here how writing transnational letters formed a social and material practice that helped recruit new migrants to the United States; then how such practices were subsumed by the state, which issued official documents for legal family reunification; and finally how the privilege of having such documents demanded more writing. This often painstaking leveraging of literacy for papers, and papers for literacy, did not result in assimilation, but rather came to be thickly associated with migratory pasts and hopes for future mobility.

Personal Letters and Transnational Souls

I begin here with personal letters, the sociomateriality of which, I later show, becomes co-opted by state practices that promise papers in exchange for literate work. In our conversations together, South Mills Azoreans mentioned letters more frequently than any other genre— the excitement at receiving them, the ritual of reading them, and the process of writing them. Letters repeatedly surfaced in accounts of families' literacy and illiteracy, of who wrote, who read, and who was written for and read to. As they have for other groups in different points in history, letters served as a meeting place on paper for those separated by wide geographical distance, a "social location for the staging of relationships."[8] And as they have for other groups, writing letters also helped Azoreans offload some of the emotional excess associated with separation.[9] For many Azoreans, letters were sociomaterial. They were social, in that their composition and interpretation were integrated into long-standing cultural practices. And they were material, in that they served as an efficient technology of communication under conditions of distance. Unlike bodies, letters relatively easily, rapidly, and cheaply moved, uniting families on paper and recruiting new migrants to the United States. Through letters, literacy came to be associated with transnational movement. Here I describe letters' sociomateriality, and in the next section show how this sociomateriality became significant in Azoreans' literacy lives, when letters interfaced with the state to produce immigration papers.

Letters, for many, were paper repositories for writers' "souls." They served as an antidote to the *saudade*, the missing or nostalgia, caused by separation. Teresa, an eighty-year-old retired factory worker and her daughter, Sofia, a fifty-six-year-old nurse's assistant, who had immigrated to the United States in the late sixties, recalled the following:

> s: [The letters to the family were] very big. It was like somebody writing a book, because then you said everything. It was their way of, um, it's like a psychiatry thing.
> t: *Contava tudo.* [We told everything.]

s: Every, every word. They would write um . . .

к: All the details?

s: Very detailed.

т: Every day, I [would say], "I go to the yard, see the flowers . . ."

s: Or . . . "Things aren't well, I'm not living well."

т: Or . . . "Today [I'm] so tired."

s: Very detailed, the letters.

т: [And] the letters to me, "Oh, [Teresa]!"

s: The letters back would be so emotional. Like you don't know how it felt to listen to you . . . So it was always emotional letters. Even though they were happy, because it was very um . . . was that *saudade*, know what I mean? When they have *saudade*, you know that? And it was like very detailed in those days. It's not like that anymore. But in those days that was the only communication, so they said their soul. They emptied their soul.

In their conversation with me, Teresa and Sofia emphasized the emotional catharsis made possible by letters' materiality. In filling the pages, in writing a "book," they were availing themselves of the "only communication" medium of "those days." They were packaging their intimate experiences, attempting to package *themselves*, in a neat envelope that would travel, tentatively bridging the physical distance between friends and family. Letters transported souls, because they were materially able to do so.

A letter that Teresa allowed me to use for this study exemplifies how the paper technology of the letter served as a transnational meeting place. Teresa was one of the few participants who, despite cheap international phone calls and the availability of the Internet, continued to write letters to Azorean friends and family. Having emerged from a coma the previous year, she almost immediately resumed letter writing, a habit of intimate connection that for her dated back to her girlhood in the Azores. (She recalled hiding in her family's outhouse to write surreptitious love letters to her boyfriend, who lived on a neighboring island. She would send the letters without her mother's knowledge by borrowing money for postage from her brother.) She showed me a recently composed letter to her Azorean childhood friend who was living in Canada at the time of our interview. The two-page letter ranged in topics: from constipation, to news of buying a new stove, to memories of going to mass together in the Azores along a road traveled by cows, to what she would have for dinner, to declarations of love for her friend.

Here is a short excerpt, of which I've translated a piece (Figure 3).

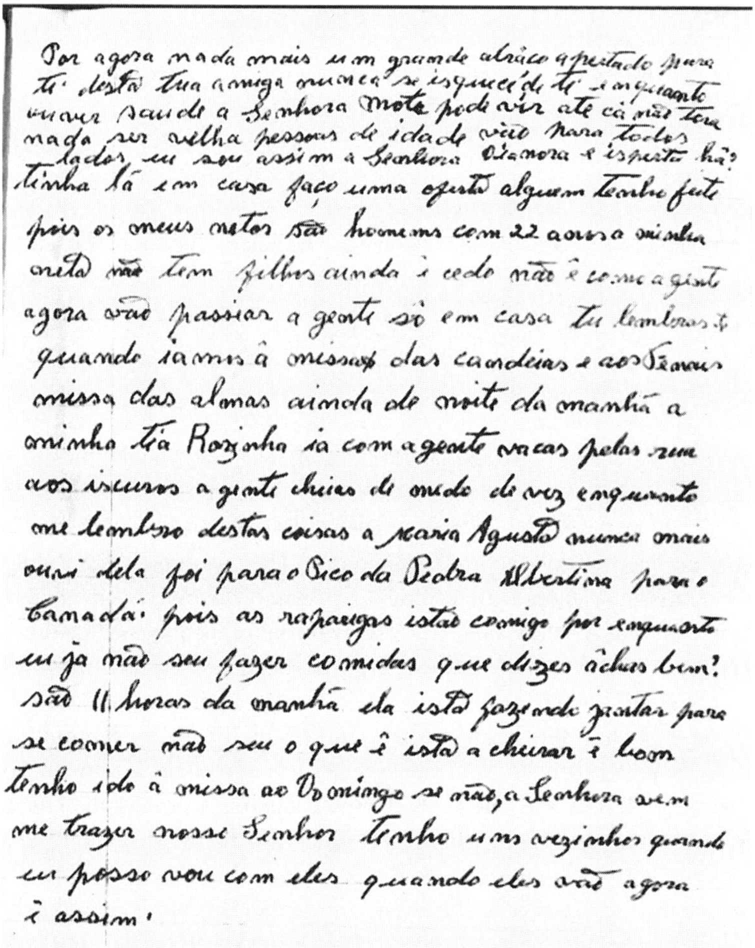
Por agora nada mais um grande abraço apertado para
ti desta tua amiga nunca se esquece de ti enquanto
viver saudade a Senhora Mota pode vir até cá não tem
nada ser velha pessoas de idade vão para todos
lados eu sou assim a Senhora Leonora é esperta há?
tinha lá em casa faço uma oferta alguém tenho feito
pois os meus netos são homens com 22 anos a minha
neta não tem filhos ainda é cedo não é como a gente
agora vão passear a gente só em casa tu lembras-te
quando íamos à missa das candeias e aos Fermais
missa das almas ainda de noite da manhã a
minha tia Rozinha ia com a gente vacas pelas rua
aos escuros a gente cheias de medo de vez enquanto
me lembro destas coisas a Maria Agusta nunca mais
ouvi dela foi para o Pico da Pedra Albertina para o
Canadá pois as raparigas estão comigo por enquanto
eu já não sei fazer comidas que dizes achas bem?
são 11 horas da manhã ela está fazendo jantar para
se comer não sei o que é está a cheirar é bom
tenho ido à missa ao Domingo se não, a Senhora vem
me trazer nosso Senhor tenho uns vezinhos quando
eu posso vou com eles quando eles vão agora
é assim.

Figure 3. In this letter, Teresa "empties her soul" to her friend. Photograph by the author.

> . . . you remember when we went to the mass of the *candeias* and to the *Fermais* mass of the souls it was still the night in the morning Aunt Rozinha went with us cows on the road in the dark and we were full of fear once in a while I remember these things Maria Agusta I never heard anything else about her she went to Pico da Pedra Albertina to Canada so the girls are with me for now and I still don't know how to cook what do you say you think it's good? It's 11 in the morning and she is making dinner to eat I don't know what it is it is smelling good I've been going to mass on Sundays if not the lady comes to bring me there . . .

The rich scope of subject matter—past, present, mundane, and philosophical—seems designed to allow Teresa's friend to participate in her inner life at the very moment of composition, as if Teresa wanted once and for all to close the irritating distance between them. Punctuating this desire, the letter concludes with an invitation: "As long as you have your health, perhaps you could come here it's nothing to be old people of age go everywhere." Letters, of course, travel more easily than do "people of age." For Teresa, their lightness, their ability to fold up into an airmail envelope, mitigated the physical challenge of distance, seeming to compress space and time into the neat two dimensions of text.

For Azoreans, letters maintained relationships not only by virtue of their technological materiality, but also because they were tied up in financial remittance exchanges, whereby they accounted for goods and money sent home. Letters I was able to view in the Ferreira–Mendes Portuguese American Archives at the University of Massachusetts Dartmouth attempted to account for the reception of other objects: I have sent a T-shirt and a money order. Please send word. Have you received it? Letters enmeshed the economic and the interpersonal, accounting for the remittances that justified such a drastic act as migration.

These circulating technological and economic objects contributed to the idea of "the better life" that Azoreans overwhelmingly told me inspired their journey to South Mills, serving as a recruitment tool for new migrants, again evidencing how literacy's sociality and materiality interacted in the transnational movement of both people and literacy. David, a forty-year-old delivery person who emigrated from the Azores as a small child, remembered his mother sending letters and packages to his cousins who still lived in the islands:

> My mother would send one of those big barrels with clothes, shoes, all kinds of stuff, paper napkins . . . The sisters, they would open it up and share whatever clothes fit the kids, and they would share everything . . . Yeah, it's a big deal down there, because it's all nice clothes . . . You send them the good stuff. Over there it was expensive to buy a pair of jeans. They couldn't afford to go buy jeans.

The packages accompanying immigrants' letters to the Azores, filled with "the good stuff," accentuated (and sometimes exaggerated) potential changes in standard of living made possible by migration. They traveled more cheaply than did people—though people often preceded them and, as readers will see in the next section, followed them.

Such a purpose, to recruit new migrants, has historical precedent: In the early twentieth century, a report by the Bureau of Labor on Southern and Eastern European workers confirmed that immigrant labor was being "effectively distributed" by the international post.[10] Accordingly, Russian Jewish immigrant and memoirist Mary Antin describes the letter she received from her father in the United States, inviting the rest of the family to join him. In his letter, "there was an elation, a hint of triumph, such as had never been in my father's letters before. I cannot tell how I knew it. I felt a stirring, a straining in my father's letter . . . My father was inspired by a vision. He saw something—he promised us something. It was this 'America.' And 'America' became my dream."[11] The letter described the "America" of which Antin would become a part. Or as various Azorean participants put it, before emigrating they harbored the notion that the United States was "paved with gold," that it promised "a better life," and that the simple "name of America" was enough to motivate them to emigrate—notions that circulated in part through letters written from family members abroad.[12] When Arjun Appadurai coined the term "media-scape" in 1996 to describe a globally dispersed imaginary that recruits migrants, he was not thinking of personal letters.[13] But for earlier waves of migrants, and for Azoreans living in the Azores when radios were a rare purchase, when only the relatively well-off subscribed to newspapers, and when the Internet hadn't yet been invented, letters accomplished the same end. Or put differently, letters were part of an earlier media-scape.[14] They entered into homes, projecting life and people elsewhere in a particularly inviting way.

Letters may have been especially powerful recruitment tools in part due to the way they were taken up as part of everyday social practices. Literacy's materiality and sociality united in letters, as they formed the center of family rituals. David recalled that letter reading was a family event:

> I remember getting the letters in the mail. Because they're all excited when they get it. "Oooh," you know, "Look, it came." They opened up the letter and started reading it. My mother would read it aloud to my father. That way they can both be there and share it. She would read it all the time to him, and I would sit there and listen. . . . And if my father wasn't there, she would wait. "Oh I'm gonna wait till your dad gets home." And she'd put the letter, wouldn't open it, and would wait until he got home. I remember that clearly. Because she would read it right after dinner. She'd wait until after dinner and then she'd read it.

The letter arrived, with the aroma of elsewhere or back home, and was saved, like dessert, for after dinner. Others described similar family rituals. One woman, for example, told of her illiterate grandmother running to their house with letters in hand to be read aloud by her mother. In being read aloud, letters assumed a central place in families, who could experience the Azores in a communal literacy event that worked to reestablish the family as an Azorean entity.

Like in other social practice accounts of literacy, letter writing was subsumed into other cultural practices, such as a gendered division of labor. Women bore the primary responsibility for maintaining the paper "meeting places" of letters. Almost all the Azoreans and Azorean Americans I interviewed recalled the writing and receiving of personal letters, yet not one research participant could recall a man writing a letter. To quote Anna, who arrived in the United States when she was four years old, "My dad wouldn't write. He would only sign his name to things. My mom did most of the writing to her family back in St. Michael."[15] As a literate manifestation of what feminist transnational theorist Uma Narayan critiques as the historic responsibility of women as culture bearers and what Rhacel Parreñas calls transnational mothering, the letters that Azorean and Azorean American women wrote upheld close connections across an ocean.[16] Like cooking or sewing, letter writing came to be a practice marked as female. Imbricated in existing social relationships, letter writing also reified the terms of these relationships, playing both a social and material role in daily life.

This discussion of letters may seem retrograde. According to the accounts Azoreans shared with me, the frequency of letter writing slowed in the late 1990s with the arrival of cheap international calling cards. And at the time of the study, many wrote e-mails, as did Brazilians, who also made use of video chat and social networking sites to communicate with family and friends, both distant and local. The presence of these new(er) digital materialities, however, did not diminish the role of paper communication in migrants' literacy pasts. Instead, as if by contrast, it further accentuated it, demanding a sociomaterial understanding of literacy that could account for how material and meaning interacted across the distance that separated migrants from homeland family members.[17]

Here, I have described how the material affordances of the transnational literacy technologies that preceded (and coexist with) the

Internet—letter writing—acted on migrants' experiences of literacy as socially and materially linked to migration. For many Azoreans, these associations among literacy, papers, and mobility were reinforced as they leveraged their literacies to write another kind of letter—an official invitation letter that promised legal family reunification in the United States. If personal letters recruited immigrants, official letters legally sanctioned their migration, imbricating literacy's sociomateriality in the state bureaucracies that regulate movement.

The *Carta de Chamada*: Letters and the State

As Azorean and Azorean American communities became established in South Mills, letters became more than transnational meeting places and/or intimacy-laden material artifacts. Here I expand research on literacy's materiality to show that letters also interacted with the state to promote family reunification.[18] The practice of writing, reading, and sending letters, *cartas*, was subsumed into state requirements to issue another kind of *carta*, an official letter of invitation that paved the way for legal migration of a family member. Both people and state organizations traded on letters' sociomateriality, heightening the meaning and valence of papers in Azoreans' literacy lives. By virtue of literacy's materiality, people and their writing practices became entangled in larger bureaucratic structures, with consequences for their lives and families.

Under family reunification laws in place since 1965, legal U.S. residents and U.S. citizens can petition for family abroad. For Azoreans, these laws have resulted in chain migration from the Azores, in which, for example, a legal resident would petition for her husband, who would then become a naturalized citizen and petition for his siblings, who would in turn petition for their parents and children, and so forth.[19] Such petitions, in local parlance, were called *cartas de chamada*, literally "calling letters." Calling letters could only be issued by those the state deemed appropriate (i.e., legal residents or citizens). Likewise, the state determined whether the callee (the "alien relative") was appropriate for tentative inclusion in the nation. Without such approval, potential migrants stayed home, went elsewhere, or bore the risks of crossing illegally. With approval, they could come, creating transnational communities within the United States. The *carta de chamada*, in short, could accomplish what personal letters consistently attempted to do through their detailed descriptions: It could collapse the ocean. It could bring families together. In doing so, it further cemented associations of literacy's sociomateriality and state regulation of transnational movement.

Azorean migrants often cited the *carta de chamada*, and the aunt or sister who "made the *carta*," as the very reason for migration, linking papers explicitly to Azoreans' transnational mobility. Even many second-generation Azorean Americans, who were not born when their parents immigrated, knew the details of who issued the official letter, making possible their legal lives in the United States. Consider the following accounts of how this official letter united the families of the participants that readers have already met in this chapter: When I asked David, the delivery worker, if his parents had family here when he emigrated with them at age four, he remarked, "My father had his sister, which is the one that called us over." Similarly, when I asked Anna, who worked as a telecommunications customer service representative, why her family emigrated, she explained, "My parents came here because of my dad. My dad's family was all here. They all migrated years before, before they were even married . . . So his family sponsored us to come over." When I asked Teresa, the eighty-year-old letter writer, why she decided to come to the United States, she simply said, "Minha cunhada chamava." My sister-in-law was calling us.

That even second-generation Azorean Americans recalled the complex web of who issued *cartas* for whom emphasizes the centrality of this letter, and their resulting legal status, to their migratory pasts and subsequent U.S. lives. Jessica, an employee at the immigration assistance office in South Mills, described the following intricate chain of migration that ended with her birth as an Azorean American:

> J: My mom was actually single, and it was an aunt of hers who petitioned for my grandmother and the rest of the family. So it was my grandmother and my grandfather and my mom and all the siblings. It was actually my godmother who was the oldest. But she was already married so she was not able to come with my grandparents and the rest of the family. So that's how they became legal here.
>
> K: And what year was that?
>
> J: In 1968. My mom came over in 1968. Several years later my mom went back to Portugal and got married to my dad. And my mom petitioned for my dad, so my dad arrived here in 1972, beginning of '73, so . . .
>
> K: And you were born here.
>
> J: Correct, I was born several years later.

From the perspective of migrants, the *carta* in both its personal and official form contributed to the development of the Azorean community on U.S. shores. For many participants, without the transnational reach of personal letters, and without *cartas* in particular, Azoreans could very well have remained Azoreans, instead of becoming Azorean Americans.

Through the logic of family reunification, the words encased in personal letters' airmail stationary were bound to the plastic authority of the green card. *Cartas*, circulated through the transnational post office and the federal government, *called* migrants to the United States, serving as the crucial mechanism through which families were reunified. For many Azoreans, this was how the global movement of texts facilitated the global movement of people under the post-1965 legal regime. This dual function of *cartas*, to both emotionally and physically connect distant family, helps explain why for many Azoreans migration was so enmeshed in papers. Transnational literacy practices and products coursed within and across the infrastructure of the nation-state, constituting and reconstituting families and communities on U.S. soil.

These functions and meanings often merged, as papers leached associations with the process of legal migration. While passage across state borders is of course granted or denied through a variety of practices and materials, the people with whom I spoke experienced such decisions largely through the literacy practices that maintained transnational connections and that resulted in literacy products—that is, papers. This relationship is perhaps best described as metonymic: In the bureaucratic interactions that are routinely demanded of migrants, the concrete meant and acted as the abstract, papers stood for passage into the nation-state, promising family reunification and national belonging. With the issuance of a *carta de chamada*, families no longer had to empty their souls into written letters. They could look their sister, mother, or son in the eye and speak.

"American by Paper": Naturalization and the Legacy of Illiteracy

In the process of writing personal letters and issuing *cartas de chamada*, many Azoreans, as readers have seen, traded on literacy's sociomateriality, exchanging it for reunification papers, one technology of state-sponsored efforts to regulate migration. Such exchanges involved more than what might seem to be simple form filling. In the context of this community's struggles with literacy, the literate production demanded by the state involved difficult and time-consuming labor, further elevating papers' status as a form of symbolic capital for Azoreans and Azorean Americans. The result of such labor, as chapter 1 suggested, was not assimilation to an American ideal, but rather the papers that attested to a complex transnational history and that promised the bureaucratic power to move.

To offer a detailed look at how these trends operated in the life of one individual, here I narrate the experiences of Cristina, a naturalized Azorean American in her forties, who described how she leveraged literacy for papers throughout her entire migration process—from writing personal letters on the Azores, to receiving a *carta de chamada*, to passing a naturalization test, to playing a role in "calling" or sponsoring another migrant. Cristina had long struggled with literacy but nonetheless undertook the high-stakes literate labor of attempting to attain papers. Practicing literacy under these charged circumstances, Cristina became, in her words, "American by paper," not culturally assimilated into the United States but recruited, via literacy's materiality, into the national bureaucracies that regulate movement.

Even before Cristina's emigration from the Azores to the United States at the age of eight, literacy, for her family, was linked to mobility. Before their immigration, Cristina traded on the sociomaterial characteristics of personal letters that I described above, dictating to her mother the goods that she wanted her U.S.-based aunt to send to them on the Azorean island of São Miguel: "Yeah, I said like this: 'Mom, tell Auntie I want a doll. I don't have a doll. Tell Auntie to send me some clogs.' I love high heel clogs. I used to steal my mother's shoes. And my aunts used to send it to us. [My mom] used to write it on the corner. And she used to say, 'Ah, the girls are asking you for this and that.'" Her mothers' inscription on the corner of the letter collapsed clogs, dolls, and written words on papers that traveled transnationally, thickening associations between literacy and movement. She recalled that the same aunt that sent her family letters and packages with clogs when she still lived in the Azores petitioned for her family's migration. Her family came to South Mills, she said, "because my aunt was here. She has been here for fifty-three years. She called everybody here. I don't know how to say. They made the invitation. We came here legal. We came here legal. We had our papers and everything."

The personal letter her aunt sent worked to recruit her family to come to the United States, where clogs represented modern life. The official invitation letter that followed drew on the role of the personal letter but was mediated by the state, to facilitate Cristina's family's legal migration. Under the powerful sponsorship of U.S. laws, Cristina's family, in her words, "came here legal. We had our papers and everything."

Like the participants described in chapter 1, Cristina's family had papers but struggled with literacy. Her mother knew how to read, having completed the fourth grade in the Azores, but her father did not, a requirement for attaining citizenship. Of her parents' literacy, she said, "Yeah, she knew how to read. She went to fourth grade. But my dad, no. And she broke her head, broke her head, for him to learn how to write his name. Because he didn't know the alphabet. She had to teach him the alphabet first." The end goal of papers motivated Cristina's mother to "break her head" to teach her father to write his name. This kind of head-breaking literate labor was part of how papers came to take on such value in the Azorean and Azorean American community of South Mills, from whom literacy had been withheld. Papers required work.

Like her father, Cristina also had to work to develop the literate capacities required for naturalization. Similar to the participants readers met in chapter 1, Cristina's literacy development was curtailed by migration and by regional labor conditions. When she moved to South Mills, she cried in the corner of the playground because she couldn't speak English. She soon learned the language but would struggle with writing well into adulthood. Like many others, she did not finish high school, and instead opted for a job in one of the city's many factories, cutting curtains, turning over each paycheck to her father to help him pay for their house until her marriage at age twenty-one. Even though her literacy education was cut short, Cristina described little trouble with workplace literacy tasks, such as the record keeping required both in her past position in the curtain factory and in her current job as a caregiver to the elderly. Her difficulties with literacy also did not keep her in the dark about international politics: She watched the news on both the U.S. and Portuguese television channels. Moreover, for everyday literacy tasks, such as reading letters and filling out forms, she called her niece for help. Not well-off, Cristina had nonetheless found a way around her struggles with literacy to stay employed and informed. Her limited literacy attainment posed a problem not so much in her work or social life, but more prominently in her interactions with the state bureaucracies that regulated migration. Papers became a site of the literacy struggle that, born of the unique circumstances surrounding migration from the Azores to South Mills, continued to plague her efforts to establish citizenship.

For Cristina, to naturalize entailed a series of literate contortions. Her aunt's *carta de chamada* had given her permanent resident status but not citizenship. Permanent resident status allowed her all the basic rights of a citizen—to leave the country and return at will, for example—without the right to vote. After maintaining permanent resident status for a certain number of years, she could apply for naturalization as a U.S. citizen. Her desire to attain citizenship after having been a permanent resident signaled her stake in her host country. As Cristina put it, "I said I'm over here in this country. I listen to everybody taking their citizen papers. So why don't I try to take the papers? It's my country. I'm over here, it's been almost thirty-six years. At that time it was thirty-two or thirty-one. I don't remember. It was a long time. I'm over here so many years, why don't I try to take my citizen papers? I'm over here. This is my country. It's more than the Azores. I said I'm gonna try it." For Cristina, naturalization would legitimize the residence she had maintained for the majority of her life. Bureaucratically tethered to her journey to the United States through the *carta de chamada*, papers (her "citizen papers") symbolized the final step on her transnational journey.

The naturalization process, however, was anything but natural for this member of a community from whom literacy had been withheld. The citizenship test required paying a hefty fee ($675), reading sentences in English, writing dictated sentences in English, and orally answering civics and history questions in English. According to staff at South Mills' immigration office, many immigrants who would like to be naturalized wait until they have been in the country three decades and pass the age of fifty-five in order to be eligible to take the test in Portuguese. But Cristina was determined not to wait that long. She paid the fee, took the test, and failed it on *three* separate occasions. Of her repeated attempts to pass this test, she said, "I used to cry a lot. I used to cry a lot. Everybody comes up and they pass, and he never let me pass." The conditions surrounding her migration—an interrupted primary school education in the Azores, the availability of blue-collar

jobs in the United States, her family's need for another income—conspired to prevent her from reaching what would seem to be migration's
successful outcome: naturalizing in the country in which she had lived
for three decades.[20] In these failures, literacy became even more sociomaterially enmeshed in the process of migration itself, through which
state officials continued to demand more (and better) writing in order
to deliver more papers.

   She described her fourth and final attempt to naturalize as a literacy
event in which the potential communicative meaning of her writing
was overtaken by the paper such writing was meant to achieve. The
test question verged on the absurd, rendering irrelevant the meaning
of the words she produced: "[The tester asked] what color was your
car? That's easy. White. I wrote 'White. My car is white.' Then he
asked me for the American flags. I said everything, the stripes and
everything . . . He asked me the questions and then I had to write. . . .
He said, 'You wrote everything good.' He said, 'I don't know why
the other people didn't let you pass.'" Nothing about writing the color
of her car, the crucial sentence in her recollection, seems to suggest
fitness (or lack thereof) for citizenship. Immigration officials did not
seem to make clear why she passed when she passed or why she failed
when she failed. Her writing was deemed insufficient for citizenship
and then again sufficient, having been devalued and then revalued by
an inscrutable system. Rather than a piece of relevant information,
the meaning made through her writing appeared to be a kind of waste
product of the literate labor she expelled to achieve the paper. "I even
still got my paper. I don't know where it is, but I got it. That I wrote
all the words and I passed. He says you can even keep this copy. Yes,
they have to keep the original, so they know I passed." The result of
this literate process was not an assimilated American identity, but
rather the papers that certified she passed. As a result, Cristina experienced papers and literacy as bureaucratic tools that managed migration, just as they had since she was a girl.

   It makes sense, then, that even after the effort and expense of naturalization, Cristina did not identify as culturally American. As she
put it, "I'm American by paper, not because I was born here. So I'm
still an immigrant. I'm like [new Brazilian immigrants]. I just have a
piece of paper that I'm American . . . I'm not American. I just have
the papers by law." Cristina was American by paper, in that she had
intimate familiarity with the system that granted her Americanness

and had the legal papers to prove it. She was not culturally American, but bureaucratically American. She was American with the condition of papers granted by the immigration authorities who demanded her writing, finally judging it, on her last try, adequate to claim the United States as her home. Being "American by paper" highlights the contingent nature of papers, so deeply entangled in both unjust educational pasts and the uncertain legal processes of migration on which so much depends.

On the one hand, there was a top-down assimilative logic at work in this process, in which if Cristina could write that her car was white, her body could be represented by a paper stating that she was a member of the nation. State-sponsored documents, in the words of passport theorist John Torpey, "impose durable identities."[21] Or in the words of political scientist James Scott, documents make identities "legible" to the state.[22] When proof of particular kinds of literacies is required for documents—such as in the literacy tests that maintained a racist quota system in pre-1965 migration law, or in the naturalization test that Cristina and many others fail—literacy and papers are bound together in an assimilationist embrace. To read and write, to be read and be written. These are the textual means by which states quell the panic induced by difference.

On the other hand, despite her leveraging of literacy for what appears to be an assimilative use, Cristina emphasized not assimilation, but instead her migratory past and her immigrant identity. As she put it, she was still "an immigrant" and was "just American by paper," accenting again literacy's connection with bureaucratically circumscribed mobility. Her citizen papers, objects that she kept in her tidy second-floor apartment in a struggling section of a struggling city, embodied layers of associations with migration, mobility, and belonging. Much like writing activities and identities are "laminated," for Cristina so, too, were papers, as they leached the meanings and actions of migration.[23] The letters requesting U.S. clogs, the *carta de chamada* her aunt issued, her mother who "broke her head" to teach her father to write his name, her own attempts to naturalize—all these experiences with literacy, so essential to Cristina's migration, legal status, and sense of home—resonated from the material of paper itself. If this layering of significant migration activities with literate labor heightened papers' significance for her (and many others), it also resulted in her forfeiting a culturally American identity, as she exchanged the prospect of assimilation, becoming "American," for a more bureaucrat-ically inflected national identification, becoming "American by paper."

Calling, Notarizing, and Silencing

The connection between literacy, papers, and state only deepened for Cristina once she naturalized—a privileged rhetorical status that de-manded even more writing. To recap Cristina's process, she was first *written* as an alien relative of her naturalized aunt, who petitioned for her, which in turn allowed her to write her way into (an ambiva-lent) citizenship and, as readers will see in this section, call others. Put another way, the path to legalization entailed a silencing, as her status was written, and a sudden envoicing from a new rhetorical–bureaucratic location, that of citizen, as she wrote to call others. This section details this process from the perspective of three people with differing legal status: one naturalized citizen, Cristina, who helped "call" another; one second-generation Azorean American, Jessica, who notarized others' documents; and one Brazilian woman in the process of being "called" or sponsored, who was silenced. In demanding dif-ferent status-dependent genres of writing, the state agencies that man-aged migration became further imbricated in migrants' experiences of literacy's sociomateriality. As they wrote (or did not write) to attain papers, many came to see literacy as a tool used to comply with larger paper-issuing institutions.

Such was the case with Cristina. Her status as naturalized led to more high-stakes bureaucratic writing, as she wrote to help "call," in the form of officially vouching for, her friend Celia, a Brazilian woman in her fifties. Cristina and Celia met when she was sweeping the stairs of the apartment building where both lived. They greeted each other in Portuguese, and after several stairwell meetings a close friendship developed. Celia, who worked at both a fast-food restaurant and a local factory, had immigrated several years before. She left three chil-dren in Brazil, promising that after six months she would send for the youngest. But her undocumented status hindered their reunification, and Celia's six-month separation from her youngest son turned into five years. She ultimately found a path to legalization and to reunifica-tion with this son (though not her two other children, one of whom had been twice deported) through a marriage with an American man, who was her boss at the factory where she worked and whom she called her "angel." Under the family reunification clause, marriage is a path toward legalization, because once a potential immigrant marries an American citizen, the immigrant becomes immediate family of that citizen. That citizen can thus petition for the immigrant's legal status through a *carta de chamada*. This was what Celia planned to do.

Cristina, as a naturalized citizen and friend, became a natural ally in Celia's process. As Cristina said, "I'm attached to her, she's attached to me. We're good friends . . . Her problems are my problems. I try to help her so she doesn't get too, how do you say, frustrated with all these papers." She helped Celia complete the *carta de chamada* by interpreting between Celia and her husband (who had no language in common).[24] And Cristina also wrote an affidavit to verify the legitimacy of Celia's marriage.

Her naturalized status lent her both the knowledge and papers that writing the affidavit required. Still, much like passing her naturalization exam, writing the letter took multiple attempts, exacting time-consuming literacy labor:

> It took me two days. But I did it . . . I did a lot of mistakes, though! . . . I ripped the paper. Then I said, "Please, God, help me a little bit. This is for my friend. She needs it, poor thing. However I can, I want to help her. Please, Jesus, help me." So many mistakes, so many mistakes. A lot of people are so smart, and me, I want to be smart. I can't. I can't write. And I did and I did. And I put things together. Then I did it.

Cristina's passionate approach to the writing process reflects its importance during a time when immigration raids in the area had resulted in the separation of families and the deportation of many Brazilians, an injustice that she described as making her cry. So much depended on this process of writing that, for Cristina, seemed out of her immediate control. She wrote, ripped up what she wrote, littered the ground with paper, and called on God and Jesus for divine intervention. Writing for immigration purposes was both vital *and* seemingly impossible. As she poignantly said, "I can't. I can't write. And I did and I did." She can't and she did. For Cristina, writing was the price of her new status as naturalized. She used her status and her literacy to attempt to maintain, and even build, community in a world organized by national borders. That she understood her literate efforts in relation to papers further embedded literacy, papers, and the regulation of migration in her overall experiences of literacy. In fact, she measured her writing in papers—the papers she used trying to get the words right

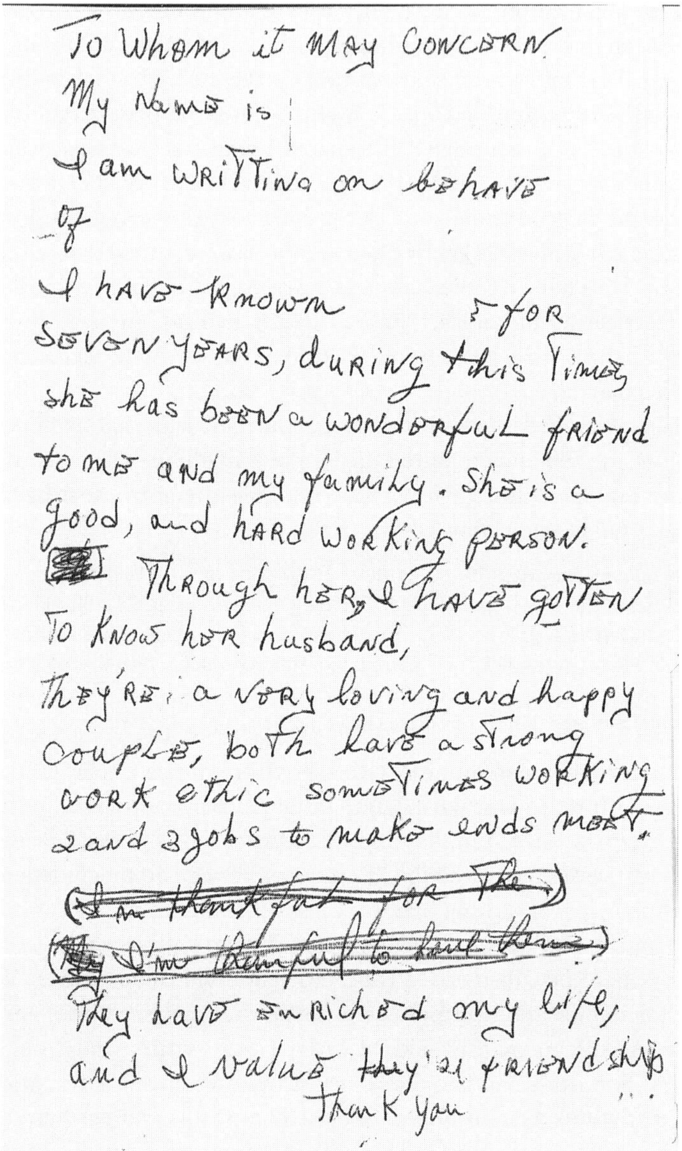

To Whom it MAy CONCERN.
My name is

I am WRITTing on behalf
of

I HAVE known
SEVEN YEARS, during this Time, for
she has been a wonderful friend
to me and my family. She is a
good, and hARD Working person.
Through her, I have gotten
To know her husband,
They're a very loving and happy
couple, both have a strong
work ethic somTimes working
2 and 3 jobs to make ends meet.
(I m thankful for the)
(They I'm thankful to have them.)
They have enriched my life,
and I value they'21 friendship
Thank you

Figure 4. Cristina's affidavit (with names redacted) exhibits both the difficulty of the writing process and her knowledge of the migration process. Photograph by the author.

in the affidavit and the papers that were to result from her efforts: "If you were to see how many papers I had on this floor! I said, 'Oh my God. But I have to do it. Because it's for a good cause and because it's for my friend.' She even started crying when I gave her the letter. She knows how to read a little bit in English. She said, 'Oh, it's so beautiful. Some words are so beautiful here.'" Papers were tied up in each stage of Cristina's writing. The social practice of literacy (writing to immigration services to help sponsor her friend) and the products of literacy (the papers that littered the floor and the papers she was hoping to attain) fueled each other. As a naturalized citizen with papers, Cristina wrote to call her friend, thereby producing more papers in compliance with the immigration regulations that manage who may write what at which stage of migration.

The letter's content reflects how papers and literacy became further enmeshed for Cristina in the process of writing the affidavit. As an American by paper, Cristina not only had the papers to be able to legally submit the affidavit but also the literacy knowledge to write it effectively (Figure 4).

By virtue of her American by paper status, Cristina knew that the official immigration authorities value the "good moral character" of potential immigrants, including their work ethic and their meeting of heterosexual familial norms.[25] Moreover, by emphasizing that she had known them for seven years, that Celia had worked during this time, and that they had "enriched" her life, Cristina also made use of her implicit knowledge of the importance of "continuous residence" in the United States and being "well disposed to the good order and happiness of the United States."[26] This letter marshaled Cristina's literate experiences with state assemblages; she knew how to use writing to get papers. To do so, she merged her interpersonal relationships with the bureaucratic definitions provided by the state, translating Celia's migrant body into a textually identifiable subject. Such is the literacy privilege of a naturalized citizen.

Even for some second-generation Azorean Americans, their status as having legal papers also compelled them to write, via regulatory apparatuses of the state, to facilitate others' migration, again compounding the associations of literacy, papers, and authority in the Azorean and Azorean American community more broadly. Consider briefly another writer whose legality was invoked in order to complete the *chain* in chain migration, Jessica, a second-generation Azorean American and a notary public in South Mills' immigration office. Readers will recall that earlier in this chapter Jessica recited a complex chain of official sponsorships that ended with her birth on U.S. soil, an American by grace of paper. Her educational trajectory was in many ways representative of the experiences of other Azoreans in South Mills that readers encountered in chapter 1: She reported "difficulty" when she started school. And when she started taking Portuguese classes in high school, she discovered that the Portuguese she spoke at home was a "slang." Still, she continued studying Portuguese through college, where she earned an associate's degree in business. At the time of our interview, she used her written Portuguese and English in e-mail interactions with her cousins on the islands, to help interpret for her parents, and in her job in the immigration assistance office, where she offered advice, translated, and notarized.

Just as Cristina's legal status allowed her to write Celia's affidavit, Jessica's legal status made possible her literate work as a notary public: According to Massachusetts' Revised Executive Order No. 445, a notary public must "reside legally or conduct business on a regular basis within Massachusetts" and "shall not use the term 'notario' or 'notario publico' or any equivalent non-English term in any business card, advertisement, notice, or sign."[27] Although one does not have to be a citizen to be a notary public, Governor Mitt Romney's executive order put the position of notary public within an exclusively English-speaking, legal-resident domain. As an American by paper, Jessica seemed to hold the almost magical gift of transforming a difficult-to-read divorce decree into an official document. Given the power to notarize, she could sign her name, stamp her stamp, and, voilà, certify documents for immigration officials. "I'm not certified in translation," she said, "but as long as it's something, I mean, I can read and understand it, we can translate it. And I'm a notary public, so that makes it an official document." Put another way, she leveraged her literate labor and her legal status to determine whether migrants held "satisfactory evidence of identification."[28] Much like Cristina signed the affidavit, Jessica signed her name alongside the notary stamp. Because of her state-sponsored rhetorical position, she could approve others' documents, inscribing immigrants' identities for the consumption of immigration services.

It is significant that even this second-generation Azorean American understood the risks of migration, the tentativeness of legality, and the importance of papers: "They don't have legal documents, a lot of them," she said of some undocumented Brazilian clients. "They don't have the proper paperwork . . . So they're always at risk that way." Such awareness of the inner textual workings of migration suggests that literacy's sociomaterial weight could be handed down, from migrant parents to second-generation children. If South Mills Azoreans struggled with a legacy of educational underachievement, they could also benefit from the legacy of a pragmatic, community-minded approach to papers. Those who could do so traded on their literacy and legal positions to achieve papers, for themselves and others.

Those who could not, however, were often silenced. I close this section with Celia, the Brazilian "alien relative" Cristina was helping to call. Though her future and her children's futures were at stake, U.S. immigration services did not ask her to write anything. In the context of such silencing, Celia perhaps perceived me, a U.S.-born university researcher wielding the technologies of bureaucracy (consent forms, a file folder, and a digital recorder) as somebody official who could advocate for her position. At the end of our interview, she departed from the narrative of her life in Brazil and her subsequent move to the United States to say the following:

> I don't want to leave. I want to die here! . . . And that God, that the Lord will bless that America will accept my son. For that I will be really happy. Because he really loves it here, too, and he's suffering there, poor thing. Just imagine, my son is here, the other is already here, and I will do the petition, in the name of Jesus, to get my citizenship for my daughter to come here. What could I want more? To continue my work peacefully, because I really like to work. And that on the day that God wants to take me, that I am here.

Being called subsumed Celia's identity under the official rubric of alien, even as it offered her the possibility that this status would change. Through the process of being called, Celia hoped to attain citizenship papers so that she could then call her children. In short, words penned or typed by the right person, with the right status, could be exchanged for the crucial papers that would abolish the distance between mother and child. For Celia, there was nothing more to ask— which is fortunate, because in her position there was nothing more she *could* ask, at least not officially.

Who writes and who is written, who calls and who is called, who is citizen and who is alien—these bureaucratic positions shifted, as people presented their literacy to the state, which issued or withheld papers.

Like the traditional Portuguese turn dance, writing begat papers begat writing. *Vira, vira, vira!* Turn, turn, turn!

Writing to Comply

The products and practices of literacy interacted in Azorean and Azorean American lives, as letter writing led to the *carta de chamada*, led to literacy tests for naturalization, led to sponsoring or notarizing or writing an affidavit, led to papers. Azoreans' and Azorean Americans' migratory histories were shot through with the exchange of literate efforts and literate outcomes among writers, readers, and state institutions. This constellation of high-stakes literacy activities and products, coordinated by a powerful institution that regulated transnational migration, caused many to imbue papers with the social meanings— legitimacy, authority, mobility—leached from the processes used to attain them. In its use by both bureaucracies and the people who engaged with them, literacy accrued symbolic capital, as a valued and often scarce resource and as a sought-after material object.

In this context, Azoreans and Azorean Americans wrote not necessarily to resist oppressive state structures, as many composition and education scholars would hope, but instead for more instrumental reasons, to comply with them, and in so doing to achieve the papers that facilitated migration and life as an immigrant. On the one hand, the blandness of identification papers, the seeming banality of writing to achieve them, does violence to the complexity of immigrant identity— identities rendered in rich nuance by many literary authors. Such is the argument of the elegant memoir *Passport Photos*, in which Amitava Kumar unpacks the lines of his identity card: name, birthplace, citizenship. The author recovers his identity by reanimating "name," for example, with narrative specificity, with its particular history and meanings. The result is a memoir that resists the reductive power of papers. In contrast, for the migrants this chapter has followed, writing and literacy were not primarily about negotiating identity or political resistance. More pragmatically, the people I spoke with used their writing, in ways both passionate and agentive, to comply with larger bureaucratic systems. Under trying educational circumstances they endeavored to achieve the papers that could authorize their migration, concretize their commitment to family and community, and promise a better future. No one presumed that papers or literacy defined their identities. Even when writers "emptied their souls" into letters, as did Teresa, writing was still also seen as a sociomaterial tool that, in the case of letters, traversed an ocean, and in the case of the *carta de chamada*, opened a legal path to migration.

In using writing as a tool to gain particular privileges, the migrants featured here distanced themselves from the longer history of assimilative uses of literacy, which would have them write themselves into culturally American identities. Instead, they wrote themselves into *bureaucratically* American identities. In this way, Cristina became not American, but "American by paper." Like Cristina, others wrote from prescribed bureaucratic positions and in complicity with state literacy demands in order to attain papers, those textual objects that certified and signified mobility. Papers mattered in Azorean and Azorean American literacy lives, then, because their matter reverberated with how history, community, education, and family were constituted in a tightly regulated migratory context.

Literacy here, then, is best understood sociomaterially, as a series of culturally and historically specific processes and material products, put into meaningful action by writers, readers, and powerful institutions, such as the state, which legislated literacy's consequences for important aspects of migrants' lives. For Cristina and others, being "American by paper" meant acknowledging that their literacy and migration histories did not have neat assimilationist ends. Instead, such histories were mobile processes, through which some of their most significant literate acts involved a kind of unequal co-authoring with mundane state agencies. For many Azoreans and Azorean Americans, whose documents peeked out of drawers, were stacked on tables, or rested inside wallets, papers carried these macrosocial meanings.

As readers will see in the next chapter, not everyone could legalize his or her status. For the undocumented, for those not *written into* but *written out of* the state, papers mattered for their literacies in different ways. If for documented Azoreans the state often mediated everyday literacy practices and products, for undocumented Brazilians who had little access to state institutions, another document-issuing bureaucracy acted on their writing: the church.

3 UNDOCUMENTED IN A DOCUMENTARY SOCIETY

Brazilian Literacy Lives

JULIANA, A BRAZILIAN WOMAN in her mid-forties, had been refused a visa on five separate occasions at an American consulate in Brazil, an eight-hour bus ride from her home. She wanted to travel to the United States to join her husband, from whom she had been separated since their son was a baby, for fourteen years. With no available legal route to migrate, she and her teenage son flew to Mexico. Under the guidance of coyotes, they made the dangerous trip across the Mexico–U.S. border on foot, during which she feared rape, drowning, dehydration, and starvation. When they arrived in a Wal-Mart parking lot in Houston, she and her son remained locked in a van until her husband paid the smugglers an appropriate sum.

Stateside in South Mills, Juliana remained fearful, this time of the law. Lacking legal papers, she was vulnerable to unemployment, deportation, imprisonment, and another familial separation. Of living undocumented in the United States she told me, "You live kind of frightened, you live worried . . . you can be here, and then you can be picked up there on the corner and be sent home with empty hands to Brazil. . . . I needed a false social [security number] to work [at a local factory]. I never did it, because I was afraid." The fear accompanying Juliana's political disenfranchisement centered, for her, around papers. To illustrate her lack of documents during our interview, Juliana took out her wallet. She first displayed her expired Brazilian driver's license, describing her anxiety about driving, an activity forbidden to the undocumented yet necessary to accomplish everyday tasks.

Then, to my surprise, she extracted a missionary card. The word "Missionária" was printed at the top, her smiling photo ID in the middle, and the name of her congregation at the bottom of the document.

She shared with me the following: "Today for the honor and glory of God I'm a missionary. I did the chaplain's course here. I don't go to American places to pray for Americans, because I don't speak English, but if there's a Hispanic that understands Portuguese well or a Brazilian, a person who understands my language, I have the *liberty*. Because I have my license. It's all *legalized*, understand? And I can go." Unlike Cristina, whom readers met in the last chapter, Juliana could not take a test or write the appropriate words to attain legal papers. Instead, she took a chaplain's course and achieved another kind of paper, a missionary card. This document, in her words, conferred liberty, legality, and mobility, many of the same privileges symbolized by state documents (though without the government enforcement that state documents enjoy). "It's all legalized," she said. "And I can go."

This chapter tells the stories of the religious literacy practices of undocumented Brazilians like Juliana. The people I spoke with read and analyzed inspirational books, religious pamphlets, denominational newsletters, Bible study guides, church service programs, and the Bible itself. They composed sermons, spiritual songs, interpretations of the Bible, religious radio shows, posters that proclaimed the glory of God, and lesson plans for catechism classes. They spoke in front of large groups of people, on street corners, through microphones, in tongues. They taped *pedidos* (supplications) to crosses, placed inscribed prayers in baskets, posted the number of souls they had saved on bulletin boards (Figure 5). In church, they engaged in deeply textually mediated worlds—worlds that in many ways paralleled the textually mediated legal infrastructure from which they were excluded.

Prohibited from leveraging their literacies for state-issued papers, many undocumented Brazilians turned to other text-based bureaucracies—churches—under whose auspices they wrote, read, and received documents. Like they have for other marginalized groups, transnational churches offered Brazilians supportive communal environments for navigating difficult U.S. conditions.[1] And like it has for other groups, religious literacy in particular became a way for Brazilian migrants to make sense of their new transnational identities.[2] But for the Brazilians who spoke with me for this study, there was more than community and identity at play in their religious literacy practices. That is, the heuristics of community and identity detailed by scholars of other groups could not fully account for the extent of undocumented Brazilians' religious literacies or for the singular passion with which they

Figure 5. Brazilian Catholics have written prayers, for themselves and others, and pinned them to this cross in the theology classroom. Photograph by the author.

pursued them. Their religious literacies, I argue here, are best understood as a sociomaterial response to the hostile textual conditions of globalization that constricted their lives. By sociomaterial response, I mean that in light of lacking state papers, many sought church papers. State documents promised the legitimacy and mobility that many undocumented Brazilians desired. Unattainable from the state, similar privileges, in similar textual forms, were made available to Brazilians via churches. In this process, the meanings papers accrued through institutionally mediated literacy practices were traded between what literacy scholar Jack Goody called the "twin bureaucracies" of state and church.[3] Put simply: written out of the state, many undocumented Brazilians wrote themselves into the church. Undocumented by the state, they documented themselves in the church.

In literacy's social history, literacy practices and products have often been traded between church and state, two long-standing "domains" of literacy.[4] To offer some limited examples: In the Middle Ages, state charters purposefully mirrored the material form and layout of more familiar religious documents, marking the transition to a state-based documentary society.[5] In France, the state wrested the power to control the movement of peasants from churches through the development of the passport.[6] Similarly, in 1970s Iran, those schooled in religious literacy used their familiarity with paper to participate in textually mediated commercial exchanges.[7] Likewise, achingly familiar with unattainable state documents, the undocumented Brazilians with whom I spoke created and accumulated church documents. Textually excluded from a powerful contemporary global institution, the nation-state, many reverted to churches, older text-based bureaucracies. In this chapter, readers see how the social meanings of papers—of authority, legitimacy, mobility—were traded between the bureaucracies of church and state. If the last chapter focused primarily on how literacy's sociomateriality was mediated by the state, leading papers to amass associations with mobility and legitimacy, here I show how such associations transferred from institution to institution, as migrants sought out larger textual infrastructures in which to situate their lives and literacies.

This chapter's argument goes as follows: I first link people's undocumented status to increased religious participation in the United States and a corresponding rise in religious writing and reading. Those who did not experience increased religious writing, I show, had documents that offered them legitimate positions in other state bureaucracies, obviating the need for bureaucratic legitimization via churches. To examine why churches in particular (and not, for example, schools or businesses) played such an important role for the undocumented, readers see how churches "documented" the undocumented through a textual infrastructure that offered an imagined mobility—that privilege so intertwined with papers—through their transnational affiliations with Brazilian homelands. In sum, as participants crossed a border and were excluded from state documentary projects, they began to write within other literacy institutions—churches—that have historically documented their subjects and whose reach extends across national borders that are otherwise textually policed.[8]

"We Live Running a Risk All the Time": Undocumented Paths to Religious Participation

Brazilian churches lined the main streets of South Mills, nestled amid Portuguese and Brazilian clothing and ethnic food shops, discount drug stores, and banks: the Igreja Missionária da Paz (Missionary Church of Peace), the Igreja Universal do Reino de Deus (Universal Church of the Kingdom of God), the Igreja Batista Missionária da Fé (Missionary Baptist Church of Faith), and the Igreja Evangelho do Quadrangular (Foursquare Gospel Church). Other evangelical churches could be found elsewhere in town, sometimes in humble storefronts and at other times in more imposing buildings. South Mills was also home to Catholic churches catering to Azoreans, as well as a Catholic church where many Brazilian Catholics found a spiritual community. These churches offered services, consultation, and child care in Portuguese, but they also promised more. *Pare de sofrer!* read a sign in red lettering atop the Igreja Universal. *Stop suffering!* This apt imperative at once acknowledged the suffering in the largely undocumented Brazilian community in South Mills and promised its relief.

In response to the increasing criminalization of migration, whereby the number of undocumented migrants in the United States has reached a historic peak, religious institutions have developed a privileged relationship to the undocumented.[9] The Conference of Catholic Bishops affirmed the right to migrate as a human right, and U.S. churches have been used as spaces of asylum to stall deportation.[10] This prioritizing of human rights, as opposed to national rights, engages in what some have called a "postnationalist discourse of universal personhood."[11] In South Mills, such discourse was present, albeit in a limited fashion (I did not meet one female leader of any religious institution, nor did I encounter any openly gay congregants). The Brazilian Catholic community actively organized for migrant political rights, and evangelical communities sought to minister to problems commonly associated with undocumented status, such as overwork, poverty, and isolation. Moreover, both Catholic and evangelical institutions offered material assistance, including money, clothes, furniture, ESL classes, and orientation to the United States. In the absence of secular support, these institutions met the pressing needs of many.

Such promises drew many undocumented Brazilians to South Mills from nearby areas.[12] One woman had been coming to South Mills weekly for Sunday services. When a friend from church offered her a job, she moved to South Mills. Another woman, who had been living in Rhode Island with her sister, was driving every weekend to South Mills for mass at the Catholic church. After a fight with her sister she said, "Forget it, I'm moving to [South Mills]." Another woman mentioned being worn down by immigrant life in Stoughton, Massachusetts. She piled her husband and three children in the car and started driving. She arrived in South Mills, saw the Universal Church of the Kingdom of God on Main Street, and even though the church was closed at the time she knew that she had found her home.[13] Along with many Brazilians, I went to church while in South Mills, regularly attending one Catholic and two evangelical churches (Assembleia de Deus and Igreja Universal). In these settings I witnessed the temporary alleviation of suffering, as pews and meeting halls filled with people clapping, singing, testifying, writing, and reading.

Undocumented status contributed to the fervor with which many participated in church. People described how, after crossing the border and becoming undocumented, they attended services more frequently, participated in prayer groups and theology classes, taught Sunday school, preached, and organized evangelical events. Sandra, a former teacher, summed up this shift in the following way. In Brazil, she said, "We didn't live in situations of such risk as we do here. So I think we feel closer to God. It's a good thing, no? Isn't it a good thing? Because we are subject to everything. We live running a risk all the time." Such vulnerability, directly and indirectly related to legal status, promoted the religious conversion of many.

For example, Jocélia, an undocumented twenty-two-year-old Brazilian woman who grew up in a *favela* (shantytown) in Brazil, held down two full-time jobs: one from 3 p.m. to midnight and another from 5 a.m. to the afternoon. One evening, exhausted from having not slept in days, she nodded off as she drove home from work, resulting in a serious accident that led her to a friend's house in South Mills and to a Catholic retreat.

> When I came here, I was not a youth who had fun. I only worked, and this made me a little frustrated, you know? Sad, lonely, understand? And nobody could change my mind. I had to work . . . But the Lord showed me something different, that I can't live only for work . . . So I went there [to the retreat] and I really felt that the Lord touched us. It was a very good experience. We sang so that the Lord would wash us with His blood. I closed my eyes and saw everything red as if it were the blood of the Lord. And I left there another person. I prayed in tongues. And I didn't even know [previously] that this existed. I didn't believe. I didn't know, and the Lord showed me.

Jocélia was Catholic in Brazil, but in the context of overwork occasioned by lack of documentation, her faith became stronger. An undocumented worker, she converted and became "another person."

Others also described paths to conversion that, directly or indirectly, resulted from their undocumented status. Consider these examples of how this conversion occurred differently across the varied lives of undocumented people: Márcio, a service worker in his early forties, described being stopped by the police multiple times because the undocumented have no access to driver's licenses ("You're persecuted. The police are on top of you"). He saw in his church possibilities for a sociopolitical answer to the human rights abuses of an unjust immigration system. Luís, a housepainter in his fifties, left his wife and infant son in Brazil when he came to the United States in 1988 to earn money, and was unable to reunite with them due to his undocumented status. Isolated, he converted to evangelical Christianity in 1994 and reconciled with his wife through long-distance telephone conversations mediated by a pastor. Even Maria Clara, an office worker with fluent English and a white phenotype that kept employers from requesting her documents, relied on churches instead of state bureaucracies in times of trauma: She avoided the police after she survived an attempted rape by one of her roommates ("The cops could, you know, go there and take me to whatever, I didn't even know"). She instead turned to a Catholic homeless shelter, where she went to mass everyday. And finally Carmém, only nineteen at the time of our interview and having just graduated from a South Mills high school, felt unable to officially complain about the discrimination she and her brother experienced in school. In contrast to her marginalization in school, she was "always in the middle" of social events at church. Time and again, people told me of life events connected to their undocumented status that led them to church.

Increased religious involvement was often precipitated by traumas (car accidents, attempted rape, persecution, debilitating anxiety) associated with undocumented status, which in turn restricted people's engagement with secular public institutions, such as the police or schools. For many, religious institutions felt culturally familiar and safe. Illuminating the conditions that led to conversion or to increased religious participation, however, is not to suggest that people's faith somehow lacked authenticity. On the contrary, many Brazilians were earnest in their beliefs. Still, their interviews revealed a striking connection between documentary marginalization—resulting in overwork, exploitation, familial separation, discrimination, and fear—and religious participation.

Religious Writing Stateside

If undocumented status promoted religious involvement, it also led to religious writing. Striking in the stories people shared with me was how their everyday writing practices, often secular while they lived in Brazil, became religious in the United States. Figure 6 illustrates, across participants, how the significant life event of migration triggered changes in literate orientation from secular to spiritual, shifts that I believe amount to a sociomaterial response to undocumented status. Of course, as participants moved across borders, other literacy practices shifted as well—just not as drastically. To put religious writing in the context of participants' other writing practices stateside—workplace writing and digital writing to family in Brazil—consider the following: With the exception of two participants with specialized degrees, most workplace literacy practices (accounting, measuring, cashiering, reporting) remained similar from Brazil to the United States, with people reporting that they quickly learned to write for work in English, and in one case, Spanish. In addition to workplace literacies, many (although not all) described increased digital literacy practices (writing on social networking sites or chatting) to communicate with distant family and friends. Most, however, did not speak of these practices with as much intensity as they did about their religious writing. They told me that they lied to family members back home to prevent worrying, that they checked in online simply to "not get lost," and that they had little time for such writing given their work schedules. Such transnational communication practices, while increased in the United States and meaningful to some, seemed to occupy the periphery of the otherwise harried lives of the undocumented people with whom I spoke.[14] In contrast, religious writing was front and center. Again and again, undocumented people told me that churches were the places where they most read and wrote.

Such religious writing was not entirely new; it often grew from participants' writing histories in Brazil. In their homeland, however, many wrote in secular genres, whereas in the United States, after having crossed the border, after having become undocumented, such genres transformed to take on religious meanings. I will offer some extended examples of this kind of genre transfer later in the chapter. For now, consider how this trend varies across the undocumented people with whom I spoke: Sandra, the former school teacher, wrote lesson plans for her job as a Portuguese teacher in Brazil, and in the United States she wrote lesson plans for the catechism class she taught at church. Márcio, the service worker in his forties, wrote rock music and a political play about the mistreatment of prisoners in Brazil, and in the United States he wrote religious ballads with a social-justice edge. Luís, the housepainter in his fifties, wrote romantic poetry and music in Brazil, and in the United States he wrote religious hymns. Finally, Rafael, a delivery person in his late twenties, described the most direct transfer from state to religious literacy practices after migration: In Brazil, he recalled loading up speakers into the back of his family's truck to campaign for his father's election as mayor of his rural hometown. Political speech making, he said, was good training for his current vocation as a missionary in the United States, in which he acts as "the loud speakers through which God speaks." In these instances, people drew on homeland genres (lesson plans, songs, speeches) and purposes for writing (social justice, persuasion, expression) to compose in the service of religion stateside.

Still others learned new religious genres in their lives stateside: For example, Jocélia, the young woman whose car crashed, learned how to

	Conditions leading to religious participation	Genres of writing in Brazil (excluding school literacies)	Genres of religious writing in the United States	Other religious literate activities in the United States
Jocélia	Overworks, falls asleep at the wheel, has an accident then becomes "a new person" at a retreat.	diary entries; letters	biblical interpretations; religious songs; sermons	Interprets from Bible to preach on subject of brotherhood, so that fellow Brazilians will not denounce each other to ICE.
Rafael	Lives recklessly in the United States, then is touched by God at a retreat.	political speeches	religious sermons	
Maria Clara	Fears police after a roommate attempts rape, so goes instead to a Christian homeless shelter where she attends mass everyday.	poetry	religious commentary for prayer group; pedidos; written confession of a sin	
Juliana	Religious faith inspires illegal crossing into the United States, leading to increased religious participation.	letters; sermons	religious radio shows; sermons; ad for house-cleaning services in religious newspaper; sermons; letters	Participated in a course to get a missionary card in the United States. Believes that national borders are human-made, not divine.
Luís	Document-enforced separation from family leads to seek pastor as mediator to reunite with wife, who demands his conversion.	rock and roll music; romantic poems	sermons; hymns	Participated in course to receive chaplain badge.
Márcio	Religious in Brazil; in the United States sees increased	rock and roll music; political plays	religious music; biblical interpretations in prayer	Seeks official status of deacon to "play a role in the

	social relevance of Catholicism to help the undocumented.	documenting social injustice	groups; comments on social networking sites to connect Catholic Brazilian community	community." Interprets Bible passage that immigrants should be treated well, and that boundaries are human-made, not divine.
Sandra	Religious in Brazil; in the United States being undocumented "puts you closer to God."	lesson plans for Portuguese classes	lesson plans for catechism classes	In explaining how undocumented daughter receives college diploma, emphasizes "faith in God."
Fábio	Religious in Brazil; in the United States undocumented status separates him from family; goes to couples prayer group with wife.	embarrassed to read aloud due to stuttering	reads Bible aloud and interprets in prayer group to overcome stuttering	Interprets Bible passage about Christian "armor" in context of work-related injury.
Aparecida	Religious in Brazil; moves from other U.S. town to South Mills because of church; goes to church every day.		extensive *pedidos*; lessons and stories for children in church school	Reads Bible in Portuguese and in English to discover different meanings.
Rafaela	Religious in Brazil; can't get job without documents to pay for ESL classes so attends them at church	romantic poems; cards; patient reports	*pedidos*	God gives her documents to come the first time to the United States.
Carmém	Cannot speak up about discrimination in school because it is "not my place," but in church is "always in the middle."	self-sponsored summaries of literature; diary entries	accounting for church events	
Washington	Infrequently attends church.	samba		

Figure 6. Religious literacy activities in the United States and in Brazil.

write biblical interpretations; Maria Clara, the woman with the white phenotype and fluent English, wrote a confession of a sin; and Aparecida, a stay-at-home mother of three, wrote extensive *pedidos* (supplications), asking for help to be a good mother to her children in a new country. In this piling up of disparate examples, I have been suggesting that often-secular homeland writing practices transformed in the United States as people oriented their writing toward religious ends.

Even those who were deeply involved in their religious institutions in Brazil stepped up their religious writing in the United States. Juliana, whose anecdote opened this chapter, evangelized for her church in Brazil and continued to do so in the United States. She showed me her *rascunhos* (notes) for a sermon, describing the formulaic structure she gleaned from her preaching experiences in Brazil: "So I take some Bible passages and did a summary of them here on the back, see? I read the conclusion of the verse, and it's all ready to go" (Figure 7).

While the genre remained the same, in the United States she expanded her audience by preaching over the radio, where she treated the theme of marital problems in the context of migration and separation. Juliana, as readers will recall, had been separated from her husband for years; he had come to the United States to work, and she could not follow him due to her repeated visa denials. In her absence, he married another woman, practicing, in Juliana's words, "bigamy," for which she eventually forgave him, crediting their reunification to God: "So I went to the radio the first time to speak about marriage . . . What God unites, man does not separate. And to speak about forgiveness. About my private life. So I gave my testimony on the radio. I came, greeted everyone with good evening, the peace of the Lord for the listeners, and began to speak. And afterwards I preached the word of God. And after that many people called to ask questions, too." Juliana acknowledged the difficulties in maintaining a fulfilling marital relationship where documentary hardships force long separations. At the same time, she offered the possibility of a return to the close family connections that many associated with Brazil, promising that through faith in God, listeners could reconstitute the family they left behind. These sermons gave her the ethos of a local celebrity, as she answered listener questions on air. Her position in her evangelical church was so central that when I returned to South Mills in 2010, the church had devoted an evening's celebration to her birthday. Congregants in formal wear sat at tables ornamented with flowers,

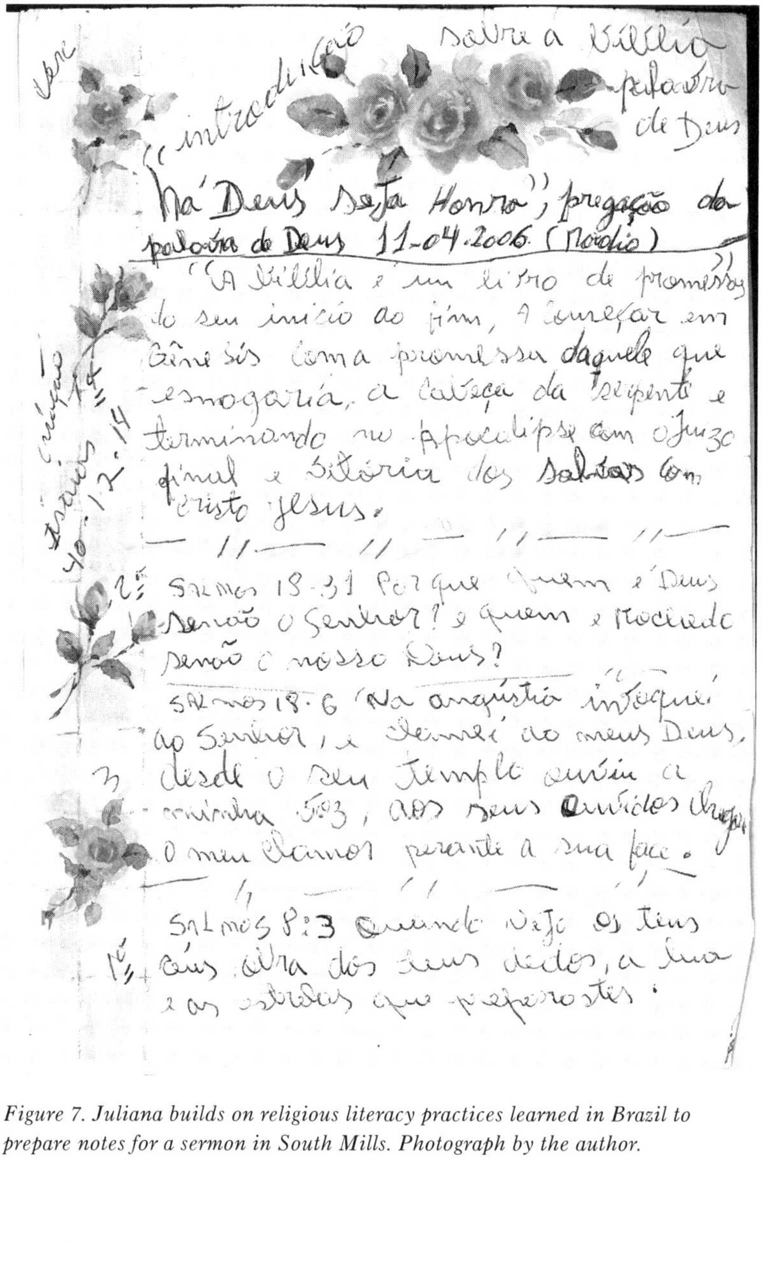

Figure 7. Juliana builds on religious literacy practices learned in Brazil to prepare notes for a sermon in South Mills. Photograph by the author.

warming trays of food lined the perimeter of the hall, presents were stacked near a large cake, and parking places were scarce. In short, the audience for and impetus behind Juliana's religious writing seemed to grow in the United States.

At the same time as Juliana's religious writing expanded stateside, her opportunities for secular writing contracted. In Brazil she worked as a salesperson and wrote for accounting purposes, whereas in the United States she had initially worked at a factory but did not return after her employer requested her documents. Instead, she turned to cleaning houses, a business for which she advertised in a religious newspaper. Juliana's undocumented status, then, enveloped even her workplace writing activities in a religious context.

In sum, across age, gender, and literacy background, undocumented people drew on their literacy resources to engage not with the state, which had excluded them, but with the church, which scaffolded their literate efforts. But what precisely accounts for this turn to largely religious writing activities experienced by so many undocumented participants?

Three Songs and Their Bureaucratic Homes

To get at the answer to this question, here I offer some telling exceptions to the trend of intensified religious writing I have been documenting thus far. Those who did *not* write in religious contexts had access to *other* authoritative bureaucracies, such as passports to other countries. There was something about the textuality of bureaucratic systems that acted on, recruited, or called for migrants' writing, especially under conditions in which legal papers were withheld. People wrote in churches, in other words, because they seemed to need a textual infrastructure within which to write. And the state was not an option.

The three undocumented people who did not increase their religious writing stateside oriented their literate production elsewhere. Such was the case with Washington, a factory worker who had been in the United States for five years to save money for his children's and wife's educations in Brazil. He was Catholic, but he did not frequent the Brazilian churches in the area and reported no religious writing whatsoever. Significantly, he had firm plans to return to Brazil in the month following our interview to reunite with his family: "There comes a time that *saudade* [nostalgia, missing] squeezes you. And family, time passes, and it's a thing you can't enjoy anymore, understand? This time that I have been here will stay behind. I won't be able to recuperate it. It's already lost." He had an opportunity to marry an American to legalize his status, but Washington balked at obtaining a divorce from his wife in Brazil, considering such a step "artificial": "I wouldn't accept it, for my part, you know. I came with the intention of one day returning." This intention to return mitigated the urgency of obtaining papers in the United States. The document he needed to reunite with his family was one he already had—his Brazilian passport.

Similarly, the two other undocumented Brazilians who did not describe intensive religious writing were also within reach of alternative documentary identities: A Brazilian of Italian descent, Carmém was the proud owner of an Italian passport and eagerly described her plans to move to Italy for college. And Rafaela, whose documentary situation I described in chapter 1, had plans to marry a U.S. citizen (though at the time of our interview she had not yet applied for a green card). Both actively participated in their respective churches but wrote little. These three participants were oriented elsewhere—to Brazil, to Italy, to the United States—suggesting that they had no need for the textual authority churches often provided the undocumented. They each had (or would soon have) documentary proof of their belonging in nation-states.

This orientation to national citizenships, as opposed to church membership, was also reflected in their secular writing. Washington, the least religious undocumented participant I spoke with, sang for me a *sambinha* (a little samba) he composed with friends in Brazil for *carnaval*, in which female Brazilian flowers compete for the love of one male flower (the rose ultimately wins). Here is a literal translation of an excerpt from the beginning:

> Of the Brazilian flower, today I want to tell,
> pay attention to the theme I will narrate,
> being born in a party of a thousand flowers, in this popular wonder,
> I will show with splendor, the beautiful dance of the flowers.

This song reminded Washington of composing with dear friends ("We were very united, really good friends, one with another, we were always together"), of his block where *carnaval* participants rehearsed, and of his nation. The *carnaval* organizers for his town had requested a song about Brazilian flowers, representing one tradition in sambas during *carnaval*, to extol Brazilian history, popular figures, geography, and culture. This song is of and about the Brazilian nation-state. Its performance stateside symbolized his commitment to his country, whose passport he legally held. Put another way, this secular literacy practice corresponded to the secular literacy product with which he identified.

This orientation toward Brazil stands in stark contrast to that in the songs composed by two other men, Luís and Márcio, who had no (or vague) plans to return to Brazil. Like that of others, their writing transformed from secular in Brazil to profoundly spiritual in the United States. Luís, readers will recall, was the housepainter who reunited with his wife after his conversion to Christianity. In Brazil, Luís had written secular poems and rock music inspired by pop icons of the 1960s and 1970s, namely, Roberto Carlos, known in Brazil as "the king." Luís won a prize at a Brazilian music festival for a song entitled "Eu sou . . ." ("I am . . ."), which he revised in the United States after converting to Christianity:

> When I came here and started to write, this was the only song that God allowed me to remember the words of. So then God told me, "Now you are going to start to write for me. So now you will put my 'D' and my 'S.'" So now the song is called . . . "Deus é . . ." ["God is . . ."]. It's the same song, only where there was "I," there is now "God." So God is, there is not an I. Before there was an I. Now God is.

While Luís's song was concerned previously with "I" or in Portuguese, "eu," stateside its subject became, with a simple addition of a "D" and an "S," God, or in Portuguese, "Deus." Here are the two first lines of his song with the original Portuguese alongside the translation:

> *Version of the song in Brazil:*
> Eu sou por tua vida [I am for your life]
> Eu sou por toda a vida [I am for your whole life]
>
> *Revised version of the song in the United States:*
> Deus é por tua vida [God is for your life]
> Deus é por toda a vida [God is for your whole life]

In the United States Luís substituted "God" for "I." From a disempowered location off the U.S. textual grid, this new writerly identity empowered Luís to speak: He performed his music regularly at his evangelical church and marketed his CDs to other Portuguese-language religious institutions in the area. The bureaucratic institution of the church undergirded his writing, allowing him to develop a writerly position, one of legitimacy and authority.

Similar to Luís's song, Márcio's writing also represents a turn away from his country of origin and toward a spiritual realm. Recall that in Brazil, Márcio wrote rock music and a political play critiquing Brazil's prison system. In the United States he wrote a song titled "The Immigrant," which described his embrace of religion in light of the loss of country and family that accompanied his migration. At the time our interview, Márcio had been in the United States for eight years, during which time he had not seen his four children, had divorced his wife, and was not able to attend the funerals of his father and sister in Brazil, despite having paid an immigration lawyer thousands of dollars for legal documents that never materialized. Here again I translate only the beginning of his song:

> Lord, when I arrived here, I only encountered sadness and didn't find peace,
> I came here on the childlike hope to change my life,
> I left everything behind, my family, my country, that I loved so much,
> I fought against my destiny, my strength disappearing, until I met You.

Like Luís, Márcio described divine authorization for his writing process ("It was something so profound, it was as if it wasn't even me that wrote"). And like Luís, Márcio oriented himself away from a secular nation ("I left everything behind, my family, my country") and directed his song instead toward "You," the "Lord." Again, similar to Luís, Márcio performed this song publicly in his church. Another participant told me it moved her to tears. For both Luís and Márcio, their religious beliefs and institutions offered them the authority, purpose, and audience for their writing that was denied to them in other contexts. Undocumented, they *documented*, or testified, under the auspices of their churches. As Márcio said of "The Immigrant," "This song is my life."

Unlike Márcio, whose writing represented a resigned commitment to living undocumented in the United States, Washington focused on his return to Brazil, singing songs about Brazilian flowers during his long night shifts to speed the days, months, and years until his reunification with his family. "Quem canta, os males espanta," he said more than once during our interview. "He who sings scares away evil." Written out of one documentary society, all three men wrote (or sang) their way toward another. Márcio and Luís largely lived their literacy lives in church, whereas Washington, soon to return home to his family, largely lived his in Brazil. In a context of profound textual disorientation, undocumented writers, it seemed, needed an infrastructure within which to textually orient. In their everyday literacy practices, then, they called on the material authority of texts, whose social meanings were buttressed by and exchanged between the domains of church and state.

Of course, in a documentary society there are many other powerful bureaucracies the undocumented could have chosen to support their literacies. Why churches?

Documenting the Undocumented

Religious institutions loom in the social history of literacy. They have sponsored the literacies of disenfranchised groups, documented people and land, and infused people with textual authority.[15] Such sponsorship, documentation, and authority were denied to undocumented participants in secular realms, a marginalization that Aparecida, the stay-at-home mother of three, described succinctly: "You don't exist." South Mills' religious institutions addressed their congregants' literal alienation, at least in part, through papers. To highlight this role is not to imply that religious writing and church documents replaced political rights. They clearly did not. Rather, for those with whom I spoke, crossing a national border and becoming undocumented shifted their literacy practices into a religious bureaucracy rife with some of the same ideologies and promises swirling around that oft-uttered word, "papers."

Missionary Cards

Juliana, whose anecdote opened this chapter, was not alone in wielding her missionary card as a partial antidote to documentary exclusion. Luís, the housepainter whose romantic ballad transformed into a hymn, and who came to the United States in 1988 on a visa that had long since expired, described the absurdity of his undocumented status: To get a driver's license, he explained, you need a social security card. But to get a social security card, you need a valid work permit, for which a certain kind of visa is required, which can depend on the amount of money in your bank account, the stamps already in your passport, and/or your marriage (or divorce) certificate. "Everything you want to do," he said, "you depend on a document you don't have." During our discussion of his documents, Luís, like Juliana, took out his wallet. He showed me a chaplain's badge—a large plastic gold-colored star set against a black faux-leather background: "I'm a chaplain, understand. Chaplains are people who do church work in hospitals, prisons. I can't go to the prison because I'm not legal. I have this barrier. But I can go to hospitals, where I go every so often for the sick. Sometimes Portuguese-speaking people who don't speak English, I go there and bring them the word, the comfort of the word of God." While those with the hopes of legalization might take a course to pass the citizenship test, Juliana and Luís took a chaplain's course sponsored by a Brazilian evangelical church. Luís wielded his document in hospitals, ministering to fellow Portuguese speakers. To be clear, these church documents did not afford the same rights as state documents, and Juliana and Luís were not duped into thinking they did. Yet these missionary cards mattered deeply in their literacy lives. The cards offered evidence of studies and of their authority to preach. Moreover, in the context of Juliana's life-threatening trip across the Mexican border and Luís's sacrifices to be in the United States undocumented for twenty years, the cards reverberated with concepts, such as liberty, legality, and mobility, that are usually reserved for the documented, for those who did not have to, as Juliana described, pluck cactus needles from their skin after running through the desert at night.

Bible Interpretations

The Bible, as the sacred text on which these churches' documentary infrastructures depend, functioned for many participants as a textual challenge to immigration law. As a result, they seemed to embrace a spiritual citizenship in lieu of the political citizenship that was, for the undocumented, more fraught.

During our interview in his apartment, Márcio, whom readers will recall authored the song "The Immigrant," gestured to his large Bible (Figure 8). Flanking the Bible were flowers, a statue of Jesus, and a photo of his deceased father, whose funeral he could not attend due to his documentary status: "Jesus said, God left the following law for Israel: Treat the immigrants well, because you were immigrants in Egypt. This was the law for everyone. And unfortunately, certain countries don't do this for the immigrants. It's in the Bible." Márcio's interpretation of the Bible replaced U.S. laws with what he saw as the more inclusive law of God. Similarly, other participants argued that while borders were "made by man," the world was made by God, allowing them passage across national borders. In the same vein, Jocélia, the young woman who became intensely religious after her car crash, interpreted a Bible passage on brotherhood to encourage those gathered at a prayer service to not denounce one another to Immigration and Customs Enforcement (ICE).

Others leveraged biblical interpretations for spiritual protection from the exploitation accompanying undocumented status. Fábio, a construction worker in his mid-thirties, and his wife migrated to the United States in 2006, leaving three children in Brazil to be raised by their grandparents as they attempted to earn enough money to provide for their kids' educations. At the time of our interview, Fábio had been out of work for two months, because a careless colleague had sliced off his finger at his construction site. While he benefited from emergency surgery, his attempts to fill his prescription for physical therapy had been thwarted. He had taken up the matter with a sympathetic

Figure 8. Márcio's Bible, flanked by a statue of Jesus, photos of family, and flowers, is placed in a prominent corner of his small apartment. Photograph by the author.

lawyer, but in the meantime, he and his wife were living on her income as a housecleaner, and it was unclear whether he would ever regain movement in his hand. He countered this vulnerability through reading a carefully chosen Bible passage in his prayer group, despite his embarrassment at stuttering when reading aloud: "It's taking away a little of my shame, thank God, my shame in participating with my comrades. It doesn't matter if you're embarrassed or not, you have to read." He repeated the passage for me, titled "The Armor of Christianity," during our interview. It developed a metaphor of spiritual protection from evil, rallying Christians to don the "armor of God . . . your waist wrapped with truth and dressed with the chest plate of justice." This reading offered him the position of a warrior for justice at a moment of profound vulnerability. Again, this text resonated with notions of law and justice that were otherwise the purview of state bureaucracies.

Despite their sociomaterial resonances across the domains of church and state, it was understood by all that biblical interpretations had little purchase in the state's legal realm. Fábio followed up his interview with this: "One has a lot of faith in God, you know? One believes and believes in God . . . But it's complicated . . . These laws, the business of this country." Or as Márcio put it to me, "The problems to get these papers, girl!"

Miracles

As Fábio and Márcio suggested, given the choice, those with whom I spoke would all gladly have legalized their status. In 2008 many held out hopes of a new U.S. president instituting another period of amnesty like that of 1986, when a path to legalization and citizenship was opened for many longtime undocumented U.S. residents. Yet most knew that no matter the results of the election, amnesty was far from guaranteed, and even if it were to come to fruition, would be a long time in coming. In this context, some prayed for documents. For Sandra, the former schoolteacher, God helped her daughter finally receive her college diploma despite the considerable trials of getting a degree while undocumented. And as readers saw in chapter 1, for Rafaela, who by all accounts had a poor chance of getting a visa, God gave her the visa (long since expired) to come to the United States for the first time. Others hoped for God to "touch the heads of politicians" to grant amnesty. In one evangelical church service I attended, the pastor implored the ten congregants to believe in the "God of the impossible." Participants dutifully presented papers handed out the previous week on which they had written their desires for God to act in their lives. As they ritually deposited the papers in a basket on an altar illuminated by red light, dramatic music played loudly and the pastor shouted into his microphone over the din: "What you wrote on this sheet will happen in your life," and then, "Do this miracle, my God, do it!" Then he turned back to the congregants, asking us to repeat, "The Lord is the God of the impossible. Do the impossible." The impossible, in this case, was to make money ("God does not want you to live poor in a country of the rich!") and to gain papers ("One day, I will have my papers. One day, I will legalize myself in this country!"). For the undocumented laboring in low-wage jobs, gaining documents seemed to require an act of God, who I hoped would respond with sympathy to the desires that congregants penned on yellow sheets of paper and offered up on the altar.

Taken together, these examples demonstrate how churches textually ministered to undocumented congregants, participating in a bureaucratic logic in which papers conferred legitimacy—a legitimacy buttressed by a sacred text and a deity. Recall that Juliana at the beginning of this chapter spoke of her fear of being picked up "on the corner." On my return trip to South Mills in 2010, she invited me to proselytize with her on one of the busiest corners in town. I declined, but I saw her with several other church members later as I was driving by. She was wearing a bright red shirt, holding a white sign with red lettering that said, in English, "Jesus is the faithful." The man driving in front of me honked at her and gave a thumbs-up. There she was on the corner, unafraid.

Transnational Textual Affiliations

In addition to echoing state uses of literacy, these churches' documentary infrastructures also bore transnational connections to Brazil, further contributing to their bureaucratic potency for undocumented participants, for whom a physical trip back to Brazil was impractical. (Returning to the United States after leaving while undocumented can be impossible or life threatening.) "Religion," as sociologist Peggy Levitt writes in her aptly titled ethnography *God Needs No Passport*, "is the ultimate boundary crosser."[16] Or as Rafael, the delivery worker who used to campaign for his father, put a similar concept, riffing on the title of a popular Brazilian film, "God is Brazilian." While the undocumented were restricted from physically crossing boundaries, their engagement with religious literacies allowed them to commune with their homeland, to spiritually travel. In this way, the association of papers, literacy, and mobility detailed in chapters 1 and 2 was extended in literacy events involving churches.

In all churches and ethnic stores I visited during my fieldwork, I found texts linking Brazil and religion. Both evangelical churches had headquarters in Rio de Janeiro, and their South Mills branches sustained strong ties to this parent institution. The South Mills Brazilian Catholic church, whose headquarters were in Rome, nonetheless maintained connections to Brazil through the liberation theology teachings of its Brazilian priest and through its written liturgy, published in São Paulo and imported to the United States. All three churches routinely sponsored the movement of pastors and priests, trained in textual interpretation and theology, to areas of Brazilian migration such as South Mills. Moreover, the Brazilian headquarters exported Brazilian-published texts and theological study guides for consumption by Brazilians abroad. Finally, as readers have seen, Brazilian immigrants themselves carried with them generic knowledge gained in Brazil, which they then used in their religious writing for migrant audiences in the United States. Transnational churches, in turn, benefited from such writing's ability to attract more congregants, whose monetary contributions traveled back to Brazil, financially solidifying ties between geographically disparate religious communities. Viewed from a functional perspective, the machinery of writing in these contexts did what it often does: maintain connections across distance.

Likewise, these religious texts accrued associations with the mobility denied to the undocumented. God does not need a passport, and neither did the religious texts that so frequently and so enviably crossed borders. Such associations were on prominent display in even ostensibly secular Brazilian ethnic stores. For example, one store, with a name signifying Brazil and a Brazilian flag in the window, offered almost exclusively religious reading material, including the Bible, Bible study guides, and inspirational titles such as *Count Your Miracles* and *Grab the Rope*. Religious books were twice pressed into my hands as gifts and were often displayed in participants' homes, suggesting that these imported texts did not linger long on stores' shelves. In fact, excluding Carmém, Rafaela, and Washington, the undocumented Brazilians who did not write in religious contexts, *all* undocumented participants described spiritual reading practices. In the context of Brazilian stores, these spiritual books functioned as markers of Brazilian nationality, as they were set alongside hard-to-find Brazilian foods as well as Brazilian flags and soccer jerseys, pointing to a symbolic mingling of nation, text, and God.

Such texts, published in Brazil and gesturing toward Brazil, also organized Brazilian religious events, where congregants and pastors adapted them to negotiate undocumented immigrant life, offering Brazilian-specific religious teaching as one answer to the literal alienation of congregants. For example, the Brazilian Catholic priest taught a theology class housed on the fifth floor of a ramshackle school building across the street from the church. The space was decked with Brazilian Catholic images, namely, a prominent poster of Brazil's black Our Lady of the Apparition and a cross, to which class members had taped *pedidos* written in Portuguese on small pieces of white paper, asking for blessings for loved ones. If the class space was framed by these Brazilian images, its content was framed by a Brazilian text, *Time to See, Time to Believe, Time to Love!* a chapter of which was assigned for the class to read and discuss. Published in Brazil for the education of "street social educators," this text drew on Latin American liberation theology principles that meld social justice and religion. As an active member of this class, Márcio, the author of "The Immigrant," articulated his desire to organize for the rights of the undocumented— a move supported by Father Pedro, whose theological education included political protesting with parishioners in the impoverished northeast of Brazil, a region at the heart of liberation theology principles. That the texts, the philosophy, the religious leader, and the ambience all hailed from Brazil allowed the class to travel, if not physically, then at least spiritually.

For many, this transnational documentary infrastructure provided imaginative access to the Brazilian homeland, allowing the undocumented to tentatively transcend a hostile documentary environment through textual participation in Brazilian spiritual realms. Religious texts functioned as transnational touchstones, cementing associations of papers, literacy, and mobility. The documentary society of South Mills Brazilian churches resonated in Brazilians' literacy lives in part because it transcended and traversed the borders that were otherwise prohibitively monitored by papers.

Counting and Being Counted

People engaged in a variety of religious literacy activities as a sociomaterial response to their undocumented status: Religious documents materially countered, and were even were wielded in protest to, state documents. Religious writing, anchored in a bureaucracy that predates the state, provided a position from which to speak. Religious reading of the Bible, whose authority, for many, superseded state laws, offered a sense of protection. And engaging in transnational religious literacy events simulated the kind of cross-border mobility that was otherwise prohibited. Those who did not participate in religious literacy had documents that promised them other bureaucratic homes. For those who did participate in religious literacy, their writing and reading offset—though did not resolve—their textual exclusion from the geographical location in which they physically lived their lives. The undocumented participants featured in this chapter met documents with documents, writing with writing, text with text. The form of their literacy activity materially matched the form taken by their disenfranchisement—a sociomaterial response to the textual conditions of their exclusion.

In some ways, the people with whom I spoke used literacy to assimilate themselves into churches in the same way that literacy has historically been used to assimilate migrants into the state. That is, instead of writing to assimilate into nationalist ideologies, they were writing to assimilate into religious ones. Though like for the Azoreans and Azorean Americans readers encountered in the last chapter, if any kind of assimilation occurred via literacy, it occurred *bureaucratically*, as undocumented Brazilians wrote themselves into religious bureaucracies. For Brazilians, that their writing was mediated by larger, more powerful, "sponsoring" institutions, such as church or state, did not dilute the personal or social consequences of their deeply felt religious literacy practices.[17] On the contrary, the textual infrastructure of these institutions weighted Brazilians' religious literate expression with authority, relevance, and community. In textually aligning themselves with larger institutions, they staked out documentary territory in which what they had to say mattered—mattered more than the lives many risked to come to the United States, mattered for their very salvation. Their writing was co-opted by the larger bureaucracy of the church, at the same time as they co-opted this bureaucracy in order to write.

The point of this chapter, then, is neither to extol nor to critique these "twin bureaucracies," the church and the state.[18] Instead, I have tried to show how literacy's sociomateriality was exchanged between them, as everyday people who were written out of one documentary society wrote their way into another. Such a conclusion points to a deeper connection between documentary infrastructures and individual writing than scholars have previously appreciated.[19] Some of the earliest recorded uses of literacy have been to sustain bureaucracies—accounting in ancient Mesopotamia or census taking to develop the modern nation-state, for example.[20] If bureaucracies have a historically documented need to *count*, undocumented Brazilians had a corresponding need to *be counted*. In a society in which belonging is textually constituted, they also wanted to textually belong. Perhaps it is only moving into a new hostile web of documentary affiliations, as people do when they become undocumented, that such desires become urgent.

Brazilians' marginalization was not only textual: It was also racial, hemispheric, economic, political, gendered. Yet people spoke to me repeatedly, and at length, about *papers*. Documents—"things that speak," that make us "legible"—seemed to crystallize their disenfranchisement.[21] To be undocumented in a society saturated with documentation is perhaps to experience alienation in ways that are uniquely textual. To write under the auspices of an alternative authoritative bureaucracy, likewise, is to textually negotiate this alienation. It is to participate in the social meanings of papers, of authority, legitimacy, and the potential for mobility. For the undocumented migrants featured in this chapter, then, texts were strong because lacking papers in the documentary society of the U.S. nation-state restricted their movement, rights, health, and well-being. Texts were also strong, though, because in the documentary society of churches, they offered solace, communion, salvation, and voice. Bolstered by potent bureaucracies and the writing practices that sustained them, papers appeared to offer humanity to those labeled aliens. In this context, the everyday undocumented writers I spoke with harnessed the social power of literacy to gain what textual capital they could. Reified in the institutions of church and state, this textual capital became symbolic capital, as people wrote and read to attain the privileges that papers promised.

The logic behind textual inclusion and exclusion is at once ineffable and coldly logical, miraculous and mundane—in other words, bureaucratic. These are the hostile, and often inscrutable, textual conditions of globalization—conditions that shape the borders of the nation state and, as readers will see in the next chapter, prospects for literacy lives led within them.

4 "IT'S NOT BECAUSE OF THE ENGLISH"

Literacy Lives of the Young

SIMONE, an undocumented college student, worried that her unauthorized status would be found out when she registered for her major's
required internship. Jocélia, also undocumented, put her childhood
dream of studying English in college on hold, since she was not eligible for school loans. Steven, an Azorean American educated in U.S.
public schools, was misplaced in an ESL community college class with
immigrants his mother's age, postponing his hopes of being the first
in his family to earn a four-year college diploma.

Documented and undocumented, born in the United States to
Azorean parents or born in Brazil, the young adults between the
ages of eighteen and twenty-eight featured in this chapter found their
mobility stalled at key points in their educational trajectories. None
spoke English as a first language, but English acquisition was not their
primary concern. Instead, they spoke of papers. They wanted green
cards to move across borders, driver's licenses to move through the
streets, diplomas to move up. Papers, they hoped, would allow passage through the checkpoints that threatened to impede their travels.

All transnational migrants have, by definition, moved.[1] But for
young people with whom I spoke, the pressures of mobility, both
social and physical, were especially potent. They (or their parents)
migrated, in the words of so many, for *uma vida melhor*, a better life.
To achieve this better life in light of disappearing blue-collar jobs,
young adults went to school, attempting to complete GEDs, high school,
associate's and bachelor's degrees. This process of schooling, in turn,
confirmed the seemingly commonsense logic of mobility as a mode of
succeeding, as a way of being in the world. Consider the titles of the
United States' most recent, as of this writing, sweeping educational

policies, No Child Left Behind and Race to the Top. If you want to make it, these programs bark, you better hustle. It is no surprise that young people often echoed this mandate. *Ir para frente*, they repeated to me, meaning *get ahead, go to the front, and move forward*, the stories of their lives.

Honing individual language and literacy skills, such a crucial part of the project of schooling, is often believed to be the key to social mobility for migrant youth, who are thought to lack the linguistic resources necessary for success. Scholars disagree over precisely which kinds of language and literacies best serve these purposes. On the one hand, educational sociologists routinely track migrant youths' assimilation through their English literacy attainment. Standardized productions of literacy, in this view, stand in for national belonging. Scholars sensitive to literacy's shifting social values, on the other hand, have argued for more diverse conceptions of what kinds of literacies can count as successful for a range of purposes. Some have emphasized ways to bridge the distance between home literacies and school literacies.[2] And others have highlighted the practices of "code-meshing" and "translanguaging" to create meanings beyond the limits of standard written English.[3] Such approaches address young writers' and readers' larger social worlds in ways that can be both pedagogically productive and humanizing for marginalized groups. But whether students' diverse linguistic resources are seen as problems to overcome or resources to be utilized, literacy research on transnational students remains fixated on language.

Yet individual language ability tells only part of the story of the literacy pressures bearing down on transnational young adults. The experiences of migrants in South Mills suggest that theories of what transnational literacy is and does must account for factors beyond individual linguistic production in any language. For South Mills young adults, the potency of language, whether English or Portuguese or translingual or code-meshed, could only be activated insofar as it coincided with or quietly subverted the agendas of more powerful institutions, such as the nation-state and the school, whose power is extended, in part, through papers. Papers appeared to wield more brute force than home or classroom language standards, impinging on the learning and future prospects of transnational young adults. In short, the promise of standard English was eclipsed by the urgency of papers.

For migrant youth in the United States, papers are nothing if not urgent. Because of the many ethical and methodological complications of conducting research with undocumented youth, findings linking legal status to educational achievement (or underachievement) have appeared slowly. But what researchers do know is striking. Summarizing the far-reaching consequences of undocumented status, Suárez-Orozco and colleagues write, "The effects of unauthorized status on development across the lifespan are uniformly negative, with millions of U.S. children and youth at risk of lower educational performance, economic stagnation, blocked mobility, and ambiguous belonging."[4] Often the negative effects of undocumented status appear later in adolescence. For those who migrated "illegally" as young children, they may only learn they are undocumented when they turn sixteen and must negotiate their ineligibility for driver's licenses, after-school jobs, and student loans. Many find going to college, that entryway to the middle class, a financial impossibility without the papers that can help them get loans.[5] And even if they can graduate from college, a degree does not promise jobs for those who cannot show their employers a social security card. In such circumstances, undocumented youth must "learn to be illegal," a process chronologically linked to their coming of age, with as yet untold implications for their social, emotional, and cognitive development.[6] Lacking the right papers can stall, or at least reroute, even the most ambitious upwardly mobile trajectories.

Not all transnational migrants are undocumented, of course; at least three-quarters of migrants in the United States, as of this writing, are authorized. Yet even for the documented, papers are a concern. As De Genova has argued, all immigrants are politically defined by the unstable position of their *deportability*.[7] For example, around the time of this study legally documented Azoreans who had committed crimes stateside were deported back to the Azores, islands many of them left as children.[8] Even many young people who have no reason to fear their own deportation often worry about that of others, such as unauthorized parents or siblings, especially when living in mixed legal status families. And even the very young may be negatively affected by a caregiver's undocumented status; a longitudinal study has shown that because undocumented status can lead to social isolation and lower earnings, mothers' documentary status can shape the cognitive development, including vocabulary acquisition, of children as early as twenty-four months of age.[9] And finally, undocumented parental status can negatively affect the educational outcomes even of young people who *remain* in their homelands, as they receive less remittance money than peers whose migrant parents are documented.[10] The textual arm of the nation-state, in sum, can have a broad reach, particularly when it comes to its most vulnerable subjects, the young.

For young people in South Mills, the textual arm of the nation-state also reached into their literacies. That is, their individual experiences with literacy often echoed the uses of literacy by the larger institutions of state and school to regulate mobility.[11] As individual and institutional uses of literacy collided in young people's lives, they came to understand and use literacy in terms of papers. Literacy practices and literacy products merged, as young people attempted to get ahead both by writing and by presenting the right papers. Literacy and papers, papers and literacy, were thus experienced as nearly interchangeable resources that one proffered to pass through border checkpoints, schools, and city streets. In chapter 2 those with the potential to be documented wrote to attain papers, and in chapter 3 the undocumented wrote in light of *not* having papers. For the young people featured in this chapter, their writing served *as* papers. They wrote to pass.

This chapter details how young people's literacy practices merged with the literacy products that managed their lives. As Deborah Brandt has written, both literacy practices and artifacts can "haunt" contemporary scenes of learning, as their traces reproduce literacy's dominant meanings.[12] Such historically produced meanings, in turn, are often taken up in individuals' writing processes, to become "sedimented" in the texts that people author.[13] Put another way, people, practices, and texts inter-animate one another in moments inflected by literacy's longer sociomaterial history in both individual and institutional lives.[14] Such processes were at work in the literacies of the young people of South Mills, and served to deprioritize English in their literacy experiences. Under the textual conditions of their marginalization, it was not English, but *papers* that more profoundly shaped their educational trajectories, migratory lives, and ultimately their writing.

To make this case in the pages that follow, I first show how mobility and literacy have been linked for young people, as many migrated to further educational goals. If literacy promoted mobility, young people found that papers often regulated it, contributing to their beliefs that to achieve their goals stateside they needed not more and better English, but more and better papers. It is here that papers and literacy began to merge for the young. Many saw them as related tools, used within the larger textual regimes of state and school, to alternately constrict or facilitate their movement. These sociomaterial meanings suffused young people's beliefs about literacy's potential for improving their lives, a process exemplified by their experiences of writing to pass the checkpoints that stood in their way.

Upwardly Mobile and U.S. Bound

Young people began to associate literacy education with social and physical mobility well before migration.[15] Young adults often migrated across the world in order to move up in the world. This narrative of mobility was remarkably consistent across the ten young adults in the larger study. Consider here how such a narrative functioned in the lives of five, who represent a range of educational accomplishments, from having dropped out of high school to having completed a four-year degree. Their migration trajectories began from remarkably similar places, with positive orientations to academic literacy and with the belief that the United States would offer the possibility to transcend limiting social positions through education.

For many first-generation Brazilian migrants, the preparation for upward social mobility via education began before they migrated. Simone, an undocumented college student in her twenties, went to private schools in Brazil to avoid what her mother, Sandra, described as the "precarious" public schools in their small town in the interior of Brazil. When Simone was in seventh grade, however, her father lost his job as a banker, with the result that her parents could no longer afford private school tuition. Determined that her daughters would receive the best possible education, and by extension more secure footing in the middle class, Sandra spoke with the former principal of Simone's private school, who had moved to South Mills two years earlier, and who advised the family to join her. Just before Simone entered eighth grade they did. When I met them, they had been living in South Mills without documents for eight years. But Sandra believed she made the right decision. "Without them studying here, we would just go home," she told me. Migration was a logical continuation of Simone's parents' efforts to ensure their children's educational success.

Similar beliefs pervaded other families' decisions to migrate, even when the parents were not as highly educated as Simone's. Twenty-one-year-old Milton, a documented community college student from Brazil, was the son of a single mother who worked in Brazil collecting bus tickets. She invested in his early literacy education by teaching him to write, her hand guiding his as he traced a pencil over a lined piece of paper, "making those little waves," and by paying for private reading classes before he started school. In her attempt to both make ends meet and educate her son, she cooked *marmitas*, heavy tins filled with layers of food, which a seven-year-old Milton would deliver to customers, a process that taught him math. In a pattern widely repeated, his mother migrated to the United States and left him with family friends in Brazil for what she said would be six months but turned into five years, while she earned money, paid off loans associated with migration, and finally was able to arrange for his legal passage. He told me he'd like to finish college and work with computers, or perhaps become a lawyer, in part because he was becoming a man. As he put it, "I won't always have my mother," the woman who harnessed the difficult conditions of his upbringing for education and migration, laying the groundwork for his social mobility stateside.

Of all the young people I spoke with, undocumented twenty-year-old Jocélia, whom readers met in the previous chapter, had the longest social distance to travel from her home in Brazil and perhaps the most passionate beliefs in the promise of education. Jocélia grew up in one of Brazil's many impoverished *favelas*, where she lived with her mother and abusive stepfather. School was her refuge. She often didn't have food at home, but at school she could eat. Once she was old enough to work at twelve, she babysat during the day and attended school at nights alongside working adults. During this time she fell in love with English, using it as a secret code to record her thoughts daily in her diary and to write worshipful love letters to her doting English teachers. School, and the English-language classroom in particular, pointed the way to possibilities that her social circumstances and family history would seem to preclude. Jocélia's mother had become a domestic servant at the age of seven ("So small! Cooking in those big pans!" Jocélia exclaimed). But through the sparkling lens of an education in English, Jocélia envisioned a different life for herself in the land of opportunity, the United States. She borrowed money from her cousins, already living in South Mills, and migrated on a student visa that expired when she didn't have enough money to continue to pay tuition. Optimistic, at the time of our interview she hoped to earn enough money both to return to school and to buy her mother a house in Brazil—two goals she believed could be accomplished stateside.

For these three Brazilians, educational goals promoted migration. Plans for their social mobility began when they were still children in Brazil, as their mothers (or in Jocélia's case, her precocious self) put them on particular literacy tracks, aiming to take them forward and ultimately to take them elsewhere. The residue of these childhood experiences continued to circulate and act on them. All were strikingly driven, in part because migration entailed sacrifice. Milton and his mother lost years of his childhood together. Simone's mother exchanged a job as a teacher for one as an undocumented factory worker, and more excruciating, she left Simone's older sister in Brazil. Jocélia felt she had abandoned her mother, who complained that she didn't help her enough (Jocélia made up for her absence by remitting money to her mother). In what Alvarez terms the "immigrant bargain," the sacrifices of migration weighed heavily on the educational success of these young adults.[16] To balance the scales, they had to make good on the American Dream. They were determined to go *para frente*.

Even for those born in the United States, social mobility seemed a logical continuation of physical mobility. For the two Azorean Americans featured in this chapter, their plans for academic achievement entailed a thinking back through the migration histories of their parents. Steven, a second-generation Azorean American who had put his community college degree temporarily on hold, described his mother's reasons for migrating as "because of school." In the United States she earned a community college degree and opened a successful travel agency. Readers will recall that Tina, from chapter 2, a second-generation Azorean American who had dropped out of high school and was taking classes toward a GED, described her mother's decision to migrate as if she were there, taking on, to an extent, her mother's hopes and dreams for the United States: As a young person in the Azores, her mother often saw planes passing overhead as she was hanging laundry and vowed to go to the United States to be "rich." This image—of a young woman in a rustic village dreaming American dreams underneath the path of an airplane—speaks to the collusion of physical and social mobility that, though they themselves did not migrate, animated the narratives of second-generation immigrants.

In light of the normative expectation of social mobility, second-generation Azorean Americans often judged their parents for their supposed underachievement. Steven's father was a truck driver who migrated at seventeen and did not continue his education stateside. In Steven's view, his father "had a lot of opportunities in this great country" that he "passed up." Steven, who thought of himself as ambitious, a doer, said he "takes after his mother," and hoped to succeed through school. And during my last interview with Tina, which occurred in the presence of her mother, the conversation turned into a family argument, as Tina derided her mother for not learning to speak English after thirty years in the United States. I read Tina's and Steven's anger with their parents as disappointment with the broken promise of upward social mobility.

They both planned to do better. Steven viewed his transnational upbringing as a positive motivator of academic achievement. Though he did not think of himself as good at literacy ("Reading is hard for me," he said), Steven described satisfying early literacy experiences linked to his transnational family life. He received children's literature in the mail from his aunt who remained on the Azorean island of São Miguel. And when he became old enough to spend the summers in the Azores with his grandparents, he learned to write letters in Portuguese back to his parents. In the future, he hoped to complete college to ensure a footing in the middle class: "Nowadays you see associate's degrees, bachelor's degrees, you have to go to college. That's why I'm at [the local community college]." For her part, Tina, after a long workday and after her children were in bed for the night, struggled to write the essays required for her GED class. "Even a high school degree doesn't get you what it used to," she said, aware of the long road ahead. Tina, with the least formal education of those in this chapter and with little, in her words, academic "help at home," saw migration and educational upward mobility as of a piece. She felt she had missed out on some early advantages, but she put her shoulder to the academic wheel anyway, gave a shove, and attempted to move forward.

Documented and undocumented, born in Brazil and in the United States, from poor and middle-class families, born to parents with formal education and those with none, these young people shared remarkably similar views of the trajectory from first- or second-generation migrant to successful middle-class U.S. resident. For all, the belief that through education, and literacy education in particular, one could better one's circumstances permeated their and their families' migration experiences. The ideology of mobility pervaded their childhood literacy experiences, during early literacy lessons, during rehearsals of familiar migration stories, during discussions of future plans. Their plan, unquestioned and widely shared, was to fulfill the narrative logic by which moving to a new country entailed moving up. Moving up, their early experiences led them to believe, was to be accomplished through literacy education.

But if literacy education was to promote mobility, many encountered roadblocks on their educational paths—roadblocks they believed (sometimes rightly and sometimes mistakenly) could be overcome not necessarily with English, but with papers. The following two sections detail these roadblocks first from the perspective of undocumented young people, and then from the perspective of documented.

The Border Thickens: The Undocumented

In my discussions with undocumented young people, they did not express concern over their English. Based on self-reports, the kinds of jobs they held, their educational credentials, and in two cases interviews that moved between English and Portuguese, I became convinced that young people's English literacy was not blocking their mobility. The educational problems they faced were linked to their undocumented status. Their stories revealed that a similar system of textual regulation that polices national borders also policed their schools. As a result, they often experienced schools —public, authoritative, bureaucratic—as extensions of the very state that sought their expulsion. In fact, at the time of this study policy makers in some states had taken advantage of schools' bureaucratic infrastructure to make them effective border guards: In Alabama, for example, migration information was collected in elementary schools. And in other states, transnational young people were restricted from entering college without documents, or had to pay out-of-state tuition. The border effectively thickened into the lives, literacies, and classrooms of undocumented young people.[17] As a result, it was not the linguistic aspect of literacy that required negotiating for the three young women I feature in this section; rather, it was literacy's material incarnation in papers.

For some, undocumented status made it financially impossible to pursue higher education. Such was the case for Jocélia, whose story of truncated educational attainment is, unfortunately, the shortest. She did not have the money to both pay back the loan that financed her migration and pay for tuition. Plus, since she had entered the United States on a student visa, she was not authorized to work, thereby limiting job prospects to low-paying, often exploitative positions. As a result, she did not continue her studies, at which point her student visa expired and she became undocumented. She hoped to go back to school at some point, but Jocélia had few options. Even if she could renew her student visa, unlikely given that she overstayed and was "illegal," she still would not be able to earn enough money to pay for her tuition. And even if she could cobble together enough under-the-table income to pay for tuition, these jobs would divert her time away from studying. Jocélia worked to continue her English education informally, by practicing her English even around fellow Portuguese speakers. "I came here," she told me, determined and cheerful, "to learn English." Yet the way state visa regulations articulated with colleges and universities meant that the higher educational trajectories of students like Jocélia—bright, motivated, from an impoverished background—were often stalled. Jocélia's academic success depended on a student visa, the renewal of which was out of reach.

Unfortunately for Simone and Carmém (another undocumented young Brazilian woman, whom readers briefly met in the previous chapter), both of whom migrated to South Mills when they were still young enough to attend public schools, school and state were aligned in K–12 contexts as well. If states systematically sought the exclusion of the undocumented, schools would ideally be spaces of inclusion, where all young people would have, in Carmém's words, a "place." The project of K–12 schooling is not, after all, to enforce immigration law. It is to educate children. Yet even as early as middle and high school, the textual regulations governing migration had thickened into their classrooms. In eighth grade, Simone entered an ESL track, which she described as "bagunçado," messy and chaotic. Students were not motivated, Simone explained to me, because so many were undocumented. What was the point of studying if your potential was already limited? Their viewpoint is entirely rational, Simone explained. There are few institutionalized rewards for completing college while undocumented, because job opportunities are restricted to those that do not demand papers—often low-paid service work, such as cleaning houses.[18] For this reason, a Brazilian mother I interviewed encouraged her teenage son to leave school. Since he wasn't doing well and didn't have documents anyway, there was no point in graduating. If one of the payoffs of completing school was attaining a well-paying job, and such jobs were off limits to the undocumented, it makes sense that young people despaired that their efforts at school were in vain. For school to be a materially worthwhile endeavor, one needed at least a valid work visa.

Lack of papers also foreclosed opportunities for potentially positive connections with teachers in schools. Both Simone and Carmém spoke of the debilitating consequences of discrimination that they linked to their legal status. For example, Carmém disliked the ESL classes in which she found herself, not because of English, but because of her "inferior" position as an ESL student: "I didn't like it. *It wasn't because of English*. I didn't feel, kind of, I don't know. I knew that there wasn't my place. So I felt very below, very *inferior*, you know? . . . The way they looked at you." In Carmém's experience, the salient problem with ESL was not the content, the English language itself. It was, instead, the context in which, as an ESL student, she felt inferior, in part because of papers.

A potential refuge from the discrimination Carmém and Simone experienced were some of the teachers who were immigrants, who "lived what we lived. They treated us different, they treated us well. But the American [students and principal] that were in the school, they never treated us well." But even the help from the immigrant Portuguese teachers had limits circumscribed by documents. I asked Carmém if she could appeal to the Portuguese teachers for assistance in negotiating her hostile school environment, to which she replied, "You can't, you know? You can't complain. You have to know your place. This is just when they told us: 'You weren't born here, go back to your country. This is not your country.'" In one way, the immigrant Portuguese teachers "lived what we lived," but Carmém and Simone could not cross the documentary border that separated them from these potential allies. The school environment, far from living up to its inclusive ideals, reaffirmed the state's view of undocumented students like Carmém as deportable. Without the papers attesting to national belonging, Carmém was told, "this is not your country"—even when English was "not a problem."

This message—"this is not your country"—seemed to be repeated at every turn within schools, reifying them as places for legals only. Consider the experiences of Carmém's younger brother, who had been effectively deported (or "self-deported") and whom Carmém sorely missed. Tall for his age at twelve, he had been misbehaving in school. He had pushed another student in line, had stepped on a carton of milk, causing it to explode on a staircase, and had missed days of school. School officials separated him from other children for the other children's "protection," called the police because he had "stolen" the milk, and took him to court for missing school, at which point the judge threatened to take him from his family and put him in foster care if he didn't straighten out, a verdict punctuated by the phrase that Carmém repeated to me as governing her experiences at school: "This is not your country." Carmém's parents, rather than face the prospect of the state taking custody of their son, made arrangements for him to return to Brazil to live with his grandparents. When he "self-deported," the United States literally ceased to be his country.

If Carmém felt that school was not "her place," it was not because she was not academically inclined: her favorite childhood games were "playing teacher," and she wrote summaries of literary novels in her diary for fun, activities that would portend a place firmly in the privileged norm for U.S. schools. But without the right papers, Carmém experienced schools differently. No longer fun, they were of a piece with courts, public institutions whose bland bureaucratic gazes belied surprising menace, and in which transnationals, and the undocumented in particular, were at risk. These legalistic consequences represent a particularly bureaucratic instantiation of discrimination, where a series of school and state regulations seemed to conspire, to make those without papers feel "inferior," and to endeavor to exclude them altogether.

This constant threat of deportation hounded undocumented young adults. During my fieldwork, the subject of nearby ICE raids threaded its way into everyday conversations, and both Jocélia and Simone spoke of their fear of being denounced to authorities. At the same time, the local Brazilian paper ran a cover story on a nineteen-year-old bride jilted just days before their wedding, not because her fiancé got cold feet but because he was detained and deported. The headline read "ICE Freezes Wedding," and the center photo pictured an empty wedding dress, near a smaller photo of someone in handcuffs—images likely potent for Carmém who, at the time of our interview, had been recently married to another undocumented Brazilian migrant.[19] The future, imagined in vivid colors by many young adults, was clouded for the undocumented by uncertainty. Exactly what one could or could not do and exactly how far one could or could not go was never clear. Carmém was appalled that the police were called to reprimand her brother ("He was just doing typical kid things") and that her family's status as migrants was invoked in court. But she was also confused. It seemed that the school/immigration authorities were capable of anything. As for Simone, she exited the ESL class that marked her as potentially undocumented, in order to, in her words, *ir para frente.*

But just how far ahead she could get without papers was in question. Simone's high school and college career were marked by misinformation and rumors that she could not clarify without revealing her status. As early as high school, classmates told her that she could not go to college if she wasn't a citizen. Once in college, a trusted friend told her she needed to have legal documents in order to complete her required internship. She was even misinformed by the head of admissions at her university, who warned her in her freshman year that she had better have her documents "ready" by the time she graduated. She worried that he was right when she found, at the end of her senior year, that she had to fill out a form to graduate: "I said, now this . . . Now they're going to ask for this, ask for that, no?" I asked Simone's mother how she and her husband persisted in encouraging their children to study, despite the expense of college, the slim prospects for employment, the fear of being found out, the uncertainty of the future. She answered by saying she had faith in God, highlighting the lack of a clear institutional path to upward social mobility via education for the undocumented. Perhaps educational institutions were the only sites in which to pursue social mobility, but they were also closely enough aligned with the state that they could plausibly demand papers. Such threats kept young undocumented transnationals running.

The border thickened into the academic lives of Jocélia, Carmém, and Simone in ways direct and indirect. On the one hand, the relationship between school and state was infrastructural: student visas, as we saw with Jocélia, were part of the official classification system of immigration services, a privileged category for transnationals who had the means to study in U.S. schools. Jocélia, it turned out, did not have the means and so lost her visa. The experiences of Carmém and Simone show that the border infiltrated K–12 classrooms in other ways as well:

Undocumented young people, understandably, felt unmotivated. They faced discrimination. They felt bereft at the deportation of family members. They did not know whom to trust to tell them how far they could go. Educational progress became labyrinthine for the undocumented, whose future prospects so heavily depended on papers.

In hours of interviews with Simone over a two-year period, she expressed little concern with the potentially daunting task of putting one word after the next in an academic essay in English. For Carmém, "the English wasn't the problem." Her English literacy was sufficient for her to land a job at an insurance agency immediately after graduating from high school, where she drafted complex car insurance policies entirely in English. And Jocélia seemingly effortlessly switched between English and Portuguese throughout our interview, and happily described how she was beginning to learn Spanish. For these young undocumented women, their success stateside was not impeded by struggles with language but by bigger textual anxieties: Would they have the right papers to pass?

The Power of Papers for the Documented

Documented young people did not usually face the threat of deportation, the anxiety of being found out, and the confusion about their futures that pervaded the lives of the undocumented. Achieving the social mobility that they desired seemed to require only that all-important immigrant ingredient, hard work. Despite their best efforts, however, young second-generation Azorean Americans found themselves struggling in school. To their indignation, their papers did not work like they were supposed to. Their diplomas and passports, their "American papers," to quote Steven, did not always allow passage through mainstream avenues toward social mobility. Steven and Tina, who were not quite white and not quite middle class, experienced discrimination throughout their educations that acted more powerfully on their progress than did papers. Yet despite this personal experience to the contrary, *they continued to believe in papers' promise.* Such beliefs, in the face of evidence to the contrary, speak to how forcefully the institutional histories of papers infused their lived experiences.

The problem of "second generation" underachievement has been attributed to downward assimilation into poor, minority communities; persistent racism; or poverty.[20] And some of these factors may have been present in Tina's and Steven's lives. From their perspectives, however, what stood out was the ways that schools equated their transnational histories with literacy deficits—deficits readers will later see they sought to overcome through papers, with far-reaching consequences for their educational success. For Tina, the school fundamentally misunderstood her background as a bilingual American when she entered kindergarten. In a move repeated throughout the United States, Tina was placed in special needs classes, in her words, "only because of the language." This legacy haunted her long after she learned adequate English, and into middle school, where it was suggested that she return to special needs. She never did rejoin the special needs program because she got pregnant with her first child and dropped out. Significantly, though, in her two interviews with me she attributed her attrition not to her pregnancy, but to her academic misplacement. The bilinguality that accompanied her transnational childhood was read as a cognitive impairment, halting her educational progress just as it was getting started.

Academic misplacement could haunt transnationals' educational trajectories even into college. Such was the case with Steven. When Steven entered kindergarten for the first time in South Mills, he was held back a year for, in his words, "speaking Portuguese." But Steven quickly picked up English, graduated from the technical high school, and proceeded to the local community college, with the goal of majoring in business administration. Although he had graduated from high school in the United States, at college he was placed in a required ESL class, where he was among recently arrived immigrants his mother's age, and which he described as the "longest class he ever took, even though it was only forty minutes": "The teacher was too slow and easy. I felt like I was taking an eighth-grade class. It was too easy for me: 'Today's word for the week is . . . Write a paragraph.' Like you know? 'On your favorite thing.' Simple things. We were taking spelling tests." Clearly, both Tina and Steven felt they were academically tracked in ways that undersold their academic competency and wasted time that they could have better spent moving forward.[21]

Maddening to both Steven and Tina was that neither their language ability nor their papers mitigated their chronic misplacement. "I don't even have an accent in English," Tina insisted. As Steven complained, "I mean I know I speak English. I've done the work." From their points of view, problems with language were attributed to them because of their transnational histories—histories including a bilingualism that only became problematic in the context of schools. "I just know how to speak two languages" was Steven's adamantly positive take on what both his school and community college read as a deficit. For Steven, if his linguistic ability in English was not a problem, his position as American-born transnational, illegible to the dualistic discursive categories that governed his placement in his college composition course, was. Steven, whose literacy education, recall, spanned the Azores and the United States, was not recognizably native, so he had to be foreign.

Both Steven and Tina, however, had the papers to prove they were *not* foreign. As Steven incredulously put it, "I have a high school diploma. I've been here for school my whole life." Having the right language and the right papers, they protested, should have been enough to ensure their legibility. Yet neither citizenship papers, nor English language competency, nor the diplomas that certified this competency protected Tina and Steven from educational misplacement. Neither papers nor language fulfilled their promise of upward social mobility. If texts are strong, and if language is power, the lesson seemed to be that xenophobia was stronger.

It is a testament to the way young people *experienced* texts as strong, and *experienced* papers as promoting mobility, however, that both Steven and Tina believed the panacea to their educational struggles was not more or better English, but more and better papers, as I explain here. Such beliefs grew from their family's histories of textually mediated migration and their literacy experiences stateside. Both young second-generation Azorean Americans and documented first-generation Brazilians came to understand their opportunities in "this great country," in Steven's words, in part through their parents' efforts to attain papers. Tina's and Steven's families followed the pattern of so many Azoreans described in chapter 2. For example, Tina's mother migrated, wrote letters to her fiancé in the Azores, and finally issued a *carta de chamada* to sponsor his migration. For documented Brazilians, a *carta de chamada* was gained similarly, through marriage to an American citizen. For example, Milton's mother (and that of another documented student from Brazil, Gabriella) was sponsored through her marriage to an American man. In Milton's mother's case, the marriage was short-lived but served its purpose. She could call for her youngest son, who would complete high school stateside. For Gabriella, her mother's marriage allowed her to live with her mother as she studied at the community college.[22] However they were attained, papers circulated in family narratives and in young people's understanding of how they had come to inhabit the particular set of rights and restrictions that accompanied their legal status. Those who migrated and those born in the United States were aware of how papers were achieved, and what privileges they could provide. The social and institutional practices accompanying papers worked their way into young people's beliefs about those papers.

That having the right papers failed to provide for their educational mobility did not override these young people's beliefs that papers could compensate for the misplacement that characterized their educational experiences. Tina's misplacement in school, justified by the nationally inflected concepts of language and literacy, extended what I understood as her feelings of national displacement, from both the Azores and the United States. She sought to shelter her young daughter from similar tribulations by enforcing that in her house "there is no Portuguese, only books." The language, Portuguese, was replaced by the material text, the paper book. Books were the key to avoiding, in Tina's words, "what Mommy did," the key to finishing college, to making good, two generations later, on the American Dream. Similarly, for Steven, the oppressive alignment between language and nation could only be broken by the more powerful logic of papers. Consider the following interview excerpt, in which I asked Steven a routine question about his father, who worked delivering imported Portuguese wines to New England retailers.

K: Does he get to use his Portuguese?
S: Yes. Of course. He's an American citizen here. He got his American papers a year after he was here, actually.

In what appears to be a non sequitur, Steven answered my question about his father's *language use* with a discussion of his *papers*. There is a logic in this association, however, that Steven's scholastic experiences bore out: One's language, connected to one's continued communication with an ethnic community, calls into question one's Americanness. And Americanness is shown most definitively for transnationals *by papers*. Papers divided Azorean Americans from newly arrived immigrants, as readers saw in chapter 1. And papers facilitated mobility. Books and diplomas, in this way, carried a similar semiotic weight as naturalization documents. They were the payoff on the investment of migration. Both were, in Steven's words, "American papers."

On the one hand, the experiences of these Azorean Americans suggest that the educational trajectories of second-generation young adults may be more profoundly impeded by the widespread misunderstanding of bilingualism than by anything else. In schools, Tina's and Steven's transnational positions were refracted back to them as language and literacy shortcomings—shortcomings that they did not recognize, but that nonetheless had devastating consequences for their educations. Yet despite the relentlessness with which schools seemed to equate linguistic assimilation and educational achievement, documented young adults continued to dwell instead on the primacy of papers, even in the face of evidence that papers did not always mean mobility. Migration papers were crucial parts of families' migration mythologies, of how they came to reside in the United States, and of how they planned to provide their children "opportunities in this great country." It was worrying to many that these opportunities were not forthcoming, highlighting the fragility of upward social mobility for those marked as transnational.

Young adults answered these concerns not with more language classes, but with more *papers*. Papers were proof of national belonging when national belonging was called into question. And papers both demanded and promised mobility when mobility was stalled. The logic that the right papers would allow one to pass was so commonsensical that evidence to the contrary was met with incredulity. Surely, the answer was simply to attain more, and more appropriate, papers. In sum, young people associated papers with the mobility that literacy education promised but rarely offered.

"Pretty Soon They Will Prohibit Us from Walking": Cars, Sandals, and Licenses

Such associations were enforced not only in schools but also in extracurricular spaces, namely, in that icon of social and physical mobility, the car. I had initially disregarded young adults' frequent mention of cars—buying them, driving them, crashing them, working with them, being stopped in them—as a curious coincidence in my fieldwork, unrelated to the larger themes of literacy that I was pursuing. Yet a closer analysis of this category revealed that the most American of vehicles, the car, crystallized the relationship between papers and physical and social mobility for transnational young adults. In a car one speeds along a route forged from available public roads, and one is also potentially stopped and asked for one's papers, which may or may not suffice to allow one to pass. This ethnographic detail, I hope, allows readers a fuller picture of papers' integration in young people's experiences of social and physical mobility, which the final part of this chapter will show sedimented into their writing processes themselves.

For many, the very attainability of cars in the United States spoke to possibilities for upward social mobility. Jocélia described wanting to stay in the United States despite her undocumented status, because, in her words, she was very "materialist": "Here I already worked and bought a car [that she subsequently crashed], my laptop, my little things that I always dreamed of having . . . I want to buy a house for me and a car for me, understand?" Milton gave a similar explanation: "Look, here you have, you have more opportunities . . . When am I going to have a car like that one there in Brazil? . . . When am I going to be able to drive [at this age], no? I have a good television. When am I going to buy this in Brazil?" Others echoed these sentiments. "I could work for fifteen years in Brazil and still never have a car," Gabriella complained. Simone spoke of buying another technology of mobility, sandals: "At least here, if I see them, I can wait for them to go on sale and buy them." The word "materialist," as a summary of the excruciating exchange of car for country, both justified the significant sacrifices made to migrate and subtly indicted a U.S. culture in which everyone, in another metaphor of mobility used by Simone's mother, was "running after money." Cars signified not only what one could buy in the United States but where one could go, and at what price.

Cars also highlighted migrants' socioeconomic vulnerability: Readers learned in the previous chapter that Jocélia crashed her car due to sleep deprivation occasioned by crushing overwork at three under-the-table jobs. Similarly Steven, who attended a trade school, watched his vocational dream as an auto-body worker disappear in the midst of deindustrialization. In his words, he had picked up a "hobby, not a trade." And recall that Carmém's first job out of high school was drafting car insurance policies. She ultimately quit, due to the "humiliating" anti-immigrant discrimination she experienced from her supervisor. For these young adults, the American Dream was more fragile than they had imagined, depending on a physical body encased in metal and glass, zipping through the streets in pursuit of cash. These traumas—a near deadly crash, the loss of a longed for career, the psychological harm of repeated discrimination—loomed in young adults' discussions of their struggles stateside. They demanded that migrants reroute: Jocélia, as we saw in chapter 3, found God, Steven went to community college, and Carmém found work in South Mills ethnic Brazilian enclave, tentatively safe from the hostile mainstream. That such traumatic life events occurred in and around cars spoke to the risks of mobility, both social and physical—risks mitigated or heightened by papers.

The anxiety of driving without papers frequently surfaced in immigrants' stories. For example, in order to get to an internship required for her college major, Simone had to drive to a town forty-five minutes away, a task she shared with a documented Azorean colleague. Forbidden to have a driver's license due to her documentary status, she drove in fear of being stopped by the police, detained, and deported: "Imagine me, on the road every day. Thank God, nothing ever . . . I was never stopped," she said. Accompanying this constant fear in the moving spaces of the car was another low-frequency anxious hum: She did not want the friend with whom she carpooled to find out her status.

Like Simone, others experienced driving as sites of profound anxiety, where papers in the form of driver's licenses that they could not renew or apply for threatened to impede their movement. Many described being pulled over by the police and getting in car crashes where they had to negotiate their lack of insurance and licenses. Father Pedro, the head of the Brazilian Catholic church, told me of a Brazilian family being picked up by police "for not looking American" at a gas station as they were filling up. ("You mean for not looking like a white American?" I pressed. Father Pedro laughed. *Obviously.*) They were detained and deported. In light of such deportations, I heard of Brazilians who had stopped driving altogether (although I never personally met them— how else was one to get around?) as an example of the stark consequences of restrictive immigration laws. To drive may not be a human right, but it is a fundamentally "American" one, representing at once the contradictory freedoms and oppressions that undocumented South Millsites experienced in the United States.

Simone's father explained the textual vulnerability of driving best.

> When you drive in your country, you have your language and your docu-
> ment. The police stop you, you have your document. You know how to talk.
> Here, the police stop you: "Your driver's license." "There, I have it." He
> starts to say one thing, say another, you end up understanding a little, but
> not understanding almost anything else. You aren't used to messing with
> the police, so it's difficult. The situation is difficult.

In this scenario he shows a document to the police. But the document
itself (legal? forged? expired? he did not say) does not clarify. The
police officer begins to speak, in a language that is not "yours" and in
a genre ("messing with the police") that is also foreign. Offering his
document seems to muddle communication rather than facilitate it,
obscure rather than clarify, rendering him illegible and the words of
the police inscrutable. This high-stakes textual interaction, one that
for many migrants ends in detention centers and deportation, reifies
his position as a migrant subject to documentary regulations, especially when on the move. The moving migrant, the one who dares
occupy the American space of a car, is one that seems to threaten the
social order.

As one young participant summed up the restrictions on immigrant
mobility, recalling Simone's mention of sandals, "Pretty soon they will
prohibit us from walking." Some participants already thought they
were restricted from walking, highlighting the dangerous visibility that
participants experienced when in motion. "In Brazil," Simone told me,
"people go out on the street, make noise on the street, stay on the street,
you know? You can stay on the street, on the sidewalk, playing." Her
mother similarly described a Brazilian social life in which families
took their chairs to the sidewalks in the evenings to sit and chat with
neighbors, following up with, "Here you can't do that. There are many
things you can't do here." Public spaces, particularly roads, were experienced as sites of intense government regulation, where one was
prohibited from socializing or loitering, depending on your perspective.
In the Latino community Ralph Cintrón describes in *Angels' Town*,
cars were ostentatious symbols of strength and cleanliness, a means of
commanding "respect in conditions of little or no respect," of keeping
at bay conditions of decay, of being visibly (and audibly, in the case of
"thumpers") masculine. Decades later, in two different Latino communities, in a context marked by mass deportations, moving through

the streets in a car invited unwanted regulatory attention. It was safer to stay still, or to buy some sensible sandals.

The experiences of young adults in cars may, for some, call into question the potency of papers. High school diplomas did not protect Stephen and Carmém, whose livelihood depended on cars, from having to find another means of supporting themselves. Similarly, lack of driver's licenses did not appear to stop most people from driving. But migrants nevertheless experienced papers as tightly regulating their movement through city streets. The undocumented drove, but they did so in fear. I witnessed them inch their ways from curbside parking spots to the street, mouthing quick prayers that they would make it to their destinations. While the textual regulation of mobility, so neatly distilled in cars, did not function absolutely, it nonetheless constituted a crucial part of the imaginary that young people had come to inhabit on U.S. soil. Papers gripped their lives, from the migration process itself to their attempts to go *para frente*—or, for that matter, to go anywhere.

Writing to Pass

Thus far readers have seen how literacy and papers accumulated associations with young people's movement across an obstacle-filled terrain. If many migrated in the hopes of educational success, in which literacy learning played a central role, many had their hopes dashed stateside, as the lives of the undocumented were restricted by papers, and the lives of the documented were believed to be bettered by papers. As young people attempted, with varying success, to leverage literacy for papers and leverage papers for literacy, the meanings of literacy and papers merged, such that literacy practices and literacy products came to be experienced as interchangeable instrumental resources to get ahead. In their writing, young people authored texts that sedimented the sociomaterial associations of literacy and papers with mobility.[23] Behind the wheel or with diploma in hand, they presented papers to pass. Likewise, behind the computer or with pen in hand, they wrote to pass. In this way, transnationals' associations with papers—associations of authority, mobility, regulation—thickened into their writing. To explain how literacy and papers merged in the process of writing to pass, I first show how *literacy* functioned as *papers* in young people's writing in college, work, and extracurricular settings, and then how *papers* functioned as *literacy* in young people's uses of diplomas and certificates, a process that muddied the distinction between literacy practices and literacy products.

For Simone, the only undocumented participant in this study who graduated from a four-year college in the United States, her college experience was punctuated with writing papers and presenting papers. These two textual tasks were required to move ahead, occupying parallel positions in the narrative of regulated mobility she shared with me. Buoyed by the financial sacrifices of her undocumented parents (her mother worked in a factory, her father in a restaurant), she was pursuing a degree in medical sciences at the time of our first interview. She described how her uncertain documentary context infused her efforts to do what college students must do to pass: write papers. For many readers, Simone's experiences of college writing may sound familiar. In the required course for her major, she encountered her toughest professor, who demanded essays that, in her words, one could not "B.S.": "If he doesn't see what he wants, or if he sees what he doesn't want, he'll take off points. . . . You write *na na na*, he will 'minus two.' It has to be exactly what he wants." Similarly, in her first-year writing course, she depended on *o penguinzinho colorido*, "the colorful little penguin book," in order to master academic citation systems: "You have to learn MLA, that P, I don't know what it is . . . APA. You have to learn it . . . they give a book that is called Penguin book, no? The colorful little penguin [*penguinzinho colorido*], and you have to read it And from there you write one time. If you do the citation wrong, he corrects it." What Simone chose to tell me about her college writing (with one significant exception that I describe shortly) speaks to her subordinate position as an undergraduate in an academic hierarchy—a position in which her words needed to be corrected, deleted, and revised, or she would face the consequences ("minus two"). As many composition scholars have pointed out, in these circumstances, written words are not necessarily taken up primarily to communicate, but instead to submit them to judgment.[24] "Passei na marra," Simone said of the required writing course in her major, a phrase that roughly translates as "I passed by the sweat of my brow." "But I passed. Everything turned out alright." In this sense, "writing to pass" is a common orientation to literacy among undergraduates, which Simone shared.

The anxiety with which Simone described such writing, however, must be understood in the larger textual context of her documentary vulnerability. She viewed college writing as a checkpoint—a perspective that aligned with the checkpoints she regularly encountered throughout college, at which her documents were demanded. Checkpoints pervaded her college experiences, strengthening connections between presenting papers and writing a paper. The only guides she had to help her through collegiate checkpoints were untrustworthy—more like the coyotes that smuggle humans across borders for pay than like colorful penguins. For instance, she described her anxiety about being able to complete a required internship for her major. Note the detail in which she recalled being asked for her papers, an everyday bureaucratic interaction that her documented classmates most likely had long forgotten.

> When classes finish, there is a day in your junior year. You make a line there, and everyone shows their ID. I showed my [Brazilian] passport to her. She said, "You have a passport. That's OK." And I was worried, not for the fact that I had a criminal record. I don't have anything, you know, but um, I don't know, you know. The check turned out OK, I don't know what. And then, there was another: the paper that was to apply, you had to put your social security number. So there was something else that I didn't have. So it was like that.
>
> In the middle of the summer, I was like this: "It is possible that I'll do the internship? Will I do the internship?" Then when I got news of the internship, it was a happiness, you know? I am going to do the internship. I was accepted.

Just as her writing for college resulted in passing (even if "na marra"), so, too, did the documents that she showed the administrator who surveyed her papers for her internship. For the moment she had been allowed to move forward.

Likewise, when she showed up for the first day of her internship, she was again asked for papers, this time her social security card. "I just froze," she said of this moment, worried that the classmate that accompanied her would overhear and denounce her to the authorities. Simone offered her phone number instead, which apparently sufficed. Just as she passed through busy intersections in her car, she passed for legal, and passed her class. In fact, Simone used the same phrase to punctuate her passing of each of these checkpoints: "Deu tudo certo," which means, "Everything turned out alright."

This concern with papers seeped into Simone's orientation to academic literacy as a whole. The only college writing she described as meaningful to her was her final research paper in her technical writing class, which detailed the fraught process of crossing a border illegally and acquiring an education. A multimodal project about migrant rights, it featured an image of migrants swimming across a river at night and another image of a cross in the desert for those who died in the journey. These images, along with the accompanying words, argued for passage of the DREAM act—which would allow a route to legal permanent residence and citizenship for the undocumented who arrived in the United States as children and who completed their educations. In this essay (which I do not quote here for fear of compromising her identity) and indeed all her college writing, Simone inscribed a risky path toward upward social mobility, ducking in and out of the shadows as she traveled. On the whole, college writing was for Simone about passing—passing classes, passing checkpoints, passing for legal. It was about giving the right-enough information to a figure of authority with the power to deny or grant her passage. Simone was, after all, on the move. This is not to denounce her attitude toward schooling as overly instrumentalist. Rather, it is to recognize that the punishing material realities that were tied up in her lived experiences with textuality could not be extricated from the literate site of the classroom, could not be extricated from her writing itself. She experienced her writing as papers.

As the only undocumented young person in the study to complete college stateside, Simone in some ways was anomalous. The experience of "writing to pass," however, was widely shared among transnational young adults, speaking to how thoroughly the social uses of papers infused everyday writing. Tina, for example, seemed to be Simone's polar demographic opposite: Azorean American and a mother of two, she had not completed high school and was taking state-sponsored GED classes for those laid off from factory work. She also wrote to pass. In her GED class she wrote an essay about being a young mom and learning to care for her daughter, to feed her, to burp her, to love her, which she read in front of her classmates ("I had people crying . . . It was amazing. It was one page front and back."). A meaningful piece of writing, yes. But it was also instrumental. She hoped to get the same question on her actual GED essay test, so that she could reproduce it verbatim, essentially turning her heartfelt essay into a standardized document that she could proffer in exchange for passing. Young people experienced literacy as papers, in part, because, much like with papers, their literacy was used by educational institutions as a regulatory tool.

Young people recounted such regulatory uses of literacy across the domains of school and work, further enmeshing literacy practices within the logic of papers. Such was the case with both Tina and Steven. When Tina left school, she went to work in the area's factories, with jobs including cutting curtains, embroidery, winding yarn, operating the frame, packing, and shipping. Here, because of increasingly systematic record-keeping processes, one day's output could be easily compared to another day's, pressuring workers to produce more ("It was all there on the computer. They were tough on you. Like a sweatshop"). Literacy was a management tool. Likewise, if her high-stakes GED test showed her improvement after a year of courses, she could continue to take state-funded classes. If not, in her words, "time's up." Tina was hustling, writing essays late at night in order to keep up in what she experienced as another kind of textually regulated sweatshop. Steven also described his literacy experiences in relation to the management of time and productivity: "When I study for school I have to sit there for a good two hours to study. Some other people can look at this," he said, gesturing toward the consent form he signed, "But not me. It's a tough time for me to read." During the course of our interview, I began to suspect that it was the bureaucratic conditions surrounding reading that contributed to his self-reported difficulties with literacy. He told me that his favorite class at the community college was his speech class, which "gave me a big turnaround in reading." His difficulty seemed not to be in reading itself, but in reading in the context of an English class (or in the context of an interview by an English professor), which deemed his literacy deficient and marked his scholastic misplacement from first grade to college. From Steven's and Tina's perspective, literacy had been used to demand taxing labor in factories and in school, to allow them to pass or to forbid them from passing. This was how literacy and papers functioned in their parents' lives, beginning with migration, and how literacy and papers had functioned in theirs.

In the practice of writing to pass, the uses and meanings of literacy and papers coalesced, sometimes taking on a more literal form. Carmém, for example, who found herself excluded from school environments, started her own lending library. She would receive books in the mail from Brazil, read them, sign her name, and pass them to a friend with the following instructions: "When you finish reading it, put your name, and pass it on to someone . . . who you know will read it. So you sign it and you can see the name of the person who has it." As opposed to her experiences in the institution of the school, in which she didn't like the way "they looked at you," in her lending library she controlled the terms of her visibility. She inscribed a literacy community in which she was a documented member, and in which other members read a book and signed their names. She did not traffic in public literacy spaces, which were cordoned off, but developed other realms of writing defined by their circulation, their very ability to be passed from one to another. In these varying forms, young people repeatedly merged literacy practices with products, often not distinguishing between the meaning of writing a paper to pass and the meaning of attaining a paper that would allow passage. In this way, writing to pass extended the logic of presenting documents to pass.

Young people's educational ventures, embedded in the larger textual regimes that regulated their mobility, reflected both their personal literacy histories and the institutional literacy histories that so constrained their lives. The meanings of literacy coursed across these sites and were activated and reactivated in their everyday writing practices. Their literacy was papers.

And their papers were also literacy. Such was the case with the way young people viewed diplomas, those papers that certified literacy knowledge. Many viewed the literacy knowledge as a byproduct of the certification itself, which was thought to have broader value. For example, as Simone completed her senior year, she became concerned that she would need a valid visa or green card in order to graduate, as the college admissions officer had warned her in her freshman year. So she was relieved when she learned her application had "passed." She received a phone call from the university's administration: "They asked how do you want to see your name on your diploma? I said *oba* [wow]. I said *oba*. And it turned out alright. My diploma arrived at home. I said, *nossa senhora* [our lady], now it really ended. *Pronto. Chega*. [It's done]." Simone did not tell me about her graduation ceremony or party or writing her final exams. Instead, she dwelled on the appearance of her name printed on her diploma. Both she and her mother spoke of checking the mail daily until this document arrived, a crucial turning point in her narrative. While at the time of our 2010 interview she still did not have immigration papers, Simone hoped to leverage her diploma for a job in Florida—a state that some Brazilian migrants jokingly referred to as *o Brasil que deu certo*, the Brazil that turned out right, in which they believed a climate and culture similar to that of Brazil existed alongside opportunities for economic advancement.[25] While diplomas do not provide the political rights that a green card would, the diploma's arrival in her mailbox, Simone hoped, was the "end." Simone had certified herself in English literacy, having graduated from a U.S. college, but what she emphasized to me was not the English literacy but the certification. Her personal literacy, and that of the institution that evaluated it and used it to regulate her progress, was distilled, or sedimented, within the diploma.

Gabriella, a documented Brazilian woman, shared a similar story. Gabriella did not have the right documentary status to take out student loans in the United States and could not afford tuition, so she decided to continue her education in Brazil. To pay for her studies there, she traded on the two valuable goods she had picked up stateside: First, she had fluency in English literacy, which she learned both through her work as a housekeeper and as a secretary, dictionary in hand to speak to employers, and through letters to an American boyfriend that he sent back to her corrected. Second, and perhaps equally useful, she had earned a certificate from an ESL class she took at Harvard. She described her most significant literacy learning as divorced from the formal educational institutions from which she earned a certificate, but she planned to use the certificate to get a job in Brazil. Her literacy knowledge could do little without the certificate to prop open the door of opportunity.

From the perspective of many young people, these distinctions between certificates and knowledge certified, between papers and literacy, hardly seemed to matter. They compiled the literacy and papers they could to get where they wanted to go. To offer a summary of the young people whose narratives I've featured here: When Steven's technical degree did not offer him work in his dream auto-body career, he did not lose faith in diplomas but tried for another. Jocélia, traumatized by the punishing conditions of undocumented life, turned to the Bible. Likewise, Milton, though without concrete plans to move back to Brazil, wielded two high school diplomas, one from the United States and one from Brazil, which he hoped would leave opportunities open for him in both countries. Carmém hoped to leverage her Italian passport to move to Europe. And Simone. For Simone, *deu tudo quase certo.* Everything almost turned out alright. She did not have a driver's license, but she attained a college diploma, which she hoped would allow her to pass.

Mobility infused the way young people understood the conditions of their past, the challenges of the present, and their plans for the future. It constituted their narratives, their cyclical life patterns. Far from liberatory, in their narratives "writing to pass" was a way to stay marginally ahead of the pack in what felt for some like a rat race, and for others like persecution. "Writing to pass" describes their literate efforts to get ahead in the way they had learned that migrants appropriately get ahead, or get *anywhere* for that matter: by presenting the right papers. At the same time, "writing to pass" resonates with the assimilationist logic that has long dogged U.S. literacy history, in which the literacies of people of color have been systematically devalued. As the border thickened into the lives of young people, they wrote to pass the political, academic, and social checkpoints that stood in their way. In so doing, they hoped to attain the upward mobility they came to the United States to pursue and that often seemed to remain, tantalizingly, a green card or a diploma away.

Strong Texts in Young People's Lives

Young people's experiences with papers saturated their experiences with literacy, such that literacy practices and literacy products became tightly fused in their imaginations and in everyday use. In the context of textually regulated literacy regimes, young people both wrote to pass and attained documents that represented their literacy knowledge, hoping to use those to pass as well. If English literacy was used at the turn of the twentieth century to "assimilate" immigrants (help them pass socially or racially), young people in this study showed little concern with English or assimilation. Their most significant experiences of literacy were more material than linguistic, more transnational than assimilative, more pragmatic than ideological. English could be learned. Leveraging the appropriate literacy to attain the papers that would allow one mobility in the United States or elsewhere? That was a much more consequential and difficult proposition. For these reasons, young adults continued to foist dreams and anxieties onto the dense locus of texts, the invaluable currency of transnational realms.

Taken together, the stories young people shared with me reveal the social conditions that can lead texts to be experienced as strong. As readers recall from the introduction, "strong text" refers to largely out-dated theories of literacy that reduced complex literacy practices to their products, and imputed civilization-changing qualities to liter-acy's technical properties. In some ways, young people's experiences of literacy as papers lead to an alignment with such theories: For them, literacy was experienced as its product, as strong texts with far-reaching consequences. At the same time, texts were experienced as strong due to the collusion of multiple deeply social factors: Nation-states and schools that used literacy to regulate populations; globalization pro-cesses that encouraged families to move for upward mobility; ide-ologies that swirled around literacy education; and everyday literacy experiences that were shaped by people's documentary status. Texts, perhaps, can only be strong in such conditions, where literacy is socio-historically enmeshed in institutions, people, practices, and the arti-facts, such as papers, that resonate with its various imbrications. For the young people of South Mills, literacy accrued meaning as it circu-lated, socially and materially, across these varied nodes.

Papers, as readers have seen here, did not function monolithically. They did not fully restrict the entrance of the unauthorized to the United States, nor did they always secure the rights of the authorized. It was, I believe, the incomplete and often unpredictable enforcement of papers' regulatory power that contributed to their tenacious hold on the lives of the young. Maybe these young people would move ahead, maybe they would be held back. Maybe they would be deported, maybe they would be allowed to stay. Such porosity may have strengthened the textual regimes of school and state in young people's lives. The result was that papers vibrated with the potential for movement. These meanings flowed through young people's literacy practices, as they wrote to move up and as they compiled documents to move elsewhere. Such beliefs about literacy and papers—that they can get you from one place to another, that they can help you pass—characterized the too-often-unfulfilled aspirations of the young. For many, the American Dream was a dream on paper only.

CONCLUSION

Lessons Learned from Transnational Lives:
Toward a Sociomaterialist Literacy

I INTERVIEWED RAFAEL, a young undocumented Brazilian man, in my rental car in the parking lot of St. Mary's Catholic Church, still crowded after the evening Brazilian mass. It was raining, painting the already gray city a deeper shade of grit, but Rafael was cheerful, playful even. Like I began most interviews, I asked him if he'd like to choose a pseudonym.

"James Bond," he replied.

"James Bond," I repeated. "No. It has to be a Brazilian name, no?"

"José," he complied.

"José?"

"In Brazil there are many Josés and Marias. Lots and lots."

"Here, too," I answered, thinking of my grandfather, father, uncles, and aunts.

"What is your husband's name?" Rafael asked.

"Ricardo."

"It can't be Ricardo . . . Ricardo is *bad*," he said, pronouncing "bad" in English. "So I have my wife. If she stays with another man, that man gets the nickname Ricardo, because he picks up married women. Get it?"

"Rafael," a name *I* finally decided on, had offered up several potential pseudonyms: James Bond, an undercover detective; José, who could be mistaken for any male at any geographic or historic location in the Lusophone diaspora; and Ricardo, a man who infringes on the institution of marriage, temporarily usurping the role of husband. I was the one who forced the issue of pseudonyms, false names I would use in this book to hide the real identities of those who made themselves vulnerable before my computer keyboard. But James Bond/

José/Ricardo/Rafael already understood this pseudonymic logic. He knew that written identification often obscures, even as it claims to illuminate, that it often excludes even as it claims to integrate, that it often fixes in place even as it promises mobility.

Like Rafael, the people featured in this book were living, reading, and writing in a contradictory moment of both rapid global movement and entrenched bureaucratic restrictions of this movement. Through the struggles and triumphs they shared with me, this book has also followed another character adapting to the rapidly globalizing, document-infused first decade of the new millennium—literacy. The people with whom I spoke did not associate literacy with cultural assimilation, that old goal of immigrant literacy instruction. Instead, they associated it with mobility. Moreover, they did not think of literacy in terms of only the practices of reading and writing. Instead, they linked such literacy practices with literacy products. For the migrant communities at the heart of this book, literacy practices and products coursed through powerful bureaucracies, regulating people's movement, in ways that, as Rafael's simultaneously playful and wary response suggests and as this conclusion will detail, has consequences for literacy's social uses, its pedagogical potential, and its longer-term role in transnational lives.

A Sociomaterial Theory of Literacy: Some Social Consequences

The sociomaterial theory of literacy I have been developing in these pages suggests that in transnational lives, literacy is best seen as a mobile complex of practices and products, instilled with meaning both by institutions and by the people under their thrall. In chapter 1 readers saw how literacy's and papers' value shifted in relation to each other, as migrants vied for upward mobility. In later chapters, literacy and papers were exchanged among people and state institutions during the migration process (chapter 2), traded between state and church bureaucracies that promised liberty (chapter 3), and fused together in individuals' literate attempts to get ahead (chapter 4). By virtue of this interplay between process and product, what I have come to call sociomateriality, literacy accumulated associations not with assimilation but with authority, legitimacy, and mobility. These associations thickened as institutions and people used literacy to attempt to

maintain or attain social power in a profoundly documentary and profoundly transnational moment, during which the United States had
chosen literacy as a first-line technology of enforcement—over other
semiotic technologies, such as song or sculpture. Such institutional
practices, for many migrants, suffused their everyday individual experiences with literacy. When migrants spoke of papers—of how they
wrote to get papers (chapter 2), wrote in light of *not* having papers
(chapter 3), wrote *as* papers (chapter 4)—they were invoking literacy's
material reach, extended by institutions such as state, school, and work,
into their social lives.

Such institutional circumscription does not mean that literacy is
fundamentally oppressive, nor does it mean that literacy is necessarily
liberatory. Such uses depend, broadly speaking, on its context. Literacy,
for some that I interviewed, was used to exert political agency: There
was the editor of the Portuguese ethnic newspaper whose rhetorical
choices both honored ethnic differences between Brazilians and Portuguese and politically allied them in issues of immigration; the university professor whose writing and academic training allowed him to
develop a scholarly program of study that would speak to working-
class Portuguese Americans; the high school graduate who wrote short
stories that allowed him an imaginative escape from a demotivating
school environment. When leveraged at the kairotic moment, by the
writer who was in a position to construct a compelling ethos (such as
some educated men), writing was used to resist social injustice, or at
least to hew one's own path through an otherwise dark forest. In other
instances, readers have seen in these pages how people wrote to sustain
connections across distance, to commune with a higher being, and to
share important life events, such as in chapter 4, when Tina described
her daughter's birth for her GED class. As a literacy educator, I have
often held up such examples to emphasize the power of writing to help
individuals influence their social realities. Such examples resonate with
my own vocation, as one who thinks about writing, who teaches writing, and who herself writes. No doubt, literacy *can* be emancipatory
in the lives of individuals and communities.[1] At the same time, the
migrants of South Mills have reminded readers that literacy's currents
also often pull toward conservation of the status quo, as individual
writing borrows literacy's power from the bureaucracies that wield it
as a regulatory tool. It is easy to underestimate the strength of this
conservative undertow.

Understanding literacy sociomaterially helps account for these seemingly contradictory social uses, a case I make in the rest of this section. By way of example, consider two different possible readings of my interview with Rafael: One could read Rafael's sly critique of my request for a pseudonym as a strategic agentive discursive moment, in which he turned the tables on my writerly authority, thereby gaining a kind of empowerment. Perhaps it was. But the fact remains that he had no papers, a social, material, and textual reality with consequences for what he could or could not reveal about himself in this book. If he used literacy resistantly, it was perhaps because literacy was also integral to the conditions of his oppression. When literacy scholar James Gee suggested that the presence of print in definitions of literacy was optional, his justification was that print is everywhere anyway.[2] It was so ubiquitous, he claimed, as to be unnecessary as a defining feature of literacy. This book has shown, however, that the infrastructural nature of literacy was precisely the factor that impinged most directly on many migrants' literacies. It shaped how and to what ends they valued and used writing.

Perhaps uniquely visible in transnational lives, this ubiquitous documentary society made texts strong in the lives of South Mills migrants. Recall the scholarly dilemma over "strong texts" outlined in the introduction. Strong texts represent theories that suggest literacy has far-reaching consequences, independent of its social context. This older theory of literacy has been replaced by views suggesting that literacy does not autonomously accomplish anything in the world; rather literacy reflects the social uses to which it is put. This book has sought to reconcile these theories by showing that migrants experienced texts as strong—as having far-reaching consequences—precisely because of the social contexts that imbued texts with power. Texts were made strong both socially and materially in migrants' lives, as literacy practices and products accrued associations with the powerful bureaucratic institutions that undergirded everyday life. Transnational contexts, such as the one described in this book, make strikingly apparent the strength of texts. Borders, after all, are mediated by fences, guns, and documents. To migrate legally, one must engage with the state's textual apparatus—an apparatus that often appears impenetrable.

In this textually policed context, many people with whom I spoke experienced texts as strong, because the state used texts to alienate them in ways that were deeply corporeal. Papers represented bodies,

sanitizing their humanity into manageable categories.[3] It is no accident that at the Mexican border in 1917 the United States simultaneously began to require passports and delousing.[4] While fumigation no
longer occurs, at this writing migrants are still required medical vac-
cines to get legal papers, making one Brazilian migrant I spoke with
feel "like a cow." Shaun Tan's haunting graphic novel *The Arrival*
offers an excellent example of such textual dehumanization. It pictures
a Kafka-esque medical inspection, the results of which are pieces of
paper with indecipherable symbols pinned to a migrant's suit jacket.
The migrant's facial expression is of perplexity bordering on despair,
a reasonable response to one's body being textually categorized, being
made legible to others and illegible ("like a cow") to oneself. As Torpey
points out, documents are meant to stand in for the body: eye color, age,
gender, weight, race, nationality.[5] The body is replaced with papers,
which are much easier to manage. In such a context, texts are strong.

At the same time, because literacy is not just material but also social,
and because its use is dispersed among people and institutions, texts'
strength is never absolute. Recent scholars of papers have pointed out
their limitations. To offer some disparate examples: Even in the auto-
cratic, centralized society of Islamabad, Pakistan, subjects took up the
technology of paper *against* the state, forging documents to gain profit.[6]
In the very different context of revolutionary France, one bureaucrat
saved heads from being severed at the guillotine by soaking damning
documents in pails of water and disposing of them in a bathhouse.[7]
In the history of migration specifically, forgeries are famous. Many
Chinese migrants at the turn of the twentieth century took advantage
of a loophole in racial exclusion by fabricating "paper sons"—scru-
pulously detailed fictional family networks designed to fool immigration officials.[8] And rhetorician Ralph Cintrón has detailed how, closer
to the turn of the twenty-first century, one undocumented migrant
wielded multiple ID cards with different names that allowed the human
behind the cards, the one not inscribable in a bureaucratic system, to
escape.[9] Forgery and water solubility are fascinating events in papers'
bureaucratic life and times, evidencing its role in both maintaining
and undermining state control. Such examples suggest that systems of
bureaucratic documentation are neither an impenetrable Foucauldian
panopticon nor a dispersed and malleable set of rules that can be re-
written at will. They are, rather, entrenched infrastructures that, one
way or another, must be faced.

Migrants often deal with such systems by trading on literacy's sociomaterial potential. Such was the case with how migrants and their allies exploited literacy's sociomateriality in the 2006 immigration marches. Both documented and undocumented protestors wore T-shirts proclaiming "I am illegal" and "I am undocumented." Texts, worn on the body, acted as a subterfuge, scrambling people and their assigned status, temporarily throwing the border guards in cities and schools off the scent. Like others, James Bond/José/Ricardo/Rafael understood the power words can wield over bodies, to remake them from humans to aliens. This managerial abstraction, of which the technology of literacy is perhaps uniquely capable, is evident in the social lives both of institutions and of the people who traverse them. In sum, literacy is neither the enemy suppressing helpless victims nor a hero of social justice. I have been suggesting that when we see literacy sociomaterially, we can more fully appreciate how it comes to have such seemingly contradictory social consequences.

The stories of the people who shared their lives with me for this book, I believe, demand this fuller accounting of literacy's consequences. From their perspective, the meaning of literacy often departs from what scholars and others have previously thought. If literacy has been theorized as a social *practice*, the people in this study also experienced literacy as its sociomaterial *product*. If literacy has been connected to *identity*, many also viewed literacy in relation to written *identification*. If literacy has been linked to its *social context*, many also saw literacy as a technology of *decontextualization*. If literacy educators have hoped that literacy *empowers* and *humanizes*, for many migrants literacy also *oppressed* and *alienated*. If policy makers have touted literacy a way to *assimilate*, many migrants hoped to use it to *move*. The stories people shared with me do not negate dominant understandings of literacy. Rather, they ask scholars, educators, and policy makers to consider the conditions under which literacy may also be experienced quite differently, expanding our theories of what literacy is and does.

Toward a Sociomaterial Pedagogy

The problem of educational failure has long been attributed to mismatches between home and school literacy contexts, as well as to the larger systems of inequality, such as racism or economic injustice, that have produced such mismatches.[10] The experiences of those who spoke with me offer the possibility that educational alienation may occur not only as a result of mismatched contexts, nor only as a result of unequal power structures—though such forces are also at work. Alienation may also inhere in texts, as sociomaterial conveyors of the larger social meanings accrued through institutional literacy practices.

If literacy's materiality accumulates associations with social practices, as this book has tried to demonstrate, when such social practices are alienating, texts themselves may be experienced as technologies of *alienation*. Consider, for example, the visa and passport that excluded Rafael from the nation, his clever choices of pseudonyms, and his ironic use of the indefinite article when he told me, "I would like a paper." Here Rafael distanced his literacy use from both academic discourses (represented by my request for a pseudonym) and national uses of literacy (represented by his ironic take on his potential for attaining legal status). Rafael, as an undocumented person, seemed to experience literacy not as contextualizing, but as *decontextualizing*—an experience made possible by literacy's sociomateriality, through which, to echo Latour, institutions "delegate" their work to texts.[11] Put crudely, the state delegated the work of alienating Rafael to the papers they denied him.

To clarify how putting texts at the center of contextual theories of literacy can help account for some migrants' educational struggles, consider three by-now-familiar examples from this book.

Cristina, readers will recall from chapter 2, wanted to naturalize but failed the English part of the naturalization test three times. We might read her situation as two different literacy contexts in conflict— that of the normative naturalization test and that of this transnational working-class woman. Due to her personal history, her class background, regional labor politics, and linguistic discrimination, she struggled with English literacy, causing her failure. The logical solution might be to make the test more culturally responsive or to bring Cristina's literacies more in line with those of immigration and naturalization services. Yes. In addition to aligning literacy contexts, however, it is also helpful to highlight the material role of texts as purveyors of literacy's larger social meanings. Such attention provides a fuller understanding of Cristina's literacy struggles. As Cristina said of the United States, "This is my home. I wanted to get my papers." But after she finally passed the test, after humiliation and after great expense, she said, "I'm not really American. I'm just American by paper." In her naturalization encounter, papers carried with them meanings of belonging and exclusion, meanings reified through institutional literacy practices, as she failed and then succeeded at attaining them. This textually mediated process ultimately distanced her from Americanness and further distanced her from literacy as a resource she could profitably wield. Readers will recall that such alienation was apparent in her process of writing an affidavit for her friend, during which, evidently distressed, she repeatedly ripped up drafts she deemed inadequate.

Such alienation can be even more profound for the undocumented. Readers will recall Carmém, from chapter 4. Her home literacy context (playing teacher, writing about literature in her diary) would seem to predict educational success in many mainstream English-language classrooms. Moreover, she described having no problem with English. School contexts and home literacy contexts apparently aligned. Yet the material reach of texts into her social life distanced her from school, negating the benefits of such alignment. Without papers, without those textual products that promised national inclusion, she was alienated: "I didn't like it. It wasn't because of English. . . . I knew that there wasn't my place." Without papers, Carmém was written out of the physical space she inhabited. This placelessness was concretized when her brother was effectively deported; his literal decontextualization was facilitated by institutional literacy practices—the use of papers to define deportability. She chose not to continue her education in the United States, and instead hoped to leverage different papers to pursue higher education elsewhere. Nonetheless, when I returned to South Mills in 2010, she had not left, nor had she continued her studies, her academic potential having been thwarted, in ways direct and indirect, by her documentary status.

And finally, recall Jocélia, who appeared in chapters 3 and 4. She grew up in one of Brazil's impoverished *favelas*. School, and the English-language classroom in particular, pointed the way to opportunities that her modest circumstances would seem to have precluded. Given her difficult social context, scholarly pursuits appeared to be a sanctuary. In order to pursue an education in English, Jocélia envisioned a life for herself in the United States, borrowed money, and migrated on a student visa. One could read her migration as a strategic use of literacy to exert agency to overcome punishing circumstances. But this reading would leave out the part of the story where her student visa expired, forcing her to drop out of school, at which point she took on several jobs, fell asleep at the wheel, and nearly died in a car crash. If literacy's use was empowering in her impoverished context in Brazil, when she crossed the border and became undocumented, she began to experience texts as technologies of alienation, forestalling an otherwise promising educational trajectory—although she did find satisfaction, if not further formal education, in later taking up the authoritative text of the Bible.

In all these cases, literacy practices and products were contextual, taking shape in homes and schools in light of individuals' social histories and the larger forces of neoliberalism, race, gender, and state politics. By emphasizing the text in these contextual forces, I am not minimizing the effect of these larger structures. Instead, I am calling attention to the way these macrosocial forces glom on to and are often perpetuated by literacy, in ways that are both social and material. A sociomaterial pedagogy, then, would begin with an understanding not just of individuals' family and community literacy practices, but also with an understanding of how practices, products, and institutions have interacted in their lives.

When we, as educators, attempt to contextualize literacy for students, I believe we are implicitly acknowledging and attempting to overcome the alienating uses of literacy adumbrated over years of students' participation in bureaucratic institutions. I recall a year of acute teacherly despair when I was teaching fifth- and sixth-grade ESL in the Dallas Independent School District. The children were eager to learn, to please the teacher, to do well in school, an institution that for all its problems they and their families respected. At the same time, their young lives were circumscribed by racism, poverty, and often violence. Young, idealistic, and shamefully wet behind the ears, I was eager to help make the change that literacy promises. But school district and state bureaucratic regulations around literacy made such promises difficult to fulfill. Teachers across the entire district were required to use the same short story on the same schedule week to week, with periodic spot-checks by administrators to make sure we were in compliance. Children's learning was continually "assessed" through standardized tests, and practice tests for those tests—practices that, we were told, had to replace library visits and after-school activities. Hours of potentially meaningful instructional time were wasted as small heads bent over desks, as hands gripped pencils and bubbled in line after line of answers in Scantron after Scantron. We were told, explicitly, to give little pedagogical attention to the low and high achievers on these tests, and instead to focus on the "bubble" kids—the ones in the middle, who could pass with a bit more attention or could fail without adequate training. Children's learning was reduced to text: the test taking and score achieving that would or would not provide them further access to literacy. In this heartbreaking scene, literacy's bureaucratic use likely helped to alienate children who were already marginalized.

This criticism is not meant to invoke a kind of utopian, pre-bureaucratic anarchy as the key to fulfilling socially just pedagogical goals. Schools and nations are irrevocably bureaucratic. Such bureaucracies make possible much that is socially good—public education, for example, and a democratic electoral system. My point is that such systems' status as bureaucracies, which by definition run on the fuel of literacy, have consequences for people's literacy learning and experiences. In some ways, these conditions are not new: Historically, bureaucracy often preceded mass individual literacy and was, perhaps, the precondition for it.[12] In our contemporary moment, literacy learning occurs under the conditions of mass literacy, in which bureaucracy scaffolds society. It is the privilege of the American, or the privilege of wealthy children with educated parents, to be so well positioned within institutions of state and school that bureaucracy is more of a nuisance than a prison, through which one must write one's way.

Consider a personal example: My four-year-old daughter underwent a prekindergarten screening for ESL, because she has been raised bilingually and thus had been "exposed" to the (viral?) forces of a language other than English. State policy, I was told. I am aware that she is the beneficiary of the class, race, and educational systems that have made me highly literate, increasing the probability of her educational success. And I also recognize that the educators conducting the screening were well-meaning, kind, and also perhaps tired. But I felt sick watching her handle a number-two pencil for seventy-five minutes, a long time for anyone, let alone a small child. After the test, I asked what the results would mean. Would they determine a specific placement? No one was quite sure. The important thing was to track those marked by language difference. This mark would follow her, necessitating yearly assessments until she graduated with her diploma, unless I certified and submitted in writing that I had been mistaken, that she in fact had been exposed only to English, a condition of linguistic narrowness that applies to fewer and fewer children in the United States. As literacy scholar Maisha Winn pointed out to me, if the great-divide theories of literacy of the past presumed that those from marginalized groups lacked literacy skills, now the assumption is that the marginalized lack the appropriate papers, or will need to undergo tests to attain the appropriate papers. My daughter's experience provides one relatively mild example of how this thesis can play out for an otherwise educationally privileged child.

Papers, so often fused to individual literacy, act as a convenient infrastructural mechanism through which social structures can be upheld. They have been demanded with particular urgency of those who, to echo the words of South Mills' liberation theology priest, "don't look American," just as they have been demanded of the United States' first African American president, just as they have been demanded of the linguistically contaminated. They can represent, manage, and attempt to control otherwise unwieldy bodies. This is one way literacy—that privileged semiotic technology that both occludes and reveals the structures that perpetuate its supremacy—presents itself in the lives of many. And this aspect of literacy is one that it behooves us, as educators and policy makers, to acknowledge.

This potential for alienation in the bureaucratic environments that characterize most literacy learning sharpens educators' challenges. Understanding the role of text in context, of literacy's materiality in the social conditions of mass literacy, provides, I believe, a fuller vision of how literacy can function in the world, and thus how to teach it effectively and compassionately to the people who use it and on whom it acts.

Beyond Language: Sociomateriality in Transnational Literacy Lives

Sociomaterial perspectives on literacy may be especially salient for transnational students, who have had the experience (or have a close family member who has had the experience) of crossing a textually mediated border. When people migrate, they enter a geographical territory demarcated in part by the bureaucratic institution that lays claim to it. They not only enter a new *literacy* regime, as sociolinguist Jan Blommaert has suggested, but a new *textual* regime.[13] If we think of literacy not only as an extension of linguistic practices but also as a sociomaterial resource entrenched in larger infrastructures, as this book has asked readers to do, we can more precisely link the defining life event of transnational experience—movement—with the technology and practice in which such movement is enmeshed—literacy. That is, sociomateriality can foster an understanding of transnational literacy that extends beyond language difference, with three implications.

First, it can help account for how changing legislation may shape immigrants' literacy learning. In 2014 the Obama administration issued an executive action that would shield the parents of citizens and some others from deportation. Like Deferred Action for Childhood Arrivals or any other immigration reform plan, this action requires eligible migrants to tangle with the state, as those eligible under particular plans must register with state agencies. While such reform widens the net of belonging in the United States, it also further distinguishes among classes of immigrants, grouping some as documented and others as undocumented. As this policy, or any future policy, is put into action, transnational migrants will be learning literacy from their particular state-defined positions, with their attendant rights and restrictions. Some will write to attain papers under new legislation, or to help family members attain papers. Others will write with the knowledge that they are, again, left out of the bureaucratic net of the nation-state. Regardless of whether this policy is sound or just, the very fact that it is a policy with consequences for the papers migrants may (or may not) hold has implications for the kinds of writing migrants may (or may not) do, as they negotiate their host country's changing textual terrain.

Second, a sociomaterial approach can redirect pedagogical energy away from linguistic assimilation and toward other goals that migrants may have, such as accessing the literacy and papers that open up transnational educational trajectories. In these pages, readers have seen how Gabriella planned to leverage an ESL diploma to pay for higher education in Brazil, and how Carmém hoped to use her Italian passport to attend school in Italy. For many like Gabriella and Carmém, education is not training to succeed only in a host country, but to acquire social mobility across countries. Many migrants use the papers they have to enter educational institutions, the learning in which yields more papers, which taken together promise different opportunities, perhaps in a third or fourth country.[14] To accurately assess the value of educational capital across a transnational field, migrants must weigh both literacy skills and the transnational exchange value of the papers that attest to such skills. From this perspective, literacy is not just what one knows, or even the context in which one practices it. It is also how such knowledge is certified, and how such certifications are evaluated across a globe partitioned into state and school bureaucracies.

Third, this approach may help researchers track the evolution of literacy technologies and their impact on transnational literacy learning. Many migrants see literacy materially in part due to their experiences of using letters, computers, and cell phones to connect with family members across borders.[15] As literacy technologies change more rapidly than researchers can theorize them, migrants and their homeland families are often at the forefront of negotiating how to communicate in ways that are both affordable and emotionally satisfying.[16] At the same time as digital communication practices spread in use and diversity, digital security technologies are also gaining traction. Border technologies are shifting from papers and stamps to digital photos, electronically encoded passports, and fingerprint scans. Alternately connecting families across borders and separating them, these paper and digital infrastructures impinge on both migrants' intimate relationships and their transnational trajectories. Given this impact, how are migrants and their families revaluing papers in relation to other technologies? And what does this array of communicative and security media mean for migrants' writing, both on paper and digitally? Sociomaterial approaches to these questions about institutions, technologies, and families can shed light on transnational literacy learning both in host countries and among migrants' family members in homelands.

Literacy's social practices and literacy's materials, coursing through the institutions that regulate migrants' lives, speak to each other. In times of rapid technological and global change, scholars might see part of our work as listening to what they are saying. For the people with whom I spoke, their literacy practices were most brightly illuminated in relation to literacy's products, papers, which snaked their way into and across migrants' determined, forward-moving lives.

EPILOGUE

MY AUNT WRITES THE FOLLOWING for inclusion in this book: "I also thought about my name, Maria do Carmo Tavares Pereira. . . . At the airport, they took our names apart. I became Maria Pereira." Later, she became "Tequila," a nickname coworkers gave her and that stuck, so that by the time we, the nieces and nephews, came along, we called her Aunt Tequila, or Tiqui. Upon marriage to my Lebanese American uncle, her name changed again, into a different language family. Her name started out one way and ended up another. Sometimes when people migrate and sometimes when they marry, the state takes apart their names. They pass through the bureaucratic machine and come out, on paper, quite different.

It is 2015, and my aunt has written this memory on a notepad advertising a local plumbing-supply company the night before my daughter and I are set to depart South Mills. Seven years have passed since my initial interviews, five since I followed up with participants, and now I have returned for a week to share findings, and to take a new, if cursory, look at South Mills' Brazilian and Azorean communities in advance of this book's publication. My aunt's note acts as a postscript to our visit, during which we convened for late dinners to discuss immigration, labor, and family, which in turn led her to think about her name—the piece of information front and center on passports and green cards, the word our earliest caregivers use to tell us who we are, simultaneously so private and so public, so immediate and so tied to our pasts.

In South Mills, I first visit some people and places in the Brazilian community, centralized along one of the town's main streets, where

Brazilian cafés, stores, restaurants, and churches were located when I conducted my research in 2008. My daughter and I enter the central Brazilian café/store, and I find it has reduced its size by half and no longer sells religious books. I have also noticed that the main street, once bustling with religious activity, is absent of Brazilian evangelical churches. One church, at least, has moved elsewhere. But perhaps the vacant storefronts and clothing stores where churches once stood also speak to a population diminishing in size or that has become more settled, less in need of the crucial just-in-time aid religious organizations used to provide. With census information on Brazilians still unreliable, it is hard to say.

My daughter and I peruse the café's crowd of goods, so casually evocative of Brazil that as I inspect a box of chocolates I feel transported. There is the national (sparkling Brazil T-shirts and flags), the everyday (soap, coffee, pans in which to steam black beans), the luxurious (perfumes from an upscale emporium, bikinis cut just so), and, reminding me that the store serves immigrants, there is also the financial—an advertisement for the café's remittance-transmittal service. I buy some pastries, and as my daughter digs into a *pão de queijo*, a doughy ball filled with cheese, I tell the proprietor who I am (she remembers) and ask her how the community has changed.

"Many have left," she tells me. She has also left but is back on business, checking in to make sure things are running smoothly, taking care of affairs. She worked for fifteen years in South Mills, earning enough to buy a house and car in Brazil, to educate her two daughters there, and to return home. As we speak, another woman enters, squealing in surprise to see the owner there after her long absence. Effusive, she comments on the owner's good looks, and they discuss her retired lifestyle—yoga twice a week, days with her grandchildren. This customer would like to retire in Brazil as well, but needs papers to be able to come and go at will. She will soon marry a Portuguese American man— for love, not for papers! she assures us—and will get them. Papers, it seems, line the path not only to successful migration, but also to successful departure.

And then there are the other kinds of departures. As we leave, I pick up a copy of the local Brazilian paper, the front page of which depicts a deportation case that has become famous, of a Brazilian man married to an American woman. My daughter buys a cheap Brazilian flag that she waves up and down the sidewalk until it detaches from its plastic base, fluttering into the street. "Your flag," someone calls. We run after it.

Across town, I visit one of the many Azorean ethnic stores in the city. Seven years ago, it was a warehouse, filled with dark nooks and crannies, crates of dried codfish, elderly Portuguese women on the lookout for certain olive oils or pickled peppers. Now a new market has been built. High-ceilinged, its walls are lined with colorful Portuguese *azulejos* (ceramic tiles), and it features a café that serves Portuguese sandwiches and pastries. This new market is welcoming, airy, chic, like a Whole Foods of Portuguese-ness. The charcuterie offers ten different kinds of Portuguese sausage (four of which I buy to bring back to Wisconsin), a temperature-controlled room for dried cod, ceramics from the island of São Miguel, octopus frozen in plastic wrap, and an expansive selection of Iberian wines. It is not gritty. It is packaged.

This store, the owner tells me, is for the second generation. He looks at my daughter, cradles her face in his hand. "Cara linda," he says to her, the same words my grandmother, long passed, used to say to me. "Pretty face," it means, but not exactly "face," something closer to "mug." "The second generation," he continues, "they come in and want to make the food their grandmother or mother made. They buy cookbooks, ask questions. This is for them." My aunt, who meets us there for a *café galão*, coffee and steamed milk, misses the shadowy hunt of the older warehouse, the chance encounters with products and people.

The owner shows us upstairs. There is an office, a stock room, a break room, and, stunning in this place of business, a bright chapel, painted light blue and gold, lined with paintings of the Passion, of Our Lady. A statue of the patron saint of refugees stands next to a holy water receptacle fashioned to look like two hands, which can be refilled from a plastic gallon jug on the floor. "Everybody has troubles," the owner says. "You can come here for fifteen minutes and ask for help."

He gives me his card, and that of his son, who is in Boston gathering banners for the upcoming day of Portugal, during which Azorean ambassadors will visit the store. He invites me to come meet them. They are to offer tastings of pastries, organic tea, specialty jams. "They are eager to have a partnership," he says. They are eager to maintain a market.

Does the marketing of ethnic identity mean that Azoreans are becoming assimilated, so indistinguishable from a mainstream that to assert ourselves as Portuguese we must buy the appropriate accoutrements, must liven up the economy cabin of our flights to the Midwest with the smoky aroma of Portuguese *chouriço?* If so, such "assimilation" must be balanced with loss—a loss of names and cultural heritage, a loss that the Azorean government and local entrepreneurs are filling with goods (like cookbooks) and services (like a trip to your father's island), marketed to members of those later generations who feel that somewhere in their transnational histories something went missing.

The original deal was that opportunities stateside would make up for the inevitable losses brought on by migration. People came to the United States, after all, to get ahead. But for many Azoreans and Azorean Americans, the American Dream has only partially fulfilled its end of the bargain, and the legacy of under-education in relation to regional labor conditions persists. The unemployment rates in predominantly Portuguese South Mills are 7.4 percent—better than the peak of 14.5 percent in 2010, but still high compared to 4 percent in Massachusetts as a whole. It is possible, of course, that such social problems may soon cease to be *Portuguese* social problems. As the population ages, and the second generation becomes third and fourth, to what extent will immigrant past or ethnic identification correlate with education and economic opportunity or lack thereof? Perhaps Azorean Americans will definitively fade to white. Perhaps they will, as I do, purchase a hand-painted *azulejo* to display on their walls, a reminder of what has come before.

There are also no easy predictions for the future of the South Mills Brazilian community. Some have done what they came to do: earned money and returned home. But the apparent simplicity of this trajectory belies more complex financial, personal, educational, and legal entanglements with the United States. For example, the owner of the Brazilian store has not returned home once and for all. She maintains a financial foot in the United States and makes frequent trips to check up on her investment. And her daughter, now a successful professional with a young son, was educated in Brazil on American remittances. While we spoke, her mother called up Facebook pictures of this daughter, smiling and stylish against a glowing sunlit backdrop. Still, if given the choice, if she had had a different kind of visa, if tuition were not too expensive, the proprietor would have liked her daughter to study in the United States. If she had succeeded in studying stateside, her mother might have shown me a different picture, perhaps framed not by the white light of Brazil but by the bright leaves of a New England fall. Which is to say, return is partial and contingent. This family lives across the educational institutions, legal bureaucracies, and financial opportunities of two countries, attempting to glean the best, or at least the most efficacious, of both.

Such transnational success, however, is not guaranteed for all. I meet another former participant in her workplace, a restaurant serving traditional Brazilian lunches by weight to a friendly and polite clientele of manual laborers. "My one son still lives with me," she says. But her other son, having been deported on two occasions, died in Brazil before he could permanently join her. "God took him a year ago" are her words. There is loss and there is loss. Still, she works to put down roots—solid, legal, deep—by preparing for her daughter's and grandchildren's eventual migration. She pours my daughter some cashew juice, and we strategize about how to get them papers.

The desire for a stable and prosperous life in the United States or elsewhere, across and between, remains potent. This desire pushed both Brazilians and Azoreans to capitalize on their extensive or limited literacy resources, to attain papers or to make do without them, to reunite with family or to accept separation, to sometimes thrive and to sometimes fail, and to sometimes adopt new names bearing only a passing resemblance to old ones. Migration is for the brave. "My parents came here for a better life," a second-generation Azorean American man tells me. "They only had a fourth-grade education," he adds, "but they had intelligence." I sit up straighter, with a fresh respect for the dignity and pain that stitch together this familiar story. "They put a statue of Our Lady on the front lawn, and they worked hard."

NOTES

Introduction

1. I use the term "migrant" as opposed to "immigrant" to emphasize the transnational mobility that informed many participants' literacy practices. Many participants wanted to, or had already, settled permanently in the United States, however, and described themselves as "immigrants." Throughout the book, to describe those who entered the United States unauthorized, I use the term "undocumented" (instead of the pejorative "illegal" or the widely used term "unauthorized") to highlight the textual dimension of their legal status, literally being without the documents that would legitimate their residence in the United States.

2. Passel and Cohn, "Unauthorized Immigrant Population."

3. On the infrastructural nature of literacy, see Vee, "Understanding Computer Programming as a Literacy."

4. For demographic information on Mexican migrants, see U.S. Census Bureau, "Selected Social Characteristics in the United States," 2007–2011 Community Survey. For Latino education, see Gándara and Contreras, *Latino Education Crisis*. Azoreans and Brazilians only sometimes fall within the fraught ethnic category of "Latino." See Marrow, "To Be or Not to Be (Hispanic or Latino)."

5. Rosas, "Thickening Borderlands," and "The Border Thickens."

6. As of this writing, some parts of these laws and efforts have been challenged and overturned. That they passed, however, nonetheless represents the larger trend of thickening borders.

7. Marston, Jones, and Woodward, "Human Geography without Scale."

8. See Appadurai, *Modernity at Large*; and Sassen, *Territory, Authority, Rights*.

9. Smith and Schryer, "On Documentary Society."

10. Brandt, *Literacy in American Lives*.

11. Hull, *Government of Paper*.

12. Zolberg, *A Nation by Design*, shows that the regulation of immigration has a much longer history.

13. Lau, *Paper Families*.

14. Torpey, *Invention of the Passport*, 12.

15. Chu, *Cosmologies of Credit*.

16. Ong, *Flexible Citizenship*.

17. See Cintrón's discussion of Don Angel in *Angels' Town*.

18. Smith, *Texts, Facts, and Femininity*, 121.

19. See Abrego, *Sacrificing Families*, about how legal status stateside shapes homeland families' lives.

20. On ancient Mesopotamia, see Schmandt-Besserat, *How Writing Came About*; on conscription, see Missiou, *Literacy and Democracy in Fifth-Century Athens*; on the Middle Ages, see Clanchy, *From Memory to Written Record*; on census taking, see Anderson, *Imagined Communities*; on colonization, see Mignolo, *Darker Side of the Renaissance*; on the Reign of Terror, see Kafka, *Demon of Paperwork*; on modern law, see Vismann, *Files*; and on immigration law, see Ngai, *Impossible Subjects*.

21. Goody, *Logic of Writing and the Organization of Society*.

22. Scott, *Seeing like a State*.

23. Many book-length ethnographic approaches to literacy devote some attention to everyday bureaucratic writing. See Barton and Hamilton, *Local Literacies*; Brandt, *Literacy in American Lives*; and Papen, *Literacy and Globalization*.

24. Duffy has documented how Hmong refugees rhetorically counter newspaper editorials that make racist assumptions (*Writing from These Roots*). Guerra has shown how oral and literate rhetorics can contest marginalization in a transnational Mexican community (*Close to Home*). Cintrón argues that for a Chicago Mexican community, such rhetorics call for respect "in conditions of little or no respect" (*Angels' Town*). Kalmar offers a linguistic answer to this issue, as the group of itinerant workers with which he works develops a "wetback dictionary" to learn English in order to respond to the racially motivated murder of one of their colleagues (*Illegal Alphabets and Adult Biliteracy*). While these studies center on race, other research has called attention to how minority status is constructed through the injustices of global capitalism, such as in Hernandez-Zamora (*Decolonizing Literacy*).

25. See Bazerman, Little, and Chavki, "Production of Information for Genred Activity Spaces," on how bureaucratic documents promote compliance with larger institutions, at the same time as people attempt to protect their own interests in the writing that accompanies such documents. They write, "Texts mediate human activity at a distance and help enlist and align people to larger social institutions and practices" (456).

26. Bourdieu, "Social Space and Symbolic Power," 17.

27. Williams, *In Pursuit of Their Dreams*.

28. Ngai, *Impossible Subjects*.

29. Nevins, *Operation Gatekeeper*.

30. Ramos-Zaya points out that racially marked Brazilians are often unfairly perceived as undocumented, regardless of their legal status (*Street Therapists*).

31. Brandt, *Literacy as Involvement*, 18, 23.

32. Heath, *Ways with Words*; Street, *Literacy in Theory and Practice*; Gee, *Social Linguistics and Literacies*.

33. Brandt, *Literacy as Involvement*, 31.

34. Robertson, *Passport in America*; Torpey, *Invention of the Passport*.

35. On surfaces, see Prendergast and Ličko, "Ethos of Paper"; and Mortensen, "Reading Material." On tools of inscription, see Baron, *A Better Pencil*; Haas, *Writing Technology*; Haas and Takayoshi, "Young People's Everyday Literacies"; and Vasudevan, "Education Remix." On scriptural systems, see Sebba, *Spelling and Society*; Cushman, *Cherokee Syllabary*; and Lillis, *Sociolinguistics of Writing*. On bodies through which people write, see Haas and Witte, "Writing as Embodied Practice"; and Owens and van Ittersum, "Writing with(out) Pain." On the infrastructures that facilitate writing's dispersal, see Vincent, *Rise of Mass Literacy*, which details the relationship between the railroad and rise of mass literacy.

36. Latour, *Pandora's Hope*, 189.

37. Brandt and Clinton, "Limits of the Local," 347.

38. Burnett et al., "(Im)materiality of Literacy," 92. Arguments about literacy's relationship to both the material and the social have been made across disciplines: in works of educational ethnography, such as Pahl's *Materializing Literacies in Communities*; in theoretical and text-based work, such as Miccicche's application of new materialism to composition studies, "Writing Material"; and in historical studies, such as Reddy, "Re-entangling Literacy." Many working in the tradition of activity theory have also addressed how literacy artifacts and practices circulate in institutions, through which process their meanings shift, are taken up in new ways, and shift again. On this approach, see, for example, Prior and Hengst, "Introduction"; and Russell, "Uses of Activity Theory in Written Communication Research."

39. Using ethnography to study literacy practices began in the 1980s. See Szwed, "Ethnography of Literacy"; and Street, *Literacy in Theory and Practice*. An ethnographic approach to literacy's materiality, however, is more recent. In this approach, I join sociolinguist Theresa Lillis, who argues that the significance attached to "any specific modal dimension of writing . . . needs to be built on a study of where and how the modes of writing figure in everyday practice" (*Sociolinguistics of Writing*, 38).

40. Alfred Lewis's *Home Is an Island* offers a literary rendering of how the stories exchanged by returning migrants of the time period recruited new migrants.

41. Taft, *Two Portuguese Communities in New England*.

42. Williams, *In Pursuit of Their Dreams*.

43. Margolis, *Little Brazil*.

44. The American Community Survey shows that there are 62,096 Brazilians in Massachusetts and 321,582 in the United States as a whole (U.S. Census Bureau, "First Ancestry Reported"). Both are likely undercounts. According to Margolis, *Goodbye, Brazil*, the Brazilian government shows that as of 2011, 1.38 million Brazilians were living in the United States—a number that may be low since many Brazilian nationals do not register at their consulates.

45. The area is also home to other Portuguese-speaking migrants, such as Madeirans, Continental Portuguese, and Cape Verdeans, who have long lived in and around South Mills—as have the descendants of French and Lebanese, who largely migrated earlier in the twentieth century. Most recent migrant groups include Central Americans, Mexicans, and Vietnamese. And the numbers of working-class African Americans in South Mills, who like Brazilians have been priced out of other cities in the region, has recently grown.

46. In an often-overlooked moment in the Goody/Street debates, Goody claimed that the difference between his work and Street's is fundamentally methodological. Goody is doing topic-based ethnography (the topic being literacy) and Street is doing "field-based" ethnography (Goody, *Logic of Writing and the Organization of Society*).

47. See Duffy, "Recalling the Letter," on the strength of subjectivity; and Brandt, *Rise of Writing*, 9, on how literacy as a macrosocial force appears in individual stories.

48. I conducted many Azorean and Azorean American interviews in English both because many Azoreans speak English fluently and because I speak Brazilian Portuguese, and the difference in dialects can cause confusion.

49. My interviews were transcribed by an assistant fluent in Brazilian Portuguese, allowing me to double-check my interpretations of oral conversations, recordings of which I listened to accompanied by the written transcript. Any doubts as to phrases or meanings were then taken up with a third Portuguese speaker for confirmation. I translated all interviews myself, attempting to account for the literal meaning of what participants said and wrote without jeopardizing what I took to be their overall meaning.

1. Literacy and Assimilation in an Age of Papers

1. On Americanization campaigns, see Carlson, *Americanization Syndrome*; Berrol, *Immigrants at School*; Antin, *Promised Land*; Graff, *Literacy Myth*; and Asato, *Teaching Mikadoism*. See Wan, *Producing Good Citizens*, on how literacy has served to incorporate immigrants into the "habits of citizenship."

2. See Prendergast, *Literacy and Racial Justice*, on how literacy is coded as a "white property right," used to keep out racially unsuitable immigrants and withhold literacy from African Americans in the United States.

3. While early theories of assimilation promoted unidirectional assimilation to a mainstream, more recent theories suggest that migrants could assimilate to multiple communities within the United States and that host country communities also change. See Portes and Rumbaut, *Immigrant America*; Zhou and Bankston, *Growing Up American*; Alba and Nee, *Remaking the American Mainstream*. Transnational theories, beginning with Schiller, Basch, and Blanc-Szanton, have shifted focus from assimilation to cross-border movement ("Transnationalism"). More recently, however, Waldinger has attempted to balance this transnational focus, which he believes has been overly emphasized in recent research, with the assimilative focus of earlier studies (*Cross-Border Connection*).

4. On rhetorics of assimilation in relation to literacy, see Baca, *Mestiz@ Scripts, Digital Migrations, and the Territories of Writing*; Duffy, *Writing from These Roots*; Villanueva, *Bootstraps*; Young, *Minor Re/visions*; and Wan, *Producing Good Citizens*.

5. In this sense, my argument about literacy and assimilation adds to that of Harvey Graff, whose historical demographic study, *The Literacy Myth*, showed that for people in Ontario in the late nineteenth century, literacy often had to be accompanied by racial, gender, and religious privilege to be leveraged for social goods. I am suggesting that in a late stage of mass literacy, in a context of both deindustrialization and the textual policing of borders, for literacy to help migrants meet their goals it also has to be accompanied by papers.

6. Sales and Loureiro, "Between Dream and Reality."

7. Martes, *New Immigrants, New Land*; Siqueira, "Emigrants from Governador Valadares."

8. Martes, "Nos EUA, o que somos Nós?"; Ramos-Zayas, "Women, Urban Erotics, and the Phantom of Blackness."

9. Siqueira and Jansen, "Updating Demographic, Geographic, and Occupational Data on Brazilians in Massachusetts"; Margolis, "Brazilian Immigration to the United States."

10. Martes, *New Immigrants, New Land*.

11. Fleischer, *Passando a América a Limpo*; Margolis, *Invisible Minority*.

12. Martes, *New Immigrants, New Land*.

13. Literacy scholars have noted that meanings often do not arrive at their intended destinations when literacies travel transnationally. See Blommaert, *Grassroots Literacy* and *Sociolinguistics of Globalization*; and Lorimer Leonard, "Traveling Literacies."

14. Martes, *New Immigrants, New Land*.

15. Taft, *Two Portuguese Communities in New England*.

16. Felix, *Through a Portagee Gate*.

17. Huff attributes this lag to three factors: ongoing Portuguese migration, low levels of home-country education compared to other foreign-born groups, and an amorphous "regional factor" ("Education and Ethnicity in Southeastern Massachusetts").

18. For immigrant Portuguese who emigrated between 1990 and 2000, the rates of high school completion were 21 percent compared to 61 percent for other groups. And only 6 percent of immigrant Portuguese held college degrees. See Center for Policy Analysis, *Education and Ethnicity in Southeastern Massachusetts II*, 34.

19. U.S. Census Bureau, "Selected Social Characteristics of the United States," 2013.

20. De Sá and Borges make this argument sociologically in "Context or Culture."

21. See Brandt, *Literacy in American Lives*, on how the value of educational credentials depreciates over generations, as the standards for literacy rise.

22. Taft, *Two Portuguese Communities in New England*, 233.

23. For an overview of how Portuguese from São Miguel differs phonetically from continental Portuguese, see Dias-Tatilon, "Influences on Portuguese Spoken in Montreal."

24. Cho, "Role of Heritage Language in Social Interactions and Relationships."

25. Nearly 45 percent of the population is of Portuguese descent, and a possible additional 10 percent is from Brazil. Plus, South Mills is located in a broader region with even more Portuguese speakers, including sizable groups from Cape Verde (who speak Crioulo), continental Portugal, Madeira, and a smaller Angolan community. One young woman who attended a lecture I gave at a local university offered a regional commonplace: "In [South Mills] you can't get a job without Portuguese." This concentration of Portuguese speakers is a function of network migration, whereby migrants are drawn through legal, family, religious, and/or economic ties to regions where family and community members have previously migrated. Hence the Portuguese and Brazilian community in South Mills (or the Arabic-speaking community in Michigan or any number of other communities concentrated in one location). Gloria, who migrated from the Azores in the 1980s, offers an apt summary of network migration. When asked why she and her husband chose to come to South Mills, of all the cities in the United States, she answered, "I think because all the families come to [South Mills]."

26. On changing literacy standards, see Brandt, *Literacy in American Lives.*

27. See Abrego, *Sacrificing Families*, on how legal status can trump the human capital and economic resources that previous scholars have shown matter most to migrant success.

28. According to Ramos-Zayas, "Brazilians appeared threatening to the Portuguese at several levels, including a threat to their racial aspirations to white privilege" ("Women, Urban Erotics, and the Phantom of Blackness," 437).

29. Jota, "Maria, Acabou-se as Batatas."

30. See Ramos-Zayas, "Between 'Cultural Excess' and Racial 'Invisibility,'" on how Brazilians attempt to develop an individual ethnicity based on nationality (as opposed to identifying as Hispanic), modeling this choice on the Portuguese, who commodify their not-quite-white identity in Portuguese restaurants and bakeries. For their part, Brazilians find no easy racial identification in the United States. On Portuguese identification as Hispanic, see Perry, "Portuguese-Americans"; and Vieira, "Traveling Fado."

31. Martes shrugs off the desire by some to develop a "Portuguese-speaking" category of ethnic identification as "exotic" and points to fundamental differences between the communities (*New Immigrants, New Land*).

32. Ramos-Zayas, "Between 'Cultural Excess' and Racial 'Invisibility.'"

33. As of July 2013, U.S. Citizenship and Immigration Services also recognizes same-sex marriages (see "Same-Sex Marriages").

34. On "literacy regimes," see Blommaert, *Grassroots Literacies.*

35. See Graff, *Literacy Myth*, for an influential study of how race, religion, and gender mattered more for socioeconomic mobility than did literacy in Ontario, Canada, in the late nineteenth century.

36. For example, Brandt shows how capitalist entities invest in and make powerful particular literacies (*Literacy in American Lives*), and Graff has demonstrated how the favorable religious or racial position of a reader or writer can enhance the value of their literacy (*Literacy Myth*).

37. See Ngai, *Impossible Subjects*, for the history of such policies and their consequences for contemporary immigration. In 1917 the United States famously mandated literacy tests to determine who was (and who was not) racially fit for entry into the country. Likewise, on the southern border of the United States, literacy tests stemmed immigration from Mexico, and shortly thereafter, in 1930, Mexicans were legislated as nonwhite. Literacies signifying "whiteness" were certified by papers; other literacies were excluded. The 1965 Hart–Cellar Act eliminated racial quotas, yet in the same stroke it required papers for Latin Americans.

2. "American by Paper"

1. This is a term coined by another Azorean American participant, Joanne.

2. Bazerman, "Speech Acts, Genres, and Activity Systems," 311.

3. See, for example, Canagarajah, *Translingual Practice*; and Velasco and García, "Translanguaging and the Writing of Bilingual Learners."

4. During the time of my research, there had been some cases of legal Azorean residents being deported, but most Azoreans and Azorean Americans were secure in their legal status. See da Silva, "O Pesadelo Continua."

5. In this sense, papers also function as what Ahmed describes as "sticky" objects, whose affective power stems from their circulation through space and time (*Cultural Politics of Emotion*, chapter 2).

6. Papers resonate with similar meanings in the scribal culture of Mexico City in the 1980s: "Both the scribes and their clients recognized the authority of writing as a means to legitimize social action . . . the inscription of deeds, petitions, and events is attributed with giving permanence to enactments, validity to actions, authority to opinion, and status to its carriers" (Kalman, *Writing on the Plaza*, 49).

7. Some scholars have focused on the interaction between practices and technologies. See Burnett et al., "(Im)materiality of Literacy"; Haas, *Writing Technologies*; Haas and Takayoshi, "Young People's Everyday Literacies"; and Pahl and Rowsell, *Artifactual Literacies*. Others have examined how such practices and technologies index larger macrosocial trends. See, for example, Brandt and Clinton, "Limits of the Local"; Lorimer Leonard, "Writing through Bureaucracy"; and Vieira, "On the Social Consequences of Literacy," and "Writing Remittances." It is the latter line of inquiry that this chapter seeks to develop.

8. Gerber, *Authors of Their Own Lives*, 155. On Polish letter writing, see Thomas and Znaniecki, *Polish Peasant in Europe and America*; on Lithuanians, see Markelis, "Talking through Letters"; on Mexicans, see Guerra, *Close to Home*; on the English, see Gerber, *Authors of Their Own Lives*; on Pacific Islanders, see Besnier, *Literacy, Emotion, and Authority*; on Filipinos, see Madianou and Miller,

Migration and New Media; on multilingual professionals, see Lorimer Leonard, "Writing through Bureaucracy."

9. As Besnier emphasizes in the letters of the Pacific Islanders (*Literacy, Emotion, and Authority*).

10. Foner, *From Ellis Island to JFK*, 22.

11. Antin, *Promised Land*, 142.

12. It is perhaps for this reason that during mass migration to the United States and Canada in the mid-nineteenth and early twentieth century, migrants tended to be more literate, or from regions with a higher literacy rate, than their counterparts who stayed behind in their homelands, as Graff points out (*Literacy Myth*). He notes that while many without literacy traveled great distances, 20 percent of the Irish in Canada were illiterate in the late nineteenth century compared to 54 percent to 56 percent in Ireland. There are several possible explanations: The skills used in literacy may somehow be connected to the skills needed for long-distance travel. Literacy education can make one "receptive to the idea of travel," as Ronald Takaki surmises about early Japanese women immigrants to the United States (*Different Mirror*, 249). Or the relationship of literacy to social class could mean that those who could afford to take the trip were more likely to have some literacy.

13. Appadurai, *Modernity at Large*.

14. Some historians have argued that individual literacy is not the cause of letter writing, but perhaps the unintended, or at least emergent, result. Historian David Henkin suggests that the very popularity of the postal system in the mid-nineteenth-century United States may have less to do with rising literacy rates and more to do with mass internal migrations that characterized the period. In a context of mobility, the increasing affordability and reliability of the postal system as a vast federally sponsored communication network allowed Americans to conceptualize and participate in "family" across time and space (*Postal Age*). Mass literacy, then, did not necessarily directly lead to mass letter writing. Instead, the accessibility of infrastructures for the rapid movement of texts and people created conditions in which letter writing was possible and desirable. More recently Martyn Lyons has argued that the rise of mass literacy among the peasantry in Europe in the late nineteenth century in part stemmed from the letter writing that occurred from physical separation due to war and migration (*Writing Culture of Ordinary People in Europe*).

15. In his study of Mexican immigrant letter writing, Juan Guerra points out that male participants did write letters, but they often stopped writing those letters once their female relatives arrived in the United States and assumed the responsibility (*Close to Home*).

16. Narayan, *Dislocating Cultures*; Parreñas, "Transnational Mothering."

17. See Vieira, "Writing Remittances," for how transnational communication technologies act sociomaterially in a Brazilian context, and how digital technologies may accentuate the materiality of paper. See also Madianou and Miller, *Migration and New Media*, on how diversity of communication practices forms a context of "polymedia" in which migrants and family members choose among media.

18. Much research on literacy's materiality examines *micro* interactions of meaning making, as students compose across modes. See, for example, Shipka, *Toward a Composition Made Whole*; Vasudevan, "Education Remix"; and Jewitt, "Multimodal Perspective on Textuality and Contexts." In contrast, I show here that literacy's materiality also makes itself available to meanings and uses imposed by macrosocial structures, in this case, the state. In this sense, this analysis extends work done by Brandt and Clinton ("Limits of the Local") and Lorimer Leonard ("Writing through Bureaucracy"), by showing how literacy's materiality enmeshes people in the mechanisms of larger social structures, with consequences for their lives and families.

19. Historian Roger Daniels explains most clearly how this law privileged family reunification. It allowed for spouses, unmarried minor children, and parents of U.S. citizens to legally immigrate to the United States without numerical restrictions. Of those subject to quota restrictions, 20 percent were allotted to unmarried adult children of U.S. citizens, 20 percent to spouses and unmarried adult children of permanent resident aliens, 10 percent to married children of U.S. citizens, and 24 percent to brothers and sisters of U.S. citizens over the age of twenty-one. The remaining 26 percent was divided among scientists and artists of "exceptional ability" (10 percent), workers in occupations for which labor is in short supply (10 percent), and refugees from communist countries or the Middle East (6 percent) (*Guarding the Golden Door*).

20. For a discussion of why the number of Portuguese immigrants who naturalize is lower in the United States than in Canada, see Bloemraad, *Becoming a Citizen*.

21. Torpey, *Invention of the Passport*, 166.

22. Scott, *Seeing like a State*.

23. For a discussion of lamination in writing, see Prior, *Writing/Disciplinarity*.

24. The official title is the Petition for Alien Relative. It required a nonrefundable fee of $355 and asked for "information about your alien relative," such as names of their spouses and children, address at which they plan to live and currently live, and information from their official arrival/departure form.

25. U.S. Citizenship and Immigration Services, "USCIS Naturalization and Eligibility Requirements," Part F. As of July 2013, U.S. Citizenship and Immigration Services also recognizes same-sex marriages (see "Same-Sex Marriages").

26. U.S. Citizenship and Immigration Services, "USCIS Naturalization and Eligibility Requirements," Part D.

27. Romney, "Standards of Conduct for Notaries Public," 5, 10.

28. Ibid., 7.

3. Undocumented in a Documentary Society

1. On the role of religious institutions in immigrant communities, see Alba, Raboteau, and DeWind, "Comparisons of Migrants and Their Religions, Past and Present"; Gálvez, *Guadalupe in New York*; Guest, *God in Chinatown*; Hirschman,

"Role of Religion in the Origins and Adaptation of Immigrant Groups in the United States"; and Levitt, *God Needs No Passport*. On the importance of religious institutions to Brazilian U.S. communities, see Martes, "Os Imigrantes Brasileiros e as Igrejas em Massachusetts."

2. Sarroub (*All-American Yemeni Girls*) shows how textual analysis of the Qur'an allowed young Yemeni girls living in the United States to construct an identity that moved between Yemeni and U.S. cultures, what she calls "in-betweenness." Other studies on transnational religious literacy education (Ek, "Language and Literacy in the Pentecostal Church and the Public High School"; Hones, "The Word") and transnational religious textual practices (Farr, "Literacy and Religion") also tend to emphasize the relationship between literacy and immigrant identity.

3. Goody, *Logic of Writing and the Organization of Society*.

4. Ibid.

5. Clanchy, *From Memory to Written Record*.

6. Torpey, *Invention of the Passport*.

7. Street, *Literacy in Theory and Practice*.

8. Here I focus only on those who reported being undocumented. Of twenty-two Brazilian research participants in the larger study, four did not reveal their documentary status, four were documented, one expected to become documented shortly, and thirteen were undocumented, one of whom was attending school. Here, then, I discuss research with twelve participants: seven women and five men between the ages of nineteen and sixty, with racial backgrounds including European, African, and Indigenous, with socioeconomic levels in Brazil ranging from impoverished to upper middle class, and with educational backgrounds spanning completion of seventh grade to completion of a bachelor's degree, who hail from eight different Brazilian states and who arrived in the United States between 1988 and 2005.

9. Suárez-Orozco et al., "Growing Up in the Shadows."

10. As in the widely publicized case of Elvira Arellano in Chicago. See also Hagan, "Making Theological Sense of the Migration Journey from Latin America."

11. Hondagneu-Sotelo et al., "There's a Spirit That Transcends the Border," 138.

12. The other reason for taking up residence in South Mills was its inexpensive rents in comparison with other cities in Rhode Island, Connecticut, and Massachusetts.

13. In contrast, Portuguese-language religious institutions did not seem vitally important for many Azoreans' immediate past or present. Many attended mass, participated in the religious *festas* (festivals), and considered themselves Catholics, or in a few instances evangelicals and in one instance Jewish. And some elderly participants recalled churches being crucial to their social lives when they first arrived. One elderly Azorean woman, for example, described the satisfying experience of writing prayers to be read aloud in a women's Portuguese prayer group. Yet churches did not seem to fill quite as urgent of a need for the Azoreans I spoke with as they did for many Brazilians.

14. Waldinger (*Cross-Border Connection*) has pointed out that migrants' digital communication with families is often compromised by work schedules, time differences, and integration into host-country communities. On digital transnational communication in other migrant communities, see Burrell and Anderson, "I Have Great Desires to Look beyond My World"; Kang, "Online Spatialisation and Embodied Experience"; Madianou and Miller, *Migration and New Media*; and Vieira, "Writing Remittances."

15. On religious institutions sponsoring the literacies of disenfranchised groups, such as African Americans, see Brandt, *Literacy in American Lives*; Cornelius, *When I Can Read My Title Clear*; and Moss, *Community Text Arises*. On churches documenting people and land in the Middle Ages, see Clanchy, *From Memory to Written Record*. On religious writing imbuing people with authority, see Besnier, *Literacy, Emotion, and Authority*.

16. Levitt, *God Needs No Passport*, 12.

17. On sponsorship, see Brandt, "Sponsors of Literacy."

18. It's worth noting that at least one of the evangelical churches mentioned here had been allegedly involved in money siphoning in Brazil, drawing the widespread critique of many Brazilians. See Goody, *Logic of Writing and the Organization of Society*, on the "twin bureaucracies" of church and state.

19. These findings extend work on bureaucratic literacy practices as necessities of everyday life (Barton and Hamilton, *Local Literacies*; Papen, *Literacy and Globalization*; and Stuckey, *Violence of Literacy*) and as an index of changing literacy standards (Brandt, *Literacy in American Lives*).

20. Schmandt-Besserat, *How Writing Came About*; Anderson, *Imagined Communities*.

21. Levy (*Scrolling Forward*) describes documents as things that speak, and Scott (*Seeing like a State*) argues they make subjects legible to states.

4. "It's Not Because of the English"

1. For research on how such mobility shapes language and literacy practices, see Canagarajah ("Negotiating Translingual Literacy"); Lorimer Leonard ("Traveling Literacies"); and Purcell-Gates ("Literacy Worlds of Children of Migrant Farmworker Communities Participating in a Migrant Head Start Program") in the special issue of *Research in the Teaching of English* on the movement of literacies.

2. See, for example: Heath, *Ways with Words*; Dyson, *Writing Superheroes*; Moll and González, "Lessons from Research with Language-Minority Children"; Sarroub, *All-American Yemeni Girls*; Sepúlveda, "Toward a Pedagogy of Acompañamiento."

3. Young, "Nah, We Straight"; Canagarajah, "Multilingual Strategies of Negotiating English"; Horner et al., "Opinion"; Lu, "Essay on the Work of Composition."

4. Suárez-Orozco et al., "Growing Up in the Shadows," 461.

5. Abrego, "I Can't Go to College Because I Don't Have Papers."

6. Gonzalez, "Learning to Be Illegal."

7. De Genova, "Deportation Regime."

8. Da Silva, "O Pesadelo Continua"; Moniz, "Exiled Home."

9. Yoshikawa, *Immigrants Raising Citizens.*

10. Abrego, *Sacrificing Families.*

11. Anthropologists Holland and Lave have put this relationship in the following terms: history in institutional structures and history in person, "come together, again and again, in conflicted practice undertaken not only in the face of changing material and social circumstances, but also in the changing terms of culturally produced forms" ("History in Person," 5).

12. Brandt, "Accumulating Literacy."

13. Pahl and Rowsell, "Sedimented Identities in Texts."

14. Prior and Shipka refer to such interactions as "chronotopic lamination" ("Chronotopic Lamination"). Prior and Hengst, addressing not only reading and writing, but multiple modes of representation, develop the aligned concept of "semiotic remediation," which aims to "reach from the fleeting worlds of inner semiosis to long, historical chains of material activity in the world" ("Introduction," 16).

15. Meyers's ethnographic study of a Mexican homeland draws attention to this relationship between literacy and migration (*Del Otro Lado*).

16. Alvarez, "Brokering the Immigrant Bargain."

17. See this book's introduction for a discussion of the "thickening borderlands," a concept developed by Rosas ("Thickening Borderlands" and "The Border Thickens").

18. Gonzales, "Learning to Be Illegal."

19. Rodrigues, "ICE Esfria Casamento."

20. On downward assimilation, see Zhou and Bankston, *Growing Up American*; on racism and the second generation, see Lee, *Up against Whiteness*; on poverty and the second generation, see Perlmann, *Italians Then, Mexicans Now.*

21. Such articulation problems between high school and college are problematic for the 1.5- and second-generation students. Valdés, for example, denounces the injustice of asking students to pay for required ESL courses that often do not count for a college degree after they have graduated from high school and exited from ESL programs (*Learning and Not Learning English*).

22. In some ways, mothers' prominence in young people's memories of migration is an extension of the gendered division of literacy labor, by which women are expected to do the heavy lifting (see chapter 2). They not only teach their children to write, as did Milton's mother and Steven's grandmother, but also legally document their children. Under the family reunification clause, the clearest way to do so is through the textual trappings of marriage. This process, which positions mothers' bodies as documentary objects traded for legal status, would, they hoped, lead to upward social mobility for their children.

23. Pahl and Roswell, "Sedimented Identities in Text."

24. See, for example, Nystrand, "What's a Teacher to Do?"

25. Marcus, "(Re)creating Spaces and Places in Two Countries."

Conclusion

1. Robert Yagelski usefully reminded me that the uses of writing are different from the act of writing ("Literacy and Consequences").

2. Gee, "What Is Literacy?"

3. Nevins has argued that contemporary bureaucracies shifted the focus from the body to papers, or from "despotic to infrastructural power" (*Operation Gatekeeper and Beyond*).

4. Ibid.

5. Torpey, *Invention of the Passport.*

6. Hull, *Government of Paper.*

7. Kafka, *Demon of Writing.* As Kafka elsewhere quips, "State power is water soluble" ("Demon of Writing," 18).

8. As legal scholar Estelle Lau (*Paper Families*) has shown, migrants developed crib sheets that detailed the exact number of plots in home villages, which lots were vacant and where, what family members liked to eat, birthdates and ages, and so forth. All of this writing took place with the goal of attaining papers—papers that, Lau shows, even after exclusion was lifted and migrants "confessed" to lying, continued to act on migrants' lives. (One man who served in the U.S. Army under his "paper" name changed his name back to his birth name—but his headstone could not be marked with the U.S. veteran seal due to the discrepancy.)

9. Cintrón, *Angels' Town.*

10. Perhaps the most famous embodiment of these claims is linguistic anthropologist Shirley Brice Heath's *Ways with Words.* Heath documented the discursive practices of working-class African American and working-class white communities in the Carolina Piedmonts. She showed how these "ways with words," embedded in culture, home, and family, differed from the middle-class "ways with words" that dominate schools, often leading to failure for groups marginalized by race and class. Prendergast followed up on her study, arguing that it was the larger context of racial inequality that promoted educational inequality (*Literacy and Racial Justice*). On racial inequality and literacy education, see also Kynard, "Literacy/Literacies Studies and the Still-Dominant White Center."

11. For a discussion of Latour, see this volume's introduction.

12. Schmandt-Besserat, *How Writing Came About.*

13. When one leaves one country and enters into another, one's language does not always change. In fact, many people move to communities, like South Mills, in which the lingua franca of home communities is the lingua franca of the host community. On "literacy regimes," see Blommaert, *Grassroots Literacy.*

14. Fong, for example, longitudinally tracks Chinese nationals who pursue higher education in various countries, depending in part on the perceived value of the degree (*Paradise Redefined*).

15. Madianou and Miller, *Migration and New Media*; Vieira, "Writing Remittances."

16. On the rate of changing literacy technologies and the necessity of new theories, see Leu et al., "New Literacies."

BIBLIOGRAPHY

Abrego, Leisy Janet. "I Can't Go to College Because I Don't Have Papers: Incorporation Patterns of Latino Undocumented Youth." *Latino Studies* 4, no. 3 (2006): 212–31.

———. *Sacrificing Families: Navigating Laws, Labor, and Love across Borders.* Stanford, Calif.: Stanford University Press, 2014.

Ahmed, Sara. *The Cultural Politics of Emotion.* New York: Routledge, 2004.

Alba, Richard, and Victor Nee. *Remaking the American Mainstream: Assimilation and Contemporary Immigration.* Cambridge, Mass.: Harvard University Press, 2003.

Alba, Richard, Albert J. Raboteau, and Josh DeWind. "Comparisons of Migrants and Their Religions, Past and Present." In *Immigration and Religion in America: Comparative and Historical Perspectives*, edited by Richard Alba, Albert J. Raboteau, and Josh DeWind, 1–24. New York: New York University Press, 2009.

Alvarez, Steven. "Brokering the Immigrant Bargain: Second-Generation Immigrant Youth Negotiating Transnational Orientations to Literacy." *Literacy in Composition Studies* 3, no. 3 (2015): 25–47.

Anderson, Benedict. *Imagined Communities: Reflections on the Origin and Spread of Nationalism.* London: Verso, 1983.

Antin, Mary. *The Promised Land.* New York: Houghton Mifflin, 1912.

Appadurai, Arjun. *Modernity at Large: Cultural Dimensions of Globalization.* Minneapolis: University of Minnesota Press, 1996.

Asato, Noriko. *Teaching Mikadoism: The Attack on Japanese Language Schools in Hawaii, California, and Washington, 1919–1927.* Honolulu: University of Hawai'i Press, 2006.

Baca, Damián. *Mestiz@ Scripts, Digital Migrations, and the Territories of Writing.* New Concepts in Latino American Cultures Series. New York: Palgrave Macmillan, 2008.

Baron, Dennis. *A Better Pencil: Readers, Writers, and the Digital Revolution.* Oxford, U.K.: Oxford University Press, 2009.

Barton, David, and Mary Hamilton. *Local Literacies: Reading and Writing in One Community.* London: Routledge, 1998.

Bazerman, Charles. "Speech Acts, Genres, and Activity Systems: How Texts Organize Activity and People." In *What Writing Does and How It Does It: An Introduction to Analyzing Texts and Textual Practices,* edited by Charles Bazerman and Paul Prior, 309–39. London: Lawrence Erlbaum Associates, 2003.

Bazerman, Charles, Joseph Little, and Teri Chavki. "The Production of Information for Genred Activity Spaces: Informational Motives and Consequences of the Environmental Impact Statement." *Written Communication* 20, no. 4 (2003): 455–77.

Berrol, Selma Cantor. *Immigrants at School: New York City, 1898–1914.* New York: Arno Press, 1967.

Besnier, Niko. *Literacy, Emotion, and Authority: Reading and Writing on a Polynesian Atoll.* Studies in the Social and Cultural Foundations of Language 16. Cambridge, U.K.: Cambridge University Press, 1995.

Bloemraad, Irene. *Becoming a Citizen: Incorporating Immigrants and Refugees in the United States and Canada.* Berkeley: University of California Press, 2006.

Blommaert, Jan. *Grassroots Literacy: Identity and Voice in South Central Africa.* Literacies. New York: Routledge, 2008.

———. *The Sociolinguistics of Globalization.* Cambridge Approaches to Language Contact. Cambridge, U.K.: Cambridge University Press, 2010.

Bourdieu, Pierre. "Social Space and Symbolic Power." *Sociological Theory* 7, no. 1 (1989): 14–25.

Brandt, Deborah. "Accumulating Literacy: Writing and Learning to Write in the Twentieth Century." *College English* 57, no. 6 (1995): 649–68.

———. *Literacy as Involvement: The Acts of Writers, Readers, and Texts.* Carbondale: Southern Illinois University Press, 1990.

———. *Literacy in American Lives.* Cambridge, U.K.: Cambridge University Press, 2001.

———. *The Rise of Writing: Redefining Mass Literacy.* Cambridge, U.K.: Cambridge University Press, 2015.

———. "Sponsors of Literacy." *College Composition and Communication* 49, no. 2 (1998): 165–85.

Brandt, Deborah, and Kate Clinton. "Limits of the Local: Expanding Perspectives on Literacy as a Social Practice." *Journal of Literacy Research* 34, no. 3 (2002): 337–56.

Burnett, Cathy, Guy Merchant, Kate Pahl, and Jennifer Roswell. "The (Im)materiality of Literacy: The Significance of Subjectivity to New Literacies Research." *Discourse in the Cultural Politics of Education* 35, no. 1 (2014): 90–103.

Burrell, Jenna, and Ken Anderson. "'I Have Great Desires to Look beyond My World': Trajectories of Information and Communication Technology Use among Ghanaians Living Abroad." *New Media and Society* 10, no. 2 (2008): 203–23.

Canagarajah, Suresh. "Multilingual Strategies of Negotiating English: From Conversation to Writing." *Journal of Advanced Composition* 29, nos. 1–2 (2009): 711–43.

————. "Negotiating Translingual Literacy: An Enactment." *Research in the Teaching of English* 48, no. 1 (2013): 40–67.

————. *Translingual Practice: Global Englishes and Cosmopolitan Relations.* Abingdon, U.K.: Routledge, 2013.

Carlson, Robert A. *The Americanization Syndrome: A Quest for Conformity.* New York: St. Martin's Press, 1987.

Center for Policy Analysis. *Education and Ethnicity in Southeastern Massachusetts II: 1980 to 2000 (A Continuing Challenge).* Economic Research Series 59. Dartmouth: Center for Policy Analysis, University of Massachusetts Dartmouth, 2005.

Chang, Aurora. "Undocumented to Hyperdocumented: A *Jornada* of Protection, Papers, and Ph.D. Status." *Harvard Educational Review* 81, no. 3 (2011): 508–20.

Cho, Grace. "The Role of Heritage Language in Social Interactions and Relationships: Reflections from a Language Minority Group." *Bilingual Research Journal: The Journal of the National Association for Bilingual Education* 24, no. 4 (2000): 369–84.

Chu, Julie Y. *Cosmologies of Credit: Transnational Mobilities and the Politics of Destination in China.* Durham, N.C.: Duke University Press, 2010.

Cintrón, Ralph. *Angels' Town: Chero Ways, Gang Life, and the Rhetoric of the Everyday.* Boston: Beacon Press, 1998.

Clanchy, M. T. *From Memory to Written Record: English, 1066–1307.* Oxford, U.K.: Wiley-Blackwell, 1993.

Collins, James, and Richard Blot. *Literacy and Literacies: Texts, Power, and Identity.* Studies in the Social and Cultural Foundations of Language. Cambridge, U.K.: Cambridge University Press, 2003.

Cornelius, Janet Duitsman. *When I Can Read My Title Clear: Literacy, Slavery, and Religion in the Antebellum South.* Columbia: University of South Carolina Press, 1991.

Cushman, Ellen. *The Cherokee Syllabary: Writing the People's Perseverance.* American Indian Literature and Critical Studies Series. Norman: University of Oklahoma Press, 2011.

————. *The Struggle and the Tools: Oral and Literate Strategies in an Inner City Community.* Albany: State University of New York Press, 1998.

Daniels, Roger. *Guarding the Golden Door: American Immigration Policy and Immigrants since 1882.* New York: Hill and Wang, 2004.

Da Silva, Lurdes. "O Pesadelo Continua: Cidadão Português Luta Contra Deportação Retroactiva." *O Jornal* 1 (June 2008): 6–7.

De Genova, Nicholas. "The Deportation Regime: Sovereignty, Space, and the Freedom of Movement." In *The Deportation Regime: Sovereignty, Space, and the Freedom of Movement,* edited by Nicholas De Genova and Nathalie Peutz, 39–69. Durham, N.C.: Duke University Press, 2010.

De Sá, M. Glória, and David Borges. "Context or Culture: Portuguese-Americans and Social Mobility." In *Community, Culture, and the Makings of Identity:*

Portuguese-Americans along the Eastern Seaboard, Portuguese in the Americas Series, edited by Kimberly DaCosta Holton and Andrea Klimt, 265–90. Dartmouth: University of Massachusetts Dartmouth Press, 2009.

Dias-Tatilon, Manuela. "Influences on Portuguese Spoken in Montreal." In *The Portuguese in Canada*, edited by Carlos Texeira and Victor M. P. Da Rosa, 145–57. Toronto: University of Toronto Press, 2000.

Duffy, John. "Letters from the Fair City: A Rhetorical Conception of Literacy." *College Composition and Communication* 56, no. 2 (2004): 223–50.

———. "Recalling the Letter: The Uses of Oral Testimony in Historical Studies of Literacy." *Written Communication* 24, no. 1 (2007): 84–107.

———. *Writing from These Roots: Literacy in a Hmong-American Community*. Honolulu: University of Hawai'i Press, 2007.

Dyson, Anne Haas. *Writing Superheroes: Contemporary Childhood, Popular Culture, and Classroom Literacy*. Language and Literacy Series. New York: Teachers College Press, 1997.

Ek, Lucila D. "Language and Literacy in the Pentecostal Church and the Public High School: A Case Study of a Mexican ESL Student." *High School Journal* 92, no. 2 (2009): 1–14.

Farr, Marcia. "Literacy and Religion: Reading, Writing, and Gender among Mexican Women in Chicago." In *Language in Action: New Studies of Language in Society*, edited by Joy Kreeft Peyton, Peg Griffin, Walt Wolfram, and Ralph Fasold, 139–54. Cresskill, N.J.: Hampton Press, 2000.

Felix, Charles Reis. *Through a Portagee Gate*. Portuguese in the Americas Series. North Dartmouth: University of Massachusetts Dartmouth, Center for Portuguese Studies and Culture, 2004.

Fleischer, Soraya R. *Passando a América a Limpo: O Trabalho de Housecleaners Brasileiras em Boston, Massachusetts*. São Paulo: Annablume, 2002.

Foner, Nancy. *From Ellis Island to JFK: New York's Two Great Waves of Immigration*. New Haven, Conn.: Yale University Press, 2000.

Foner, Nancy, and Richard Alba. "Immigrant Religion in the U.S. and Western Europe: Bridge or Barrier to Inclusion?" *International Migration Review* 42, no. 2 (2008): 360–92.

Fong, Vanessa L. *Paradise Redefined: Transnational Chinese Students and the Quest for Flexible Citizenship in the Developed World*. Stanford, Calif.: Stanford Univeristy Press, 2011.

Gálvez, Alyshia. *Guadalupe in New York: Devotion and the Struggle for Citizenship Rights among Mexican Immigrants*. New York: New York University Press, 2010.

Gándara, Patricia, and Frances Contreras. *The Latino Education Crisis: The Consequences of Failed Social Policies*. Cambridge, Mass.: Harvard University Press, 2009.

Gee, James Paul. *Social Linguistics and Literacies: Ideologies in Discourse*. New York: Routledge, 1996.

———. "What Is Literacy?" *Journal of Education* 171, no. 1 (1989): 18–25.

Gerber, David A. *Authors of Their Own Lives: The Personal Correspondence of British Immigrants to North America in the Nineteenth Century.* New York: New York University Press, 2006.

Gonzales, Roberto G. "Learning to Be Illegal: Undocumented Youth and Shifting Legal Context in the Transition to Adulthood." *American Sociological Review* 76, no. 4 (2011): 602–19.

Goody, Jack. *The Logic of Writing and the Organization of Society.* Cambridge, U.K.: Cambridge University Press, 1986.

Goody, Jack, and Ian Watt. "The Consequences of Literacy." *Comparative Studies in Society and History* 5, no. 3 (1963): 304–45.

Graff, Harvey. *The Literacy Myth: Literacy and Social Structure in a Nineteenth Century City.* Studies in Social Discontinuity. New York: Academic Press, 1979.

Guerra, Juan C. *Close to Home: Oral and Literate Practices in a Transnational Mexicano Community.* Language and Literacy Series. New York: Teachers College Press, 1998.

Guest, Kenneth J. *God in Chinatown: Religion and Survival in New York's Evolving Immigrant Community.* Religion, Race, and Ethnicity. New York: New York University Press, 2003.

Haas, Christina. *Writing Technology: Studies on the Materiality of Literacy.* London: Routledge, 1996.

Haas, Christina, and Pamela Takayoshi. "Young People's Everyday Literacies: The Language Features of Instant Messaging." *Research in the Teaching of English* 45, no. 4 (2011): 378–404.

Haas, Christina, and Stephen P. Witte. "Writing as Embodied Practice: The Case of Engineering Standards." *Journal of Business and Technical Communication* 15, no. 4 (2001): 413–57.

Hagan, Jacqueline. "Making Theological Sense of the Migration Journey from Latin America: Catholic, Protestant, and Interfaith Perspectives." *American Behavioral Scientist* 49, no. 11 (2006): 1554–73.

Heath, Shirley Brice. *Ways with Words: Language, Life, and Work in Communities and Classrooms.* Cambridge, U.K.: Cambridge University Press, 1983.

Henkin, David M. *The Postal Age: The Emergence of Modern Communications in Nineteenth-Century America.* Chicago: University of Chicago Press, 2006.

Hernández, David Manuel. "Pursuant to Deportation: Latinos and Immigrant Detention." *Latino Studies* 6 (2008): 35–63.

Hernandez-Zamora, Gregorio. *Decolonizing Literacy: Mexican Lives in the Era of Global Capitalism.* Critical Language and Literacy Studies. Bristol, U.K.: Multilingual Matters, 2010.

Hirschman, Charles. "The Role of Religion in the Origins and Adaptation of Immigrant Groups in the United States." *International Migration Review* 38, no. 3 (2004): 1206–33.

Holland, Dorothy, and Jean Lave. "History in Person: An Introduction." In *History in Person: Enduring Struggles, Contentious Practice, Intimate Identities,* School of American Research Advanced Seminar Series, edited by Dorothy Holland and Jean Lave, 3–33. Santa Fe, N.M.: School of American Research Press, 2001.

Hondagneu-Sotelo, Pierrette, Genelle Gaudinez, Hector Lara, and Billie C. Ortiz. "'There's a Spirit That Transcends the Border': Faith, Ritual, and Postnational Protest at the U.S.–Mexico Border." *Sociological Perspectives* 47, no. 2 (2004): 133–59.

Hones, Donald F. "The Word: Religion and Literacy in the Life of a Hmong American." *Religious Education* 96, no. 4 (2001): 489–509.

Horner, Bruce, Min-Zhan Lu, Jacqueline Jones Royster, and John Trimbur. "Opinion: Language Difference in Writing—Toward a Translingual Approach." *College English* 73, no. 3 (2011): 303–21.

Huff, Toby E. "Education and Ethnicity in Southeastern Massachusetts. Issues in Planning and Policymaking." *New England Board of Higher Education Bulletin*, August 1989.

Hull, Matthew S. *Government of Paper: The Materiality of Bureaucracy in Urban Pakistan*. Berkeley: University of California Press, 2012.

Jewitt, Carey. "A Multimodal Perspective on Textuality and Contexts." *Pedagogy, Culture and Society* 15, no. 3 (2007): 275–89.

Jota. "Acabou-se as Batatas." *O Jornal* 14 (April 2007): 1619.

Kaestle, Carl F. "Standardization and Diversity in American Print Culture, 1880 to the Present." In *Literacy in the United States: Readers and Reading since 1880*, edited by Carl F. Kaestle, Helen Damon-Moore, Lawrence C. Stedman, and Katherine Tinsley, 272–93. New Haven, Conn.: Yale University Press, 1991.

Kafka, Ben. "The Demon of Writing: Paperwork, Public Safety, and the Reign of Terror." *Representations* 98, no. 1 (2007): 1–24.

———. *The Demon of Writing: Powers and Failures of Paperwork*. New York: Zone Books, 2012.

Kalman, Judy. *Writing on the Plaza: Mediated Literacy Practice among Scribes and Clients in Mexico City*. Written Language. Cresskill, N.J.: Hampton Press, 1999.

Kalmar, Tomás Mario. *Illegal Alphabets and Adult Biliteracy: Latino Migrants Crossing the Linguistic Border*. Mahwah, N.J.: Lawrence Erlbaum Associates, 2001.

Kang, Tingyu. "Online Spatialisation and Embodied Experiences: The London-Based Chinese Community." *Journal of Intercultural Studies* 32, no. 5 (2011): 465–77.

Kumar, Amitava. *Passport Photos*. Berkeley: University of California Press, 2000.

Kynard, Carmen. "Literacy/Literacies Studies and the Still-Dominant White Center." *Literacy in Composition Studies* 1, no. 1 (2013): 63–65.

Latour, Bruno. *Pandora's Hope: Essays on the Reality of Science Studies*. Durham, N.C.: Duke University Press, 1999.

———. *Reassembling the Social: An Introduction to Actor-Network-Theory*. Clarendon Lectures in Management Studies. Oxford, U.K.: Oxford University Press, 2005.

Lau, Estelle T. *Paper Families: Identity, Immigration Administration, and Chinese Exclusion*. Politics, History, and Culture. Durham, N.C.: Duke University Press, 2006.

Lee, Stacey J. *Up against Whiteness: Race, School, and Immigrant Youth*. New York: Teachers College Press, 2005.

Leu, Donald J., Charles K. Kinzer, Julie Coiro, Jill Castek, and Laurie A. Henry. "New Literacies: A Dual-Level Theory of the Changing Nature of Literacy, Instruction, and Assessment." In *Theoretical Models and Processes of Reading*, 6th ed., edited by Donna E. Alvermann, Norman J. Unrau, and Robert B. Ruddell, 1150–81. Newark, N.J.: International Reading Association, 2013.

Levitt, Peggy. *God Needs No Passport: Immigrants and the Changing American Religious Landscape*. New York: New Press, 2007.

Levy, David M. *Scrolling Forward: Making Sense of Documents in the Digital Age*. New York: Arcade Publishing, 2001.

Lewis, Alfred. *Home Is an Island: A Novel*. Portuguese in the Americas Series. Dartmouth, Mass.: Tagus Press, 2012.

Lillis, Theresa. *The Sociolinguistics of Writing*. Edinburgh Sociolinguistics. Edinburgh: Edinburgh University Press, 2013.

Lorimer Leonard, Rebecca. "Traveling Literacies: Multilingual Writing on the Move." *Research in the Teaching of English* 48, no. 1 (2013): 13–39.

———. "Writing through Bureaucracy: Migrant Correspondence and Managed Mobility." *Written Communication* 32, no. 1 (2015): 87–113.

Lu, Min-Zhan. "An Essay on the Work of Composition: Composing English against the Order of Fast Capitalism." *College Composition and Communication* 56, no. 1 (2004): 16–50.

Lyons, Martyn. *The Writing Culture of Ordinary People in Europe, c. 1860–1920*. Cambridge, U.K.: Cambridge University Press, 2013.

Madianou, Mirca, and Daniel Miller. *Migration and New Media: Transnational Families and Polymedia*. London: Routledge, 2012.

Marcus, Alan Patrick. "(Re)creating Places and Spaces in Two Countries: Brazilian Transnational Migration Processes." *Journal of Cultural Geography* 26, no. 2 (2009): 173–98.

Margolis, Maxine L. "Brazilian Immigration to the United States: Research and Issues for the New Millennium." In *Becoming Brazuca: Brazilian Immigration to the United States*, David Rockefeller Center Series on Latin American Studies, edited by Clémence Jouët-Pastré and Leticia J. Braga, 339–63. Cambridge, Mass.: Harvard University Press, 2008.

———. *Goodbye, Brazil: Émigrés from the Land of Soccer and Samba*. Madison: University of Wisconsin Press, 2013.

———. *An Invisible Minority: Brazilians in New York City*. Boston: Allyn and Bacon, 1998.

———. *Little Brazil: An Ethnography of Brazilian Immigrants in New York City*. Princeton, N.J.: Princeton University Press, 1994.

Markelis, Daiva. "'Talking through Letters': Collaborative Writing in Early Lithuanian Immigrant Life." *Written Communication* 20, no. 2 (2003): 153–69.

Marrow, Helen. "To Be or Not to Be (Hispanic or Latino): Brazilian Racial and Ethnic Identity in the United States." *Ethnicities* 3, no. 4 (2003): 427–64.

Marston, Sallie A., John Paul Jones III, and Keith Woodward. "Human Geography without Scale." *Transactions of the Institute of British Geographers* 30, no. 4 (2005): 416–32.

Martes, Ana Cristina Braga. "The Commitment of Return: Remittances of Brazilian Émigrés." In *Becoming Brazuca: Brazilian Immigration to the United States*, David Rockefeller Center Series on Latin American Studies, edited by Clémence Jouët-Pastré and Leticia J. Braga, 125–50. Cambridge, Mass.: Harvard University Press, 2008.

———. *New Immigrants, New Land: A Study of Brazilians in Massachusetts*. Translated by Beth Ransdell Vinkler. Gainesville: University Press of Florida, 2011.

———. "Nos EUA, o que somos Nós? Latinos, Hispanics, Brancos ou 'Others'?" In *Psicologia, E/Imigração e Cultura*, edited by Sylvia Dantes DeBiaggi and Geraldo José de Paiva, 97–110. São Paulo: Casa de Psicólogo Livraria e Editora Ltda, 2004.

———. "Os Imigrantes Brasileiros e as Igrejas em Massachusetts." In *Cenas de Brasil Migrante*, edited by Teresa Sales and Rosana Reis, 87–122. São Paulo: Jinkings Editores Associados, 1999.

Massey, Douglas S., Joaquin Arango, Graeme Hugo, Ali Kouaouci, Adela Pellegrino, and J. Edward Taylor. "Theories of International Migration: A Review and Appraisal." *Population and Development Review* 19, no. 3 (1993): 431–46.

Menjívar, Cecilia. *Fragmented Ties: Salvadoran Immigrant Networks in America*. Berkeley: University of California Press, 2000.

Meyers, Susan V. *Del Otro Lado: Literacy and Migration across the U.S.–Mexico Border*. Carbondale: Southern Illinois University Press, 2014.

Micciche, Laura. "Writing Material." *College English* 76, no. 6 (2014): 488–505.

Mignolo, Walter D. *The Darker Side of the Renaissance: Literacy, Territoriality, and Colonization*. Ann Arbor: University of Michigan Press, 1995.

Missiou, Anna. *Literacy and Democracy in Fifth-Century Athens*. Cambridge, U.K.: Cambridge University Press, 2011.

Moll, Luis C., and Norma González. "Lessons from Research with Language-Minority Children." *Journal of Reading Behavior* 26, no. 4 (1994): 439–56.

Moniz, Miguel. "Exiled Home: Criminal Forced Return Migration and Adaptive Transnational Identity, the Azores Example." Ph.D. diss., Brown University, 2004.

Mortensen, Peter. "Reading Material." *Written Communication* 18, no. 4 (2001): 395–439.

Moss, Beverly J. *A Community Text Arises: A Literate Text and a Literacy Tradition in African-American Churches*. Language and Social Processes. Cresskill, N.J.: Hampton Press, 2003.

Mulcahey, Gloria. "Old-Timers and Newcomers: Portuguese and Brazilians in New Bedford and Fall River." Unpublished manuscript. Microsoft Word file.

Narayan, Uma. *Dislocating Cultures: Identities, Traditions, and Third World Feminism.* Thinking Gender. New York: Routledge, 1997.

Nevins, Joseph. *Operation Gatekeeper and Beyond: The War on "Illegals" and the Remaking of the U.S.–Mexico Boundary.* New York: Routledge, 2010.

Ngai, Mae M. *Impossible Subjects: Illegal Aliens and the Making of Modern America.* Politics and Society in Twentieth-Century America. Princeton, N.J.: Princeton University Press, 2004.

Nystrand, Martin. "What's a Teacher to Do? Dialogism in the Classroom." In *Opening Dialogue: Understanding the Dynamics of Language and Learning in the English Classroom,* edited by Martin Nystrand, with Adam Gamoran, Robert Kachur, and Catherine Prendergast, 89–110. New York: Teachers College Press, 1997.

Ong, Aihwa. *Flexible Citizenship: The Cultural Logics of Transnationality.* Durham, N.C.: Duke University Press, 1999.

Owens, Kim Hensley, and Derek van Ittersum. "Writing with(out) Pain: Computing Injuries and the Role of the Body in Writing Activity." *Computers and Composition* 30, no. 2 (2013): 87–100.

Pahl, Kate. *Materializing Literacies in Communities: The Uses of Literacy Revisited.* London: Bloomsbury, 2014.

Pahl, Kate, and Jennifer Rowsell. *Artifactual Literacies: Every Object Tells a Story.* Language and Literacy Series. New York: Teachers College Press, 2010.

———. "Sedimented Identities in Texts: Instances of Practice." *Reading Research Quarterly* 42, no. 3 (2007): 388–404.

Papen, Uta. *Literacy and Globalization: Reading and Writing in Times of Social and Cultural Change.* Routledge Research in Literacy. London: Routledge, 2007.

Parreñas, Rhacel Salazar. "Transnational Mothering: A Source of Gender Conflicts in the Family." *North Carolina Law Review* 88 (2010): 1825–56.

Passel, Jeffrey S., and D'Vera Cohn. "Unauthorized Immigrant Population: National and State Trends, 2010." *Pew Research Center: Hispanic Trends,* February 1, 2011. http://www.pewhispanic.org/2011/02/01/unauthorized-immigrant-population-brnational-and-state-trends-2010/.

———. "U.S. Unauthorized Immigration Flows Are Down Sharply since Mid-Decade." *Pew Research Center: Hispanic Trends,* September 1, 2010. http://www.pewhispanic.org/2010/09/01/us-unauthorized-immigration-flows-are-down-sharply-since-mid-decade/.

Perlmann, Joel. *Italians Then, Mexicans Now: Immigrant Origins and Second-Generation Progress, 1890 to 2000.* New York: Russell Sage Foundation, 2005.

Perry, George. "Portuguese-Americans: The Lost Hispanics." *The Portuguese American Historical and Research Foundation,* 1998–2001. http://portuguesefoundation.org/gp_portuguese_americans.html.

Portes, Alejandro, and Rubén G. Rumbaut. *Immigrant America: A Portrait.* Berkeley: University of California Press, 2006.

Prendergast, Catherine. *Buying into English: Language and Investment in the New Capitalist World.* Pitt Comp Literacy Culture. Pittsburgh: University of Pittsburgh Press, 2008.

————. *Literacy and Racial Justice: The Politics of Learning after* Brown v. Board of Education. Carbondale: Southern Illinois University Press, 2003.

Prendergast, Catherine, and Roman Ličko. "The Ethos of Paper: Here and There." *Journal of Advanced Composition* 29, nos. 1–2 (2009): 199–228.

Prior, Paul. *Writing/Disciplinarity: A Sociohistoric Account of Literate Activity in the Academy.* Rhetoric, Knowledge, and Society Series. Mahwah, N.J.: Lawrence Erlbaum Associates, 1998.

Prior, Paul, and Julie Hengst. "Introduction: Exploring Semiotic Remediation." In *Exploring Semiotic Remediation as Discourse Practice,* edited by Paul Prior and Julie Hengst, 1–23. New York: Palgrave Macmillan, 2010.

Prior, Paul, and Jody Shipka. "Chronotopic Lamination: Tracing the Contours of Literate Activity." In *Writing Selves, Writing Societies: Research from Activity Perspectives,* Perspectives on Writing, edited by Charles Bazerman and David R. Russell, 180–238. Fort Collins, Colo.: WAC Clearinghouse and Mind, Culture, and Activity, 2003.

Purcell-Gates, Victoria. "Literacy Worlds of Children of Migrant Farmworker Communities Participating in a Migrant Head Start Program." *Research in the Teaching of English* 48, no. 1 (2013): 68–97.

Ramos-Zayas, Ana Y. "Between 'Cultural Excess' and Racial 'Invisibility': Brazilians and the Commercialization of Culture in Newark." In *Becoming Brazuca: Brazilian Immigration to the United States,* David Rockefeller Center Series on Latin American Studies, edited by Clémence Jouët-Pastré and Leticia J. Braga, 271–86. Cambridge, Mass.: Harvard University Press, 2008.

————. *Street Therapists: Race, Affect, and Neoliberal Personhood in Latino Newark.* Chicago: University of Chicago Press, 2012.

————. "Women, Urban Erotics, and the Phantom of Blackness." In *Community, Culture, and the Makings of Identity: Portuguese-Americans along the Eastern Seaboard,* Portuguese in the Americas Series, edited by Kimberly DaCosta Holton and Andrea Klimt, 431–60. Dartmouth: University of Massachusetts Dartmouth, 2009.

Reddy, Nancy. "Re-entangling Literacy: A Historical Study of Extra-Curricular Writing Practices." Ph.D. diss., University of Wisconsin–Madison, 2015.

Robertson, Craig. *The Passport in America: The History of a Document.* Oxford, U.K.: Oxford University Press, 2010.

Rodrigues, I. "ICE Esfria Casamento." *O Jornal* 1, no. 43 (2008): 1–6.

Romney, Mitt. "Standards of Conduct for Notaries Public." Executive Order 445, April 2004. http://www.mass.gov/courts/docs/lawlib/eo400-499/eo455rev.pdf.

Rosas, Gilberto. "The Border Thickens: In-Securing Communities after IRCA." *International Migration* (2015): 1–12.

————. "The Thickening Borderlands: Diffused Exceptionality and 'Immigrant' Social Struggles during the 'War on Terror.'" *Cultural Dynamics* 18, no. 3 (2006): 335–49.

Royster, Jacqueline Jones. *Traces of a Stream: Literacy and Social Change among African American Women.* Pittsburgh: University of Pittsburgh Press, 2000.

Russell, David. "Uses of Activity Theory in Written Communication Research." In *Learning and Expanding with Activity Theory*, edited by Annalisa Sannino, Harry Daniels, and Kris D. Gutiérrez, 40–52. Cambridge, U.K.: Cambridge University Press, 2009.

Sales, Teresa, and Marcia Loureiro. "Between Dream and Reality: Adolescent and Second-Generation Brazilian Immigrants in Massachusetts." In *Becoming Brazuca: Brazilian Immigration to the United States*, David Rockefeller Center Series on Latin American Studies, edited by Clémence Jouët-Pastré and Leticia J. Braga, 287–312. Cambridge, Mass.: Harvard University Press, 2008.

"Same-Sex Marriages." *U.S. Citizenship and Immigration Services*, April 3, 2014. http://www.uscis.gov/family/same-sex-marriages.

Sarroub, Loukia K. *All-American Yemeni Girls: Being Muslim in a Public School*. Philadelphia: University of Pennsylvania Press, 2005.

Sassen, Saskia. *Territory, Authority, Rights: From Medieval to Global Assemblages*. Princeton, N.J.: Princeton University Press, 2006.

Schiller, Nina Glick, Linda Basch, and Cristina Blanc-Szanton. "Transnationalism: A New Analytic Framework for Understanding Migration." *Annals of the New York Academy of Sciences* 645, no. 1 (1992): 1–24.

Schmandt-Besserat, Denise. *How Writing Came About*. Austin: University of Texas Press, 1996.

Scott, James C. *Seeing like a State: How Certain Schemes to Improve the Human Condition Have Failed*. New Haven, Conn.: Yale University Press, 1998.

Scribner, Sylvia, and Michael Cole. *The Psychology of Literacy*. Cambridge, Mass.: Harvard University Press, 1981.

Sebba, Mark. *Spelling and Society: The Culture and Politics of Orthography around the World*. Cambridge, U.K.: Cambridge University Press, 2007.

Sepúlveda, Enrique, III. "Toward a Pedagogy of *Acompañamiento*: Mexican Migrant Youth Writing from the Underside of Modernity." *Harvard Educational Review* 81, no. 3 (2011): 550–72.

Shipka, Jody. *Toward a Composition Made Whole*. Pittsburgh: University of Pittsburgh Press, 2011.

Siqueira, Carlos Eduardo, and Tiago Jansen. "Updating Demographic, Geographic, and Occupational Data on Brazilians in Massachusetts." In *Becoming Brazuca: Brazilian Immigration to the United States*, David Rockefeller Center Series on Latin American Studies, edited by Clémence Jouët-Pastré and Leticia J. Braga, 105–24. Cambridge, Mass.: Harvard University Press, 2008.

Siqueira, Sueli. "Emigrants from Governador Valadares: Projects of Return and Investment." In *Becoming Brazuca: Brazilian Immigration to the United States*, David Rockefeller Center Series on Latin American Studies, edited by Clémence Jouët-Pastré and Leticia J. Braga, 175–94. Cambridge, Mass.: Harvard University Press, 2008.

Smith, Dorothy E. *Texts, Facts, and Femininity: Exploring the Relations of Ruling*. London: Routledge, 1990.

Smith, Dorothy E., and Catherine F. Schryer. "On Documentary Society." In *Handbook of Research on Writing: History, Society, School, Individual, Text*, edited by Charles Bazerman, 113–27. Mahwah, N.J.: Lawrence Erlbaum Associates, 2008.

Street, Brian. *Literacy in Theory and Practice*. Cambridge, U.K.: Cambridge University Press, 1984.

———. "What's 'New' in New Literacy Studies? Critical Approaches to Literacy in Theory and Practice." *Current Issues in Comparative Education* 5, no. 2 (2003): 77–91.

Stuckey, J. Elspeth. *The Violence of Literacy*. Portsmouth, N.H.: Boynton/Cook Publishers, 1991.

Suárez-Orozco, Carola, Marcelo M. Suárez-Orozco, and Irina Todorova. *Learning a New Land: Immigrant Students in American Society*. Cambridge, Mass.: Harvard University Press, 2008.

Suárez-Orozco, Carola, Hirokazu Yoshikawa, Robert T. Teranishi, and Marcelo M. Suárez-Orozco. "Growing Up in the Shadows: The Developmental Implications of Unauthorized Status." *Harvard Educational Review* 81, no. 3 (2011): 438–72.

Szwed, John. "The Ethnography of Literacy." In *Writing: The Nature, Development, and Teaching of Written Communication*, edited by Marcia Farr Whiteman, 13–24. New York: Routledge, 1981.

Taft, Donald Reed. *Two Portuguese Communities in New England*. New York: Columbia University Press, 1923.

Takaki, Ronald. *A Different Mirror: A History of Multicultural America*. Boston: Little, Brown, 1993.

Tan, Shaun. *The Arrival*. New York: Arthur Levine, 2006.

Thomas, William I., and Florian Znaniecki. *The Polish Peasant in Europe and America: A Classic Work in Immigration History*. Edited by Eli Zaretsky. Urbana: University of Illinois Press, 1996.

Torpey, John. *The Invention of the Passport: Surveillance, Citizenship, and the State*. Cambridge Studies in Law and Society. Cambridge, U.K.: Cambridge University Press, 2000.

U.S. Census Bureau. "First Ancestry Reported." *2013 American Community Survey*. http://factfinder.census.gov/faces/tableservices/jsf/pages/productview.xhtml?pid=ACS_13_1YR_B04001&prodType=table.

———. "Place of Birth for Foreign-Born Population in the United States." *2011 American Community Survey*. http://factfinder.census.gov/faces/tableservices/jsf/pages/productview.xhtml?pid=ACS_13_1YR_B05006&prodType=table.

———. "Selected Social Characteristics in the United States." *2007–2011 American Community Survey*. http://factfinder.census.gov/faces/tableservices/jsf/pages/productview.xhtml?src=bkmk.

———. "Selected Social Characteristics in the United States." *2013 American Community Survey*. http://factfinder.census.gov/faces/tableservices/jsf/pages/productview.xhtml?pid=ACS_13_1YR_DP02&prodType=table.

U.S. Citizenship and Immigration Services. "Volume 12, Part D: General Natural-
ization Requirements." *USCIS Policy Manual,* October 28, 2014. http://www
.uscis.gov/policymanual/HTML/PolicyManual-Volume12-PartD.html.
———. "Volume 12, Part F: Good Moral Character." *USCIS Policy Manual,*
October 28, 2014. http://www.uscis.gov/policymanual/HTML/PolicyManual
-Volume12-PartF.html.

Valdés, Guadalupe. *Expanding Definitions of Giftedness: The Case of Young Inter-
preters from Immigrant Communities.* Educational Psychology Series. Mahwah,
N.J.: Lawrence Erlbaum Associates, 2003.
———. *Learning and Not Learning English: Latino Students in American Schools.*
Multicultural Education. New York: Teachers College Press, 2001.

Valenzuela, Angela. *Subtractive Schooling: U.S.–Mexican Youth and the Politics
of Caring.* Albany: State University of New York Press, 1999.

Vasudevan, Lalitha. "Education Remix: New Media, Literacies, and the Emerging
Digital Geographies." *Digital Culture and Education* 2, no. 1 (2010): 62–82.

Vee, Annette. "Understanding Computer Programming as a Literacy." *Literacy in
Composition Studies* 1, no. 2 (2013): 42–64.

Velasco, Patricia, and Ofelia García. "Translanguaging and the Writing of Bilingual Learners." *Bilingual Research Journal: The Journal of the National Association for Bilingual Education* 37, no. 1 (2014): 6–23.

Vieira, Kate Elizabeth. "'American by Paper': Assimilation and Documentation in
a Biliterate Bi-ethnic Immigrant Community." *College English* 73, no. 1 (2010):
50–72.
———. "On the Social Consequences of Literacy." *Literacy in Composition Stud-
ies* 1, no. 1 (2013): 26–32.
———. "The Traveling Fado." In *Feminist Rhetorical Resilience,* edited by Eliz-
abeth A. Flynn, Patricia Sotirin, and Ann Brady, 59–81. Logan: Utah State
University Press, 2012.
———. "Writing Remittances: Migration-Driven Literacy Learning in a Brazilian
Homeland." *Research in the Teaching of English* 50 (forthcoming).

Villanueva, Victor. *Bootstraps: From an American Academic of Color.* Urbana, Ill.:
National Council of Teachers of English, 1993.

Vincent, David. *The Rise of Mass Literacy: Reading and Writing in Modern Europe.*
Cambridge, U.K.: Polity Press, 2000.

Vismann, Cornelia. *Files: Law and Media Technology.* Meridian: Crossing Aesthet-
ics. Translated by Geoffrey Winthrop-Young. Stanford, Calif.: Stanford University Press, 2008.

Waldinger, Roger. *The Cross-Border Connection: Immigrants, Emigrants, and
Their Homelands.* Cambridge: Harvard University Press, 2015.

Wan, Amy J. *Producing Good Citizens: Literacy Training in Anxious Times.* Pitt
Comp Literacy and Culture. Pittsburgh: University of Pittsburgh Press, 2014.

Williams, Jerry R. *In Pursuit of Their Dreams: A History of Azorean Immigration
to the United States.* Portuguese in the Americas. North Dartmouth: University of Massachusetts Dartmouth, Center for Portuguese Studies and Culture,
2005.

Yagelski, Robert P. "Literacy and Consequences: A Response to Kate Vieira." *Literacy in Composition Studies* 1, no. 1 (2013): 56–59.

Yoshikawa, Hirokazu. *Immigrants Raising Citizens: Undocumented Parents and Their Young Children.* New York: Russell Sage Foundation, 2011.

Young, Morris. *Minor Re/Visions: Asian American Literacy Narratives as a Rhetoric of Citizenship.* Studies in Writing and Rhetoric. Carbondale: Southern Illinois University Press, 2004.

Young, Vershawn Ashanti. "'Nah, We Straight': An Argument against Code Switching." *Journal of Advanced Composition* 29, nos. 1–2 (2009): 49–76.

Zhou, Min, and Carl L. Bankston. *Growing Up American: How Vietnamese Children Adapt to Life in the United States.* New York: Russell Sage Foundation, 1998.

Zolberg, Aristide R. *A Nation by Design: Immigration Policy in the Fashioning of America.* New York: Russell Sage Foundation, 2006.

INDEX

122; use of term, 161n1. *See also*
undocumented status
minimum wage laws, 23
miracles, 103–4
missionary cards, 2, 83–84, 100–101
mobility: and legal papers, 2, 52–53,
59; and literacy, 21, 25–28, 29, 33,
69, 142, 146; migration journeys,
55, 60; regulation of, 20, 131;
transnational, 21; of youth, 111–12,
138–39. *See also* upward mobility

Narayan, Uma, 65
national belonging: and legal papers,
11, 24, 48, 59, 108, 121, 128, 148;
and literacy, 2, 54, 112
naturalization, 68–74, 80
New Literacy Studies, 12–13
No Child Left Behind program,
111–12
nostalgia, 60–61, 96–97
notarizing, 74, 78, 80

Obama, Barack, 53–54, 151, 152
oppression and writing, 9

paper: materiality of, 57–58, 65;
personal letters, 60–66. *See also*
legal papers
Parreñas, Rhacel, 65
passports, 7, 13, 96, 145
pedagogy, 25, 146–51
permanent resident status, 71
Portuguese language, 10, 47, 71, 127
Prior, Paul, 172n14

quotas. *See* immigration laws

Race to the Top program, 111–12
racial privilege, 48
reading. *See* literacy
religious literacy. *See under* churches
religious organizations. *See* churches
Romney, Mitt, 78

saudade. See nostalgia
schools, 28, 35, 41–42, 119–23, 128,
140
Schryer, Catherine, 7
Scott, James, 73
SER Jobs for Progress, 37
Shipka, Jody, 172n14
silencing, 74, 79
Smith, Dorothy, 7, 8
social security cards, 1
sociomateriality, 4, 10, 12–14, 60,
66–68, 72, 86, 107–8, 114–15,
142–53
Street, Brian, 12
strong text theories, 11–13, 108,
139–40, 144, 145
student visas, 37, 120, 123, 148
Suárez-Orozco, Carola, 113

Taft, Don, 39
Tan, Shaun, 145
teaching. *See* pedagogy
textual objects. *See* legal papers;
specific document types
time sheets, 3
Torpey, John, 73, 145
tourist visas, 1, 7, 49–52
transnationalism: and Americanness,
127–28; church documentary
practices, 104–7; and literacy, 68,
152; literacy research, 112; and
sociomaterality, 151–53; and
upward mobility, 111, 128; of youth,
127, 139

undocumented status: criminalization
of, 87–88; and driving, 130–32; and
education, 23, 119–24; and
exclusion, 11, 108, 148; and legal
papers, 26, 81; and literacy, 26, 81;
percentages, 3; reforms in, 53–54,
152; and religious literacy, 84–87;
and religious participation, 87–90;
and religious writing, 90–96; and

A former elementary and high school ESL teacher, **KATE VIEIRA** is assistant professor of English in the program in Composition and Rhetoric at the University of Wisconsin–Madison.